Early Childhood and Compulsory Education

D1534702

What should be the relationship between early childhood and compulsory education? What can they learn from one another and by working together?

The rapid expansion of early childhood services means that most children in affluent countries now have several years of early childhood education before compulsory schooling. This raises an important question about the relationship between the two. Whilst it is widely assumed that the former should prepare children for the latter, there are alternatives. This book contests the 'readying for school' relationship as neither self-evident nor unproblematic; and explores some alternative relationships, including a strong and equal partnership and the vision of a meeting place.

In this ground-breaking book, Professor Peter Moss discusses the issue with leading early childhood figures – from Belgium, France, Italy, New Zealand, Norway, Sweden and the United States – who bring very different perspectives to this contentious relationship. The book starts with an extended essay by Peter Moss, to which the other contributors are invited to respond critically, as well as offering their own thinking about the relationship between early childhood and compulsory education.

Students, teachers, researchers and other academics in the field of early childhood education will find this an insightful and timely text. But so too will their peers in compulsory education, since the book time and again raises searching questions about pedagogical purpose and practice in this sector.

Peter Moss is Emeritus Professor of Early Childhood Provision at the Institute of Education, University of London, UK.

Contesting Early Childhood series
Series Editors: Gunilla Dahlberg and Peter Moss

This groundbreaking series questions the current dominant discourses surrounding early childhood, and offers instead alternative narratives of an area that is now made up of a multitude of perspectives and debates.

The series examines the possibilities and risks arising from the accelerated development of early childhood services and policies, and illustrates how it has become increasingly steeped in regulation and control. Insightfully, this collection of books shows how early childhood services can in fact contribute to ethical and democratic practices. The authors explore new ideas taken from alternative working practices in both the western and developing world, and from other academic disciplines such as developmental psychology. Current theories and best practice are placed in relation to the major processes of political, social, economic, cultural and technological change occurring in the world today.

Titles in the *Contesting Early Childhood* series include:

Early Childhood and Compulsory Education

Reconceptualising the relationship

Edited by Peter Moss

With Lucia Balduzzi, John Bennett, Margaret Carr, Gunilla Dahlberg, Hildegard Gobeyn, Peder Haug, Sharon Lynn Kagan, Arianna Lazzari, Nadine De Stercke and Michel Vandenbroeck

Routledge
Taylor & Francis Group

LONDON AND NEW YORK

First published 2013
by Routledge
2 Park Square, Milton Park, Abingdon, Oxon OX14 4RN

Simultaneously published in the USA and Canada
by Routledge
711 Third Avenue, New York, NY 10017

Routledge is an imprint of the Taylor & Francis Group, an informa business

© 2013 Peter Moss

British Library Cataloguing in Publication Data
A catalogue record for this book is available from the British Library

Library of Congress Cataloging-in-Publication Data
Early childhood and compulsory education : reconceptualising the
relationship / edited by Peter Moss.
p. cm.
ISBN 978-0-415-68773-7 (hardback) – ISBN 978-0-415-68774-4
(paperback) – ISBN 978-0-203-08075-7 (ebook) 1. Early childhood
education. 2. Education, Compulsory. I. Moss, Peter, 1945–
LB1139.23.E24 2013
372.21–dc23
2012024457

ISBN: 978-0-415-68773-7 (hbk)
ISBN: 978-0-415-68774-4 (pbk)
ISBN: 978-0-203-08075-7 (ebk)

Typeset in Garamond
by FiSH Books Ltd, Enfield

MIX
Paper from
responsible sources
FSC® C004839

Printed and bound in Great Britain by the MPG Books Group

Contents

Notes on contributors

Lucia Balduzzi (Italy) is a Senior Researcher at the Department of Education Science, University of Bologna. Her main area of interest is the professional profile of practitioners in conventional and experimental early childhood services. She has recently co-edited, with Milena Manini, *La cura della professionalità di educatrici e insegnanti nei servizi per l'infanzia*, about practitioners' professionalism in early childhood education and care settings.

John Bennett (France) was the co-author of the first two *Starting Strong* reports, published by the OECD. Currently, he is a member of the editorial board of the *European Early Childhood Education Research Journal*. His latest publication is the *Roma Early Childhood Inclusion (RECI) Overview Report,* published conjointly by the Open Society Foundation, the Roma Education Fund and UNICEF (2012).

Margaret Carr (New Zealand) is Professor of Education at the University of Waikato. Her main areas of interest are curriculum and pedagogy in the early years and the ways in which assessment practices shape learner identities. Her latest book, co-authored with Wendy Lee, is *Learning Stories: Constructing Learner Identities in Early Years Education* (2012, Sage).

Gunilla Dahlberg (Sweden) is Professor of Education with a specific focus on early childhood education at Stockholm University. Her main areas of interest are transculturalism, the magic of language and children's dialogue with nature from a transformative and immanent perspective. She co-edits the series *Contesting Early Childhood*, with Peter Moss.

Hildegard Gobeyn (Belgium) has worked as a social worker. She is currently a researcher and teacher at the Faculty of Health, Education and Social Work at University College Ghent. Her main area of research is the professionalisation of social work.

Peder Haug (Norway) is Professor of Education at the Faculty of Humanities and Education, Volda University College. His main area of interest is educational reforms and classroom activities, and he is also engaged in research about kindergartens. His latest book is *Quality of Education: Teaching in School Observed and Evaluated* (2012).

Sharon Lynn Kagan (United States) is the Virginia and Leonard Marx Professor of Early Childhood and Family Policy, and the Co-Director of the National Centre for Children and Families at Teachers College, Columbia University and a Professor Adjunct at Yale University. She is a member of the National Academy of Education, a fellow of the American Educational Research Association and a former president of NAEYC. Her areas of interest include building early childhood systems, early learning standards and assessment, early childhood quality and transitions, and social equity.

Arianna Lazzari (Italy) is a Research Fellow at the Department of Education Science, University of Bologna. She has worked as a pre-school teacher and has recently been part of the research team on the CORE project, a study of competence requirements for staff in early childhood education and care. Her main area of interest is professional-ism and professional development of early childhood practitioners within a cross-national perspective.

Peter Moss (United Kingdom) is Emeritus Professor of Early Childhood Provision at the Institute of Education University of London. His areas of interest include democracy in education and the relationship between care, gender and employment. He co-edits the series *Contesting Early Childhood*, with Gunilla Dahlberg. His latest book is *Radical Education and the Common School: a Democratic Alternative* (2011), co-authored with Michael Fielding.

Nadine De Stercke (Belgium) has worked as a social worker. She is currently a researcher and teacher at the Faculty of Health, Education and Social Work at University College Ghent, teaching communication and systemic therapy to social workers. Her main area of research is the professionalisation of social work.

Michel Vandenbroeck (Belgium) is Professor at the Department of Social Welfare Studies, Ghent University. He is also president of the VBJK Research and Resource Centre on early childhood education and care and a member of the board of trustees of the European Early Childhood Education Research Association. His main area of interest is ECEC and parent support programmes, with a focus on diversity and social inclusion.

Part I

Introductory essay

Chapter I

The relationship between early childhood and compulsory education

A properly political question

Peter Moss

> Properly political questions always involve decisions which require us to make a choice between conflicting alternatives.
>
> (Mouffe, 2005, p. 10)

This book is about a 'properly political question', the relationship between two parts of the education system: that part providing for children up to compulsory school age, termed below 'early childhood education' or ECE; and that part providing compulsory schooling, termed below 'compulsory school education' or CSE. To describe the relationship as 'political' is to call attention to the conflicting alternatives available, some of which will be explored in this and subsequent chapters, with each alternative inscribed with particular constructs, values and assumptions, and each therefore contestable. It is also to draw a distinction between political (or some might say critical) questions and technical questions. Technical questions, epitomised by the much touted 'what works?', seek to find good solutions to achieving particular agreed purposes or goals; but political questions seek to elicit what those purposes or goals should be.

This book comes in a series titled 'Contesting Early Childhood', reflecting the many possible perspectives on and understandings of early childhood education, which produce many possible answers to the political questions generated within this sector of education. Other books in the series have demonstrated repeatedly the contested nature of early childhood, arising from different paradigmatic and theoretical perspectives. What this book aims to do is to extend the space of educational contestation to include compulsory schooling and the relationship between ECE and CSE. It insists that early childhood education cannot be considered in isolation from education in general, not only because ECE is inescapably in relationship with and affected by CSE, but also I would argue because the values, goals, concepts, understandings and practices of education should extend across the whole field – a contention I will seek to explain and justify later.

The relationship between ECE and CSE has been a long-standing issue.

But it has come increasingly on to policy agendas for several reasons. Concerns have grown in many countries about standards of performance in CSE, especially for certain groups of children, which are traced back to the earliest years in CSE and the struggle such children have to gain certain basic skills and competencies; they seem to start compulsory schooling unready to learn and often never get over this initial disadvantage, hamstrung for the rest of their school lives. International assessment studies, such as OECD's Programme for International Student Assessment (PISA) – a cross-national comparison of 15-year-olds' performance in reading, maths and science – and intensifying global economic competition bring such problems and their consequences to the fore. But other developments mean that solutions are no longer sought solely in compulsory schooling itself: CSE is no longer viewed as the first act in the theatre of education.

Early childhood education has been around a long time, emerging as a significant field in the nineteenth century. But it is only recently that it has been generally recognised as an important educational player. There is a growing awareness of the educational and social importance of the early years before compulsory school, an issue discussed further below. At the same time, early education has emerged increasingly clearly as the subject of a growing discourse of children's rights: the UN Committee on the Rights of the Child has, for example, interpreted 'the right to education during early childhood as beginning at birth and (as) closely linked to young children's right to maximum development (art. 6.2)' (2005, para.7). ECE has expanded, in almost all parts of the world, so that increasing numbers of children move to compulsory school not from home but from ECE:

> Worldwide access to pre-school facilities [for children from 3 years of age] has been steadily increasing. Some 139 million children were in ECCE programmes in 2006, up from 112 million in 1999. The global pre-primary gross enrolment rate (GER) in 2006 averaged 79% in developed countries and 36% in developing countries.
>
> (UNESCO, 2008, p. 50)

It should also be noted that ECE does not necessarily begin only at 3 years of age. Increasing numbers of children under that age are to be found in formal services, and though often labelled 'childcare', these services are increasingly recognised as having an 'educational' purpose; indeed in some countries today (such as the Nordic states, New Zealand and Slovenia) all early childhood services for children from birth are part of the education system, with administrative and policy-making responsibility placed in the education ministry, an integrated workforce, a single curriculum from birth to compulsory school age and, often, age-integrated centres. In such cases, there is continuity through the 'early years'. More often, though, there are transitions to be made at around the age of 3 between a 'childcare' sector (usually located in welfare) and an 'early education' sector (usually located in education), raising a whole set of issues about the relationship between these two parts: ECE itself could be said to be split in these cases (for a fuller discussion of integrated and split approaches to ECE, see Kaga *et al.*, 2010). I return to this issue in the next section.

In such conditions, of expanding ECE and growing concern about CSE, the relationship between these two parts of the education system has become more salient, indeed inescapable. It is this particular relationship that is the subject of this book. But it deals with matters that are germane to relationships between *all* parts of education, in particular what sorts of relationship are possible between one part and another, what influences the relationships that actually emerge, what relationship should be pursued and how should that relationship be negotiated and implemented. As the two Swedish researchers whose work I draw on extensively for this chapter put the matter, their vision is 'not only for the co-operation between pre-school and school, but also between all forms of education and lifelong learning' (Dahlberg and Lenz-Taguchi, 1994, p. 1).

Often, relationships within the education system are spoken of in terms of one part preparing and delivering students 'ready' for the next part. The 'readiness to learn' or 'school readiness' role often attributed to early childhood education will feature much in this book, but the same discourse can be heard elsewhere, for example when universities complain that schools are not sufficiently preparing students for the demands of higher education. The assumption with which such 'readiness' discourses are often inscribed is that education is necessarily hierarchical, often expressed in the language of education systems (e.g. 'primary', 'secondary', 'further' and 'higher'), with learning and knowledge becoming successively more demanding, more complex and more important and with learners developing, stage by stage, towards a maturity marked by becoming an autonomous subject, a flexible worker and calculating consumer, able to make out in the various market places that constitute the neoliberal world.

Occasionally, however, this often taken-for-granted relationship is put into question, the familiar made strange, by a new conceptualisation of the relationship. One such occasion is *Starting Strong*, the review of early childhood policies in 20 countries conducted by the Organisation for Economic Cooperation and Development (OECD), the results of which appear in two major reports, *Starting Strong I* and *Starting Strong II* (OECD, 2001, 2006). Both reports speak of the possibility of a 'strong and equal partnership' between ECE and CSE.

A second occasion is a paper by Swedish researchers Gunilla Dahlberg and Hillevi Lenz-Taguchi (1994), *Förskola och skola – om två skilda traditioner och om visionen om en mötesplats* (Preschool and school – two different traditions and the vision of a meeting place). This paper originally appeared in a 1994 Swedish government committee report, whose title suggests a questioning of the hierarchical idea of readiness: *Grunden för livslångt lärande: En barnmogen skola* (The foundation for lifelong learning: a school ready for children). It offers another conceptualisation, envisioning a new relationship between ECE and CSE emerging through creating 'a meeting place' between these two parts of the education system.

In this introductory essay, I will explore further these three relationships – 'readying', a 'strong and equal partnership' and 'the vision of a meeting place'. They do not, though, necessarily exhaust the possibilities; further relationships are possible. It is not my intention to replace a single dictatorship with a triumvirate.

The first relationship – 'readying' – has had and continues to receive most attention, fitting a dominant narrative of normativity and performativity, in which the purpose of education is conformity to predetermined performance criteria. In this narrative, ECE is talked of as an intervention that can improve the performance of children in CSE, in particular those at high risk of 'under achievement'. As I shall discuss, variants of the readiness discourse can be more nuanced, placing compulsory schooling under more critical scrutiny, and shading in some respects into the other two relationships: but such nuanced interpretations struggle to make their presence felt in a public arena increasingly dominated by a cruder view of readiness.

The other two relationships have had far less policy and research attention. I shall give most space to presenting the ideas in the Swedish paper, both because this document is less accessible to most readers (being published only in Swedish[1]) and because it provides a deeper analysis than the OECD reports of the *problematique* and a more elaborated discussion of one possible solution. The OECD reports do, however, draw on a wide-ranging review of developments in 20 countries, offering cross-national breadth in contrast to the greater depth of the Swedish paper. *Starting Strong* I and II paint a broad picture of what is going on in the relationship between ECE and CSE, at least in more affluent countries, highlight some potential benefits and concerns about what is happening, and argue for a shift in the relationship from 'schoolification', an expressive term for CSE 'taking over early childhood institutions in a colonising manner' (OECD, 2006, p. 62), to a 'strong and equal partnership.' The Swedish paper goes into the reasons why trying to forge such a partnership can prove problematic, whilst also offering a possible way out of the dilemma through co-construction of shared understandings and practices.

Following this essay, highlighting a number of possibilities for the relationship between ECE and CSE, there are contributions from the co-authors of the *Starting Strong* reports and the Swedish paper: John Bennett and Gunilla Dahlberg. Subsequent chapters provide further reflections on the relationship by authors from five countries: Margaret Carr (Aotearoa New Zealand); Peder Haug (Norway); Sharon Lynn Kagan (United States of

America); Arianna Lazzari and Lucia Balduzzi (Italy); and Michel Vandenbroeck, Nadine De Stercke and Hildegard Gobeyn (Belgium). Prior to writing, they were offered this essay as a stimulus or provocation, but have not been confined to responding to it, being free to open up other lines of argument. The book finishes with a chapter in which I offer some further reflections on the relationship in the light of the preceding contributions.

The omission of authors from the CSE field is acknowledged. My main justification is that this book is in a series taking an early childhood perspective. My hope is that the book will provoke responses from other educational perspectives.

But before moving to the three relationships between ECE and CSE, which are the main focus of this essay, it is important to make passing reference to what might be termed the structural context that both defines certain facets of the relationship and influences possibilities for change.

The structural context

Despite the growing influence of international organisations and private providers on education, the nation state remains a key player, not least because it continues to determine important parts of the structural context within which ECE and CSE are situated, operate and relate to each other. There are many nation states, nearly 200 at the last count, but this book will focus on a minority, the most affluent. Generalising is always fraught, and no more so than from the affluent world to those countries where even guaranteeing a minimum standard of compulsory education for all children remains an issue and where basic material and human resources are often lacking. I make no claim to do so.

Among the many dimensions that form the structural context, three stand out: the age at which children move from ECE to CSE; the structuring of ECE; and the organisation of education in ECE and CSE, especially the workforces.

The *age at which children move from ECE into CSE* varies considerably. In most affluent countries, the compulsory school age (CSA) is 6 years, but in some cases it is 5 and, in a few cases, 7. In some countries, parents may choose to start their children at primary school before the CSA, for example between 4 and 5 in Ireland (CSA 6), the Netherlands and the United Kingdom (CSA 5), and at 6 in Denmark and Sweden (CSA 7); in most cases, parents take this option where it is available. A few countries, too, are making the later years of ECE compulsory (e.g. Poland from 6; Austria, Hungary and Latvia from 5, Luxembourg from 4), blurring the distinction between early childhood and compulsory education.

As already indicated, *the structuring of ECE* is mostly as a split system, by which I mean there are two separate sectors providing services for children before they enter compulsory schooling: 'childcare' and 'early education'. Often these serve different age groups, 'childcare' under 3s, 'early education' over 3s, though in some countries, such as England, 'childcare' services may run up to CSA, often in parallel with 'early education' for children over 3. The sectors typically differ in important respects: administration, regulation, curriculum, access, funding, workforce and types of provision. This is not a case of different but equal, but different and unequal, with 'childcare' and services for under 3s less favourably treated than education and services for over 3s. Typically, over 3s have an entitlement or at least widespread access to service, under 3s do not; over 3s get free provision for some or all of their hours of attendance, under 3s do not; and over 3s have a better qualified and paid workforce than under 3s. The provision of services is split, with one set of 'childcare' services (e.g. nurseries, crèches) and another set of 'education' services (e.g. nursery classes or schools, kindergartens), often requiring children to transfer from one type of provision to another at around 3 years of age.

Within countries where ECE is split, there are some variations. A few countries, such as England, have integrated administrative responsibility for all ECE within education, as well as an integrated regulatory system and curriculum; but they have not gone further, remaining split in key areas such as access, funding, workforce and type of provision. There is also an important difference between countries in the relative balance between 'childcare' and 'early education'. Countries in the English-speaking world typically have an 'early education' system limited to one or two years of part-time attendance, often in a primary school-based nursery or kindergarten class; the 'childcare' system takes children up to 3 and often beyond, being available for a full day. By contrast, many countries in Continental Europe have a three year 'early education' system, often available for a full school day, and a 'childcare' system confined to children under 3; France is a well-known example of this arrangement. The 'childcare' system dominates in the former countries, the 'early education' system in the latter.

There are, however, a few exceptions to this widespread pattern of 'split' ECE, countries that have achieved a fully integrated ECE system, with no distinction between 'childcare' and 'education', or between services for under and over 3s. The main examples are the five Nordic countries and Slovenia. In each case, the ECE system is today located in education. Here you find not only administrative integration, a 0–6 curriculum and single regulatory regime. You also find a universal entitlement to services from at least 12 months of age; a common system of service funding (tax-based and paid direct to services); a core 0–6 graduate professional (either a teacher or pedagogue) accounting for up to half the workforce; and most provision made in mixed-age centres, for children under and over 3 years. Underpinning this is an integrated way of thinking about ECE, which has long since got beyond the 'childcare'/'education' divide. As the Swedish preschool curriculum puts it, 'The pre-school should be characterised by a pedagogical approach, where care, nurturing and learning form a coherent whole'.

The *organisation of ECE and CSE* – in such areas as group sizes, child:adult ratios, the qualification of workers, the length of the day, the curriculum framework – varies considerably between countries, shaping the relationship between the two sectors. For example, in Denmark a 6-year-old will transfer to school from a kindergarten or age-integrated centre. The average staff:child ratio in these pre-school centres is about 1:6, and children are in groups of 20 to 22 with a mix of pedagogues[2] and assistants. The first year at school is in a 'kindergarten class', which children attend for 15–20 hours a week, with similar staffing to kindergartens or age-integrated institutions, i.e. pedagogues. Moving up to the first year of compulsory school at 7, children still attend for only about 20 hours a week. Children now are with teachers during this school time, but spend the rest of their day (as do kindergarten class children) in 'free-time services' with pedagogues. Children in ECE and CSE are covered by different curricula, the one for ECE being a brief framework document.

The experience of a French child is very different. She will move at the age of 6 years from one school, the *école maternelle*, to another, the *école élémentaire*, both in the education system and the responsibility of the Ministry of National Education. The average child:staff ratio is about 26:1 in an *école maternelle*, with one teacher and, in some cases though not always, an assistant. The teacher is qualified to work with children from 3 to 11 years of age. Moving straight into the *école élémentaire*, the child is again with a school teacher, and attends (as she did in *école maternelle)* for around 32 hours a week (an 8-hour day, with closure on Wednesday). Continuity between the two schools is further emphasised by a very detailed curriculum (*cycle des apprentissages fondamentaux*, cycle of foundation learning) that covers the last year in *école maternelle* and the first two years of *école élémentaire* (Oberhuemer *et al.*, 2010).

How might this structural context affect the ECE/CSE relationship? First, an ECE system that is split is also weakened, and this weakness is further exacerbated where the whole ECE period is reduced to just four or five years. Arguably, therefore, the chances of developing a 'strong and equal partnership' with CSE are greater – though definitely not guaranteed – where there is a strong ECE system and that, in turn, is more likely in those countries with a fully integrated system of ECE, which takes children up to at least 6 years, and includes an integrated 0–6 profession.

Second, countries where ECE is split usually add another transition to children's lives, from 'childcare' to 'early education', often around the age of 3 years. Furthermore, the 'early education' part, being often closely associated with CSE or even situated in primary schools, is already strongly influenced by or partly subsumed into CSE – there is a built-in tendency to schoolification. The relationship between ECE and CSE becomes further differentiated: there is a relationship issue *within* ECE – between 'childcare' and 'early education' – as well as *between* 'early education' (ECE) and 'primary education' (CSE). The 'early education' system then becomes very liable to a 'readiness for (big) school' role, offering a sort of 'preparatory schooling' for primary schools, to which it is tightly tied by strong gravitational forces. The consequence may be a widening gap between 'childcare' and 'early education'.

Relationship 1: readying for school

In this relationship, ECE assumes a subordinate role of preparing young children to perform well in CSE, by governing the child effectively to ensure that he or she acquires the knowledge, skills and dispositions required to be a successful learner in compulsory education, for example ready for the rapid acquisition of literacy and numeracy and able to participate in classroom regimes. ECE is, in this formulation, the lowest rung on the educational ladder, the first step of a linear process of educational progression consisting of a sequence of predefined goals, each needing to be achieved before moving on to the next. Primary or elementary education becomes the frame of reference for ECE, especially the nearer children move to compulsory school age, just as 'secondary' or 'high' school becomes the frame of reference for the upper years of primary education, and university or college becomes the frame of reference for the upper years of secondary school. Not just standards and expectations, but pedagogical ideas and practices cascade down the system, from top to bottom.

This relationship of ECE readying children for CSE – preparing the young child to the specification of primary or elementary school – is not new. But it has been reinforced in recent years by increasingly dominant discourses of lifelong learning and early intervention. Policy makers have been persuaded that children have the capacity to learn from birth or soon after; early childhood, it is argued, is 'an important phase for developing important dispositions and attitudes towards learning' (OECD, 2001, p. 128). The early years are, therefore, a necessary part of lifelong learning which, at a time of growing global competition, is seen as a necessary condition for national survival strategies. Education across the lifecourse sustaining 'knowledge economies' has been grasped as the answer to maintaining a continuing place in the sun, especially in the former industrialised 'West' as the storm clouds of competition and economic power blow in from the East.

In some quarters, ECE has moved from being just one stage in lifelong learning to being the most important. Human capital theorists have asserted that the most productive form of educational investment, bearing the best returns, is to be made in children below compulsory school age. For example, the work of James Heckman is widely quoted, with its conclusion that,

viewed purely as an economic development strategy, the return on investment to the public of early childhood development programmes 'far
exceeds the return on most projects that are currently funded as economic
development' (Heckman and Masterov, 2004), and represents a better
return than investment in later stages of education. Inspired by such asser-
tions, the European Commission has argued for ECE on the grounds that:

> Pre-primary education has the highest returns in terms of the achieve-
> ment and social adaptation of children. Member States should invest
> more in pre-primary education as an effective means to establish the
> basis for further learning, preventing school drop-out, increasing equity
> of outcomes and overall skill levels.
>
> (2006, p. 5)

But the interest in ECE is bolstered by further considerations, in particular
its perceived potential as an early intervention technology for children vari-
ously described as poor, vulnerable, excluded or disadvantaged, which, it
is argued, can determine later performance, be it in school, employment or
wider society, so reducing the inequalities that remain stubbornly persistent or are even growing. This hope, that human technology such as 'good
quality' ECE can reduce or remove profound social and economic problems, has been particularly appealing to those (often Anglophone)
countries that have some of the highest levels of social and health problems in the affluent world (Wilkinson and Pickett, 2009), whilst having
lagged behind Continental Europe in the development of ECE. ECE seems
to offer a modern day philosopher's stone that can achieve fundamental
transformations through applying human technologies[3] (usually described
under the heading of 'good quality') at an early age, obviating the need to
tackle directly deep-rooted inequalities and other injustices.

The discourses of lifelong learning and of early intervention are often
linked with, indeed subsumed into, the standards-based reform movement in
education, with its focus on setting clear, measurable standards for what
students should know and be able to do and which determine all other
features of the education system. This represents a view of education that is
strongly instrumental in rationality, strongly reproductive and transmissive in
pedagogy, and strongly technical in practice. For education to 'deliver' on
'efficiency and equity', precise and predefined standards of performance must
be set at each stage of the educational process, 'effective' (evidence-based)
technologies must be applied to achieve them and to assess achievement, and
each part of the education system must be devoted to preparing students for
the next stage of progression. ECE is then locked into a system that expects
children to achieve a succession of prescribed standards, serving as a 'foundation' that readies children for the stage of education that is to follow.

This particular 'school readiness' relationship, liable to lead to schoolification of ECE, can be found in many countries, and according to *Starting Strong II* is spreading: 'in the early childhood field, an instrumental and narrow discourse about readiness for school is increasingly heard' (OECD 2006, p. 219). The OECD report argues that this type of relationship is most prominent in countries that have adopted what it terms a 'pre-primary approach to early education', for example France, the Netherlands and several English-speaking countries including Australia, Canada, Ireland, the UK and the USA. These countries, the report says 'tend to introduce the contents and methods of primary schooling into early education' (p. 61). This approach is contrasted by OECD to what it terms the 'social pedagogy tradition', found in Nordic and Central European countries, which adopts a broad pedagogical approach 'combining care, upbringing and learning, without hierarchy... [with centres] seen as a broad preparation for life... [and in which] a more holistic approach to learning is practiced and greater emphasis is placed on learning to live together' (pp. 59–60).

Starting Strong II pays particular attention to the 'readiness to learn' relationship between ECE and CSE in the United States, which it argues contributes to making this particular relationship 'a powerful one [in other countries], as it is carried by American (English-language) research to all countries... [holding] out the promise to education ministries of children entering primary school prepared to read and write' (OECD 2006, p. 63). This readiness relationship appears in the National Education Goals set out in 1992 and incorporated into the 1994 Educate America Act, which states that 'by the year 2000, all children in America will start school ready to learn' to be achieved through all children having 'access to high-quality and developmentally appropriate preschool programs that help prepare children for school' (Section 102). In 2002, the *Good Start, Grow Smart* early learning initiative encouraged individual states to develop early learning guidelines to promote literacy and school readiness. While one of the main goals for the Head Start programme for young children, targeted at low income families, is to get children ready for school.

The result of this 'readiness for school' discourse, as reported by *Starting Strong II*, is that most states in the USA have adopted learning standards for pre-kindergarten and kindergarten children.

> These standards announce a range of knowledge, skills and dispositions that children are expected to develop as a result of classroom experiences, and focus increasingly on knowledge and skills useful for school, *viz.*, literacy, math and scientific thinking. There is a growing consensus among American educators and public policy makers that programme standards are needed in early education, and should include child outcomes – what children should know and be able to do after participating in pre-school programmes.
>
> (OECD, 2006, p. 63)

The report notes some expressed reservations. Various 'reputable bodies' have called for 'a broad interpretation of standards', but to little effect since 'current American policy values a "readiness for school" approach, which the administration sees as ensuring that all young children acquire basic knowledge and skills, and that continuity is provided between elementary school, kindergartens and pre-kindergartens' (ibid.).

The same readiness discourse is apparent elsewhere. An active example is England. The English Department for Education, in its 'Business Plan 2011–2015', announced plans to develop new indicators of 'readiness to progress to the next stage of schooling', including one set for early years to primary, as well as another for primary to secondary school (English Department for Education, 2010a, p. 22). The same department, when instituting in 2010 a review of the Early Years Foundation Stage (EYFS), the 'statutory framework for setting the standards for learning, development and care for children from 0–5 years', announced that they wanted 'to shift the focus to getting children ready for education' and that they had requested the review to look at 'the latest evidence about children's development and what is needed to give them the best start at school' (English Department for Education, 2010b, p. 1). The subsequent revised EYFS, published in 2012, 'defines what providers must do...to ensure [children] are ready for school' (English Department for Education, 2012, p. 4). This readiness discourse is also apparent in a 2011 report on early intervention commissioned by the UK government, which recommends that

> the United Kingdom should adopt the concept of the *foundation years from 0 to 5* (including pregnancy), and give it at least the same status and recognition as primary or secondary stages. Its prime objective should be to produce high levels of *'school readiness'* for all children regardless of family income.
>
> (Allen, 2011, p. 46, original emphasis)

It should, however, be recognised that despite this increasingly dominant 'readiness for school' discourse, 'readiness' itself can have wider meanings, including some that are far from the crude but influential concept of ECE preparing children for education in CSE. Even in the USA, the meaning of school readiness is contested, with different meanings having different implications for the relationship between ECE and CSE. The reader may have noted already some potentially significant variations in terminology: ready to learn, ready for education, ready for school. Sharon Lynn Kagan, a leading figure in American early education and author of Chapter 6, picks up on these distinctions in her summary of the situation from an American perspective:

From its earliest use, the word 'readiness' has amassed scores of different meanings, provoked legions of debates, and confused parents and
teachers (Kagan, 1990). It appeared in print in the 1920s, with two
constructs vying for prominence – readiness for learning and readiness
for school. Advanced by developmentalists, readiness for learning was
regarded as the level of development at which the individual has the
capacity to undertake the learning of specific material – interpreted as
the age at which the average group of individuals has acquired the
specified capacity (May and Campbell, 1981).

Readiness for school is a more finite construct, embracing specific
cognitive and linguistic skills (such as identifying colours, distinguishing a triangle from a square). Irrespective of academic domain, school
readiness typically sanctions standards of physical, intellectual and
social development sufficient to enable children to fulfil school requirements (Wincenty-Okon and Wilgocka-Okon, 1973).

To complicate matters, a third construct, that of maturational readiness, has evolved. Accepting the school readiness tenet that children
should be expected to achieve a fixed standard prior to school entry,
maturationists also acknowledge children's individual time clocks. They
believe that, because children do not develop at the same pace, they
will not achieve the school readiness standard at the same time.
Readiness, then, is not determined by chronological age but by developmental capacity (Ilg and Ames, 1965). Quite popular until recently,
this perspective has given way to other approaches, especially through
the influence of Vygotsky's theories (Vygotsky, 1978). He noted that
children grow into the intellectual life around them and that development is actually stimulated by the learning experiences offered in
formal settings. Rather than keeping children out of school until they
are ready, children need to be in learning environments where adults
and peers will nurture their learning and development. This model of
'guided participation' has now been elaborated in relation to early
childhood (Rogoff, 1990, 2003) and offers an alternative to readiness
concepts.

(Kagan, 2007, p. 14)

Christopher Brown, in the prelude to his account of a study of how ECE
'stakeholders' in a Texas school district sought to align their work with the
expectations of a standards-based system of CSE, also acknowledges
diverse understandings of the concept of readiness. Drawing on Meisels
(1999), he identifies four that are particularly prominent in educational and
political debates in the United States:

An idealist/nativist conception of readiness frames this construct as
being 'a within-the-child phenomenon', and the child is ready for

school depending upon 'a function of maturational processes inherent in [each] child', which leaves little room for the role of environment in explaining a child's readiness...

[An empiricist/environmental conception of readiness] views 'readiness [as] something that lies outside the child'...[emphasising] that the child needs to engage in a particular set of experiences to be ready for school [with ECE being a means for providing these experiences]...

The social constructionist framework views readiness as a fluid construct that is defined by the social setting in which the child resides...and as such, a child can be ready in one community but not another.

[The] interactionist perspective frames readiness as a 'bidirectional concept', meaning that readiness is co-constructed from the child's contribution to schooling and the school's contribution to the child.

(Brown, 2010, pp. 136–137)

The 'bidirectional concept' has had some impact, in particular an increased discussion in the United States of the need for a ready school for a school ready child. The same National Education Goals Panel that in 1992 set children's readiness to learn on school entry as a national goal, 'recognized [in 1998] that expecting all children to be ready to learn was not sufficient; we also needed all schools to be ready for all children' (Ritchie *et al.*, p. 162). Individual states, private foundations and national educational associations have given support to a Ready Schools movement, whose focus is 'smooth transitions' and 'sustained coherence and alignment in the education of children across ages 3–8' (ibid., p. 163), to be achieved on the basis of 'sound principles of child development' (p. 320).

Such nuanced and varied understandings of 'readiness' may influence current research in the United States and 'across the globe'. But as long as the tide of standards-based educational reform flows strong, it is 'child readiness' that will continue to have more sway in policy, locating the problem in the child and in an insufficiently schoolified ECE whose future role must be presenting children to the presumed starting line for education, compulsory schooling, ready to succeed in a standards-based system. From this perspective, the only productive communication to be had across each successive stage of the system is for educators to make clear to those in the stage below them what they expect and need from children when passed up to them: in effect, a monologue.

Relationship II: a strong and equal partnership

The first report of OECD's major cross-national thematic review of early childhood education and care, *Starting Strong I*, notes a 'welcome trend towards increased co-operation between ECEC and the school system in

terms of both policy and practice' (p. 128). But the report also acknowledges a darker side to this 'welcome trend': 'a risk of downward pressure
from a school-based agenda to teach specific skills and knowledge in early
years' (p. 41), leading to a 'school-like approach to the organisation of early
childhood provision' and the adoption of 'the content and methods of the
primary school' with a 'detrimental effect on young children's learning'
(OECD, 2001, p. 129). This schoolification process, the report warned,
threatens to bring inappropriate practice into early childhood education,
narrowing the education on offer as a focus on literacy and numeracy leads
'to neglect of other important areas of early learning and development' (p.
42): in short, subjecting ECE to a conservative and impoverished form of
education.

So co-operation with schools is to be welcomed – but only as long as
ECE is 'viewed not only as a preparation for the next stage of education...but also as a distinctive period where children live out their own
lives' and if 'the specific character and traditions of quality early childhood
practice are preserved' (ibid.). This leads to one of the review's eight policy
lessons, which together constitute 'key elements in a successful ECEC
policy': the need for 'a strong and equal partnership [of ECEC] with the
education system' (OECD, 2001, p. 128). The way this policy lesson is
expressed – not only a strong partnership but also an equal one – introduces a second dimension into the relationship, that it is not just a matter
of closeness but also one of power. A strong partnership may not necessarily be an equal one, especially given the powerful gravitational pull of
the compulsory school, established for many years and a central institution
in modern nation states: the partnership can bring benefits, but it may also
entail dangers.

The report goes on to characterise the kind of partnership it advocates
in rather more detail, making it clear that ECE has much to offer CSE:

> Strong partnerships with the education system provide the opportunity
> to bring together the diverse perspectives and methods of both ECEC
> and schools, *focusing on the strengths of both approaches,* such as the
> emphasis on parental involvement and social development in ECEC
> and the focus on educational goals and outcomes in schools...ECEC
> and primary education could *benefit from the knowledge and experi-
> ence of young children accumulated in each sector,* and in the process
> help children and families negotiate the transition from ECEC to school
> (p. 129, emphasis added).

There is, in short, a mutually beneficial dialogue to be had between ECE
and CSE in a strong and equal partnership based on each sector having
something to offer the other.

A number of more specific recommendations are made to promote 'equality of relationship and a strong continuity between early childhood provision and the education system' (OECD, 2001, p. 58). These include: the recognition of early childhood services as a public good and an important part of the education process, putting them on a par with compulsory schooling; the adoption of a 'more unified approach to learning [across both parts], recognising the contribution that the early childhood approach brings to fostering key dispositions and attitudes to learning'; and paying attention to 'transition challenges faced by young children as they enter school [with a greater focus on] building bridges across administrative departments, staff-training, regulations and curricula in both systems' (OECD, 2001, pp. 58–59).

These themes are repeated and developed in the review's second and final report, *Starting Strong II*. Picking up on the theme of 'a more unified approach' to learning in order to bring ECE and CSE closer together, the report identifies different options, underpinned by different premises:

> Broadly, one can distinguish two different approaches across countries. France and the English-speaking countries see the question of partnership from the point of view of the [compulsory] school: early education should serve the objectives of public education and provide children with 'readiness for school' skills. In contrast, countries inheriting a social pedagogy tradition (the Nordic and Central European countries) see kindergarten as a specific institution turned more to supporting families and the broad developmental needs of young children.
>
> (OECD, 2006, p. 59)

While the relationship between ECE and CSE is spelt out for the first option – the school dominates the relationship – it is less clearly defined for the social pedagogical approach. Later reference is made to continuity being established through 'agreement on fundamental values and concepts, and through the identification of general learning areas' (p. 60), as well as through the institution in the Nordic countries of classes for 6-year-olds in school, usually attended on a voluntary basis but which have in effect served to transfer this whole age group from early childhood centres into school:

> This class for children 6 to 7 years old serves as a bridge into compulsory primary schooling (which begins at 7 years), and generally takes place within the school. The pedagogy employed in these classes remains active and experiential, and learning is generated not only by adults but through peer relationships, group projects and active pedagogy…In addition, pre-schools and schools, particularly in Sweden, are forging together agreed values and pedagogical approaches.
>
> (pp. 60–1)

This seems to describe an equal relationship based on shared thinking, with even some influence by ECE on CSE via the 'pre-school class' for 6-year-olds and the introduction into school of pre-school educators: 'Rather than 'schoolifying' ECEC services, there is a strong belief that early childhood pedagogy should permeate the lower classes of primary school' (OECD, 2006, p. 59). This upward influence, the opposite of 'schoolification', has something in common with the hopes expressed by the Swedish Prime Minister Göran Persson, when announcing in 1996 the transfer of ECE from welfare into education, 'that the pre-school should influence at least the early years of compulsory school' (Korpi, 2005, p. 10).

Having raised these two options, *Starting Strong II* is at pains to moderate the impression of a simple either/or dualism: 'rather than making too sharp a contrast between the two approaches, it may be more accurate to see them as different curricular emphases, one merging into the other as part of the same continuum' (OECD, 2006, p. 63). At the same time, the report raises the question of how far 'schoolification' is taking place. Examples of this, it is argued, can be found in some countries where 'early education was absorbed early on...by a knowledge-transfer, primary education model, and was conceived chiefly as a "junior school"'. Signs of this include:

> Teachers (who) are trained predominantly in primary school methods and have little or no certification in early childhood pedagogy. Classes are organised – as in primary school – according to year of age, with young children spending much of their time indoors, doing their letters and numbers in preparation for school...Teacher instruction is considered essential...with a pronounced downward dynamic toward the group class. Less attention is given to horizontal dynamics that encourage peer exchanges and children's own discovery and meaning-making. The natural learning strategies of young children – play, exploration of the outdoors and freedom of movement, relations and discussion with other children within the classroom – are not always encouraged.
>
> (OECD, 2006, p. 62)

While the report provides no explicit answer to its question about 'schoolification' taking place, the implication of its discussion seems to be that (a) it is and (b) this is problematic.

The report reserves its most outspoken comments on the ECE/CSE relationship for the final part of the final chapter – the final word of the whole project. It makes it clear that what should be at stake, the focus of educational concern, is the future of the compulsory school. What is needed is profound change in the pedagogical thinking and practice of CSE, and ECE has a potentially important contribution to make to that change. What becomes clear is that the concept of a 'strong and equal partnership' envisages the prospect of a new and better relationship between ECE and a *reformed* compulsory school.

> Hargreaves (1994), in his critical work on teachers, is at pains to point out that the response of public education systems [to the cultural revolution brought about by globalisation and its effects] has been deeply anachronistic. Organisation, curriculum and decision-making in schools continue to resemble 19th century patterns: curricula imbibed with the certainties of the past, formal testing of discrete skills and knowledge items, and the 'balkanisation' of teachers into separate classrooms and disciplines. The school as an education institution cannot continue in this way. Knowledge is inter-disciplinary and increasingly produced in small networks. In the future, it will be constructed through personal investigation, exchange and discussion with many sources, and co-constructed in communities of learning characterised by team teaching. This approach to knowledge can begin in early childhood and, in fact, fits well with the child's natural learning strategies, which are fundamentally enquiry based and social.
>
> (OECD, 2006, pp. 221–2)

What both *Starting Strong* reports do is to set out the importance and the dangers of the relationship between early childhood and compulsory school education. They indicate there are choices to be made in the relationship, but imply there is a move underway towards a particular choice – 'schoolification'. The drawbacks and dangers of this choice are made increasingly clear, ending with a stark warning about pushing down an educational model that is not only inappropriate for younger children but also for older children, being unsuited to the times we live in and our understandings of knowledge and learning. Our attention, the report implies, should turn away from ECE readying children for CSE, and focus instead on the reform of compulsory school.

The *Starting Strong* reports, with their advocacy of a 'strong and equal partnership', envisage a 'bidirectional concept' for the relationship between ECE and CSE. But unlike the 'interactionist perspective' in the school readiness approach, referred to above, the bidirectionality foregrounded here is between two sectors of the education system, rather than between child and school. The emphasis is strongly on change in institutional relationships. But while *Starting Strong* alerts us to issues involved in the relationship between ECE and CSE, and offers a second possible future direction for that relationship, it does not go far into the causes of current problematic relationships, the potential obstacles to achieving a 'strong and equal partnership', or what forging such a partnership might require. For such a critical analysis, we must turn to Sweden.

Relationship III: the vision of a meeting place

A third possible relationship between ECE and CSE is the central theme of another key text. As already noted, *Förskola och skola – om två skilda traditioner och om visionen om en mötesplats* (Preschool and school – two different traditions and the vision of a meeting place) is a paper prepared by two Swedish academics (Dahlberg and Lenz-Taguchi, 1994) for a 1994 Swedish government committee report *Grunden för livslångt lärande: En barnmogen skola* (The foundation for lifelong learning: a school ready for children). It appears as Appendix 3 in that report and was also separately published. The focus is very much on Sweden: Swedish history, traditions, education systems and so on. But its analytical method offers an approach to the ECE/CSE relationship that is more widely applicable, and its solution to the *problematique* that the analysis reveals provides possibilities that can inform discussion beyond the borders of Sweden.

The paper and report were written in the context of discussions in Sweden about the relationship between ECE services (called *förskolan* or 'pre-school', a centre for children from 1 to 6 years of age), then situated in the welfare system under the Ministry of Social Affairs, and schools. It was a period of major structural changes with implications for that relationship. In 1990, local authorities, already responsible for ECE, also assumed full responsibility for CSE, when national government decentralised employment of school teachers to them. A year later, new legislation gave local authorities more freedom, which many used to integrate pre-schooling and schooling into one department; in 1996, national responsibility for ECE was transferred from welfare to education, where it sat alongside CSE. The 1990s also saw major changes in the organisation of services: 6-year-olds moved out of pre-schools and into 'pre-school classes' in schools; 'free-time centres', for school-age children outside school hours, also moved into schools and became the responsibility, locally and nationally, of education; team working developed in schools, involving pre-school and school teachers and free-time pedagogues,[4] three distinct and graduate professions working together with mixed-age groups of children.[5] At the same time, there was a strong discourse on the need to develop 'lifelong learning' as the basis for Sweden's successful survival as a 'knowledge economy' in the global marketplace, with the early years recognised in that discourse as 'the first step towards realising a vision of lifelong learning' (Korpi, 2005, p. 10).

For all these reasons, the relationship between ECE and CSE was very much on the policy and political agenda in 1990s Sweden. But that relationship was conditioned by one other important feature of the Swedish ECE system. By the 1990s, Sweden had a very well developed ECE system. Provision was extensive, following major expansion of services since the 1970s. Furthermore, instead of being split between 'childcare' and 'early education' or between services for children under and over 3, a widespread arrangement as already noted outside the Nordic countries, Swedish ECE for children from 1 to 6 years was fully integrated, including a workforce organised around a core graduate professional – the pre-school teacher working across the early childhood age range. Moreover, this integrated system had developed and found its identity outside the education system, very different from a split system (like France) with a nursery education sector (the *école maternelle*) that had grown up as part of the school system. If not equal in power and status to the school, ECE in Sweden as it entered the 1990s was stronger, more distinctive and more coherent than in most other countries, contributing to a very particular climate in which debate about the relationships between it and CSE took place.

It was in this context that Dahlberg and Lenz-Taguchi were commissioned to prepare their paper. Their brief is set out at the beginning: 'to illuminate the cultural encounter between school and pre-school, as well as the pedagogical possibilities and risks involved in an integration of the two school forms.' The authors are clear that their purpose is not 'to present a new pedagogical method', but rather 'to invite a discussion about children's learning and creation of knowledge, the contents and working methods of the pre-school and school, as well as the pedagogical value base'. Their paper is organised into two main parts, the first dealing with the 'pedagogical traditions' of pre-school and school, and containing an 'analysis of the defined problem'; the second setting out a new relationship, 'a vision of a possible meeting place'.

The importance of traditions

Dahlberg and Lenz-Taguchi note the same general tendency in the relationship between ECE and CSE as did *Starting Strong* a few years later: 'one can clearly see internationally...that the [compulsory] education system tends to go further down in age.' Previous expansion of the school system upwards in age has now left countries to concentrate on 'the possibilities to teach children at an even earlier age.' This downward pressure on ECE, 'schoolification', has potentially serious consequences – for children, for curriculum and for pedagogical work:

> There is a great risk that children may be labelled at an earlier age than today, if they are not able to manage the increased requirements. In this situation, the problem is put onto the children, in terms of their lack of ability and competence...Many children learn even when they are thought not able to learn, and unfortunately what they are going to learn at an even earlier age is that they cannot learn...From international studies, we know that national tests and evaluations seem to be standardising not only the curriculum, but also the teaching content

and working methods...[T]he demand for measurable learning outcomes at such an early age can easily lead to a very narrow and simple view of knowledge. One fears that increasing emphasis on evaluation of the child's competence is going to change the view of what is indicative of good pedagogical activity. There is also a fear that the upper levels of the education system would, to an even greater degree, be able to define the content and way of working in the lower levels.

The starting point for Dahlberg and Lenz-Taguchi is this inequality in the ECE/CSE relationship, so that 'the school's culture clearly dominates over the pre-school's when it comes to prestige and status'. To exemplify the point, they draw on the work of Norwegian researcher Peder Haug, author of Chapter 5 in this volume, and his study of a Norwegian experiment involving closer co-operation between pre-schools and schools in the education of 6-year-olds. What emerged was the gravitational pull of schools on pre-schools and their educators: 'during the four years of the experiment in Norway, Peder Haug was able to observe that the number of situations which were adult steered increased...[and] the possibility for free play was reduced'.

> Both in Haug's own and other studies, it was shown that pre-school teachers who come into the school teach, instruct and explain more for the children than school teachers do when they teach! The pre-school teachers over-emphasise what they believe to be the school's methods, with a teacher in front of the classroom speaking while children are listening.

During the course of the Norwegian experiment, pre-school activities and pre-school teachers were in effect increasingly schoolified, at the same time that an 'academic pre-school' was increasingly favoured in political and societal debates. What seems to be happening here is an example of what Foucault terms 'governmentality', the way in which power is exercised not directly and coercively, but through individuals embodying dominant discourses – including concepts, rationalities, techniques and practices – and then governing themselves in conformity with these discourses. In such ways, far from pre-school pedagogy influencing the first few grades of school, as some have hoped, the powerful school comes to control the pedagogical processes of pre-school classes introduced into the school. It may be that, as a recent UK report puts it, 'there is no reason why good quality play-based learning...cannot be provided in primary schools' (Cambridge Primary Review, 2009, p. 17) – but in practice it can prove hard to achieve because of the pervasive, powerful and distinctive influence of the pedagogical traditions of CSE.

Traditions play a crucial role. What Haug's work shows, and what becomes central to Dahlberg's and Lenz-Taguchi's analysis of the ECE/CSE relationship, is the significance of the traditions of each sector, both to their current ways of working and to any prospect of changed relationships. Educational reform is not just a matter of political intent and top-down implementation: it is the product, too, of a variety of economic, political, cultural and social influences, including the traditions of educational institutions and their workforces that find expression in values, social constructions, identities and practices. Such traditions cannot be ignored or simply opposed: 'reforms which involve too large a conflict with the routines and values and, therefore, the identity of institutions have little chance of being successful'. It is important, therefore, for reform to show some understanding of traditions, and the identities they help constitute, a theme to which the researchers return in proposing their solution to the need for a new relationship.

But first, the authors develop their analysis of the pedagogical traditions of ECE and CSE. In doing so, they pay particular attention to the social construction of the child inscribed in each tradition. For as they emphasise, 'the child is always a social construction and not the actual child'.[6] Central to their analysis is that ECE and CSE in Sweden have two separate constructions of the child – 'the child as nature' and 'the child as a re-producer of culture and knowledge' – so that 'the pre-school has taken a position opposite to that of the school'.

The 'child as nature', or 'the scientific child', in the ECE tradition draws both on Enlightenment thinkers such as Rousseau and on psychological theories, in particular child development. In a later book, Dahlberg describes this image of the child as 'an essential being of universal properties and inherent capabilities whose development is viewed as an innate "natural" process – biologically determined, following general laws ... [in] a standard sequence of biological stages that constitute a path to full realisation' (Dahlberg *et al.*, 2007, p. 46). Inscribed with this construction, the ECE tradition values a holistic view of the child; free play and creativity, giving rise to free and self-confident people; free expression of ideas and feelings; fun; and the here-and-now. Put simply, 'one could say that the construction of the child as nature is naturally in the child – everything is in the child, and must be given the freedom to be expressed, reworked and developed'; and that 'today's pre-school is permeated with this type of thinking'.

By contrast the tradition in the Swedish compulsory school, despite its international reputation as relatively child-centred, is 'dominated by the reproduction of the prevailing culture and knowledge', and hence a social construction of the child as 'a re-producer of culture and knowledge.' With this construction, as Dahlberg has written later, the child is 'understood as starting life with and from nothing – as an empty vessel or tabula rasa ... [needing] to be filled with knowledge, skills and dominant cultural values which are already determined, socially determined and ready to administer – a process of reproduction or transmission' (ibid., p. 44). There is greater emphasis than in the pre-school's child on the future and economic life. The school is subject centred, meaning that 'the basis for all activities is linked to the learning of concrete subject knowledge ... with the transfer of concrete and assessable knowledge as the goal.' These subjects are mostly decided and organised by others, and not the children, in contrast to the 'pre-school's tradition of child-centredness, where the ideal is that the child, as much as possible, should choose the contents and forms of expression'.

The construction of the child as re-producer and the centrality of subjects in the CSE tradition are associated with a teacher-directed learning in which teachers dominate classroom interactions:

> Of all sentences spoken in the classroom, the teacher speaks half. The teacher's sentences are also much longer. The teacher's role is to struc-ture the contents, the activities and the situations, as well as ask questions and comment on the children's answers. The child's role is to answer the teacher's questions. The teacher has the authority, while the children are more passive and are expected to do what is expected of them ... This coherent view of knowledge means that the adult has the knowledge which should be conveyed to the child. The adult talks and accounts for the knowledge with the expectation that the child should take the knowledge in an active way, learn it by heart and be able to repeat it ...
>
> The time division of subjects and breaks in the school mean that the time factor strongly steers both the choice of content and quality in the question-answer pattern and other contact between the individuals in the classroom. A great deal of time in the school is dedicated to the teacher asking questions of the students to which she already knows the answer.

This social construction of the child in the CSE tradition sits very well with a 'readiness for school' discourse. From this perspective, the task of ECE is to get this empty vessel sufficiently filled that she or he is ready to learn by the time of entry to compulsory school, meaning ready for teacher-directed learning and the compartmentalised, subject-centred life of the school regime.

Towards a common view of the child and teacher, learning and knowledge

The first part of the paper by Dahlberg and Lenz-Taguchi, through its crit-ical analysis, introduces an important insight into the relationship between ECE and CSE. Relations of power are important: but so too – at least in the

Swedish case – is the difference in tradition, since '[d]uring any period of change, it is usually clear that institutional traditions and culture are unavoidable components affecting or hindering the process of change'. The influence of tradition resides in large part in its capacity to give rise to different ways of understanding or constructing the child and the teacher, learning and knowledge – leading to a relationship between ECE and CSE of mutual incomprehension.

But given these two different traditions, of pre-school and school, the two different constructions of the child and teacher and the two different approaches to learning, how might the pre-school and the school come 'closer together in ways that maximise the pedagogical possibilities while reducing the risks involved?' Simply bringing ECE and CSE into closer proximity and calling for more co-operation without addressing differences in tradition and power runs a number of risks. One is a relationship based on a simple division of tasks: 'the pre-school teachers [will] take care of the play and the children's social development, while the school teachers take care of the intellect'. Another is confronting the children with two separate approaches, leaving them to encounter 'two or more separate traditions and thereby also meeting different ways to view learning and knowledge'. This is a recipe for fragmentation and confusion!

A better basis for a closer relationship, the authors argue, is the creation of shared understandings:

> If one wants to reach a long-term development of the pre-school and school's pedagogical work, then *a work of change, according to our way of thinking, begins with a common view of the child, learning and knowledge.* Such a work of change requires a conscious effort towards *reaching a true meeting place.* A meeting place where pre-school and school have a similar view of the learning child, pedagogy's role, and the pedagogical work and which is built on the same value base (emphases added).

In sum, a close and productive relationship, avoiding domination of one sector by the other, starts with co-constructing new and shared understandings: a 'common view' produced in a 'true meeting place.' This 'common view', they propose, might be based on an understanding or construction of the child neither as nature nor re-producer – but as a constructor of culture and knowledge and an investigative child:

> The idea that the child is a constructor of culture and knowledge builds a respect for the child as competent and curious – a child who is filled with a desire to learn, to research and develop as a human being in an interactive relationship with other people. It is a rich child. A child who takes an active part in the process of constructing knowledge. This child

is also active in the construction – the creation – of itself, their person-ality and their abilities, through interaction with the environment.

This view of the child is matched by an understanding or construction of the teacher, pre-school and school, similar in many respects to the view of the child, as a constructor of culture and knowledge.

> It is the teacher who sees her task in the process of knowledge construction to be *part co-driver, part guide or counsellor* who gives information about the journey's direction and stimulus for the rest of the journey, and *part driving force*, even if the direction is not always the one she had thought. This assumes a reflective practitioner who can function as an inspiration and through her documentation, and together with her colleagues, can create the possibility and the room for a living and critical discussion about pedagogical practices and their conditions (emphasis added).

The idea of the teacher with many roles is returned to later in the paper, when the authors also highlight the importance of listening:

> The view of the investigative teacher means a divided yet integrated professional responsibility, which partly has to do with joining in a dialogue and in communicative action with the child or the children's group, and partly has to do with a reflective and investigative attitude towards the child's working process and their own work . . . [T]he teacher takes on many roles. Sometimes a director, presenting a problem and initiating work around specific pre-planned material or introducing new information to continue the work. Sometimes prompting and assisting in the learning process as the child's own efforts begin to take a direction. Sometimes an adult voice is needed, or approving encouragement or help to go further when the process for some reason seems to have stalled. *The most difficult part of the teacher's work is to listen and let themselves be inspired by the children's questions and curiosity,* to keep all of their questions alive and to follow and study how the children search for answers to their own questions. The ideal, even if it is not always possible to attain, is for the teacher to understand the art of the listener and questioner, and not to give the child answers before the child has asked the questions. When the child asks a question, he is also saying: 'I know something! I want something!' Or in the apt expression of Maria Montessori: 'Help me to do it myself' (emphasis added).

This relationship between the investigative and co-constructing child and teacher is very different from the teacher-dominated, knowledge-transmitting relationship when the view of the child is as a knowledge re-producer. For it is based on the premise that the directions and outcomes of learning are not always pre-determined. This is (to borrow a term from Reggio Emilia) a pedagogy of relationships and listening (Rinaldi, 2006), not a pedagogy of transmission and question-answer.

The new relationship between teacher and child and the role of reflective practitioner calls for new tools and processes, in particular documentation. This should not be confused with 'so-called child observations, whose purpose was, first of all, to observe the child's psychological development'. Instead the purpose of documentation is to understand better the construction of learning and knowledge and indeed to contribute better to that process of construction.

> Documentation is about making the practice visible. It is a reflective way of relating to the practice...Through documenting what the child does and what one as the teacher does together with the child, one can see an increase in consciousness about the consequences of their [teachers'] actions, and thereby also gain a basis for change and development in their own work...In such a way, the practicing teacher can join in the development of new theories of children's socialisation, learning and construction of knowledge, with documentation providing the basis for this. In other words, the teachers can participate in the production of new knowledge. This places high demands on the teacher's professionalism, but that is also a challenge that can inspire, create enthusiasm and increase commitment. A pedagogical practice demands continual self-reflection and re-working if it is to be able to develop and change. The documentation is a resource, but without communication and dialogue around the documentation, there is no change.

Documentation can serve various purposes, including learning, assessment, the creation of a culture of investigation and reflection, and generating legitimacy for education, in both the pre-school and the school, legitimacy that is created 'when documentation is used in different ways as a visualisation of the pedagogy for the public'. The visualisation of pedagogical work made possible by documentation is important for fostering co-operation with parents, for 'public discussion about the pre-school and the school', and for giving every pre-school and school 'a public voice and a visual identity.'

This idea of documentation as visualisation for the public, as well as for the educators, has much in common with the thinking and practice of documentation in Reggio Emilia.[7] The biographer of Loris Malaguzzi, the first director of ECE in that city, argues that documenting was central to Malaguzzi's philosophy because behind this practice, I believe, is the ideological and ethical concept of a transparent school and transparent education...A political idea also emerges, which is what schools do must have public visibility; thus 'giving back' to the city what the city has invested in them... Documentation in all its different forms represents an extraordinary tool for dialogue, for exchange, for sharing. For Malaguzzi it means the possibility to discuss and dialogue 'everything with everyone'... [S]haring opinions by means of documentation presupposes being able to discuss real, concrete things – not just theories or words, about which it is easy to reach easy and naive agreement.

> (Hoyuelos, 2004, p. 7)

A shared use of documentation in ECE and CSE, therefore, provides multiple benefits. This is not only the opportunity for professionals to develop and deepen shared views or understandings, vital to a new relationship between ECE and CSE, but also the opportunity to develop and deepen education as a democratic practice and a community project.

But to create a new relationship between ECE and CSE, through a true meeting place, requires at least one more condition: for educators in both sectors to be 'equal colleagues', given that currently (even in Sweden) there are often significant discrepancies in education, pay and status to the detriment of those working in ECE. Such inequalities, bound up with issues of power and status, also need to be the subject of discussion and change, to reflect and support other changes in the relationship:

> In order for it to be possible to implement some form of co-operation between the pre-school and school, it is necessary to examine and make clear the value and power relationships which form the basis of both institutional forms. [This involves] questions on status, prestige, salary negotiations and other agreements, [questions which] are very important to discuss in the introductory phase.

A co-operative relationship or partnership calls, as far as possible, for a meeting between equals or, at the very least, clarity by all concerned about power relations and recognition that work needs to be done to reduce power differentials.

The meeting place

What Dahlberg and Lenz-Taguchi propose as the basis for a new relationship between ECE and CSE, a relationship that might be typified in *Starting Strong*'s terms as a 'strong and equal partnership', is not the dominance of one or other of the partners, not downward pressure from CSE or upward pressure from ECE, neither schoolification nor pre-schoolification. What they suggest instead is the creation, through co-construction, of new, shared understandings – of the child, of the teacher and her role, of knowledge, of learning – since what is done in any educational institution 'must always have a close connection to the view of the child and the view of knowledge that one wants the organisation to evoke'. The two parts of the educational system – ECE and CSE – must 'gather round a living pedagogical value-base and a practically applied philosophy... which has wide support from the personnel, parents, leadership, and politicians in the municipalities'.

Such goals are not easily achieved. Common understandings, the foundation for a new closer relationship, cannot be imposed. Dahlberg and Lenz-Taguchi propose, instead, that 'such a work of change requires a conscious effort towards reaching a true meeting place ... where pre-school and school settle on a similar view of the learning child, pedagogy's role and the pedagogical work, and which is built on the same value base'. This is a meeting place not only for co-constructing shared understandings, but to which both pre-school and school teachers can 'mutually contribute their professional knowledge, their culture, and their tradition ... each respective teacher group should bring new ideas to the other' (p. 21).

The meeting place is a space for reflecting on and constructing not only values, traditions, images and ideas, but also pedagogical practice. 'With a starting point of the view of the child as a constructor of culture and knowledge', Dahlberg and Lenz-Taguchi envision a meeting place 'where both the pre-school teachers and the primary school teachers are given the possibility to develop their pedagogical practices'. Their vision of a meeting place is, therefore, about creating a 'way of relating' between ECE and CSE, which is characterised by an approach that not only shows respect for and understanding of past traditions, but also is researching, reflective and analytical, an approach therefore that is dynamic and open.

Difficult as this may be, the authors believe that 'such a meeting is fully possible'. Several reasons give them hope. Despite their ontological and epistemological differences, the Swedish pre-school and school have much in common. There is the 'experience we have from the discussions going on today in both institutions (Swedish pre-schools and schools)'. There are the curriculum and goal documents, 'which build the foundation for the pedagogical work in the pre-school and school' including values for both ECE and CSE 'which are all about children's rights to equal life opportunities and education, to develop their resources and potential', as well as highlighting democracy as a fundamental value. Last but not least, and despite the differences in tradition and culture, there is a 'common heritage of ideas in the pre-school and school tradition' in Sweden, in particular 'the classic concept of *bildung*, progressivism and the philosophy of dialogue'.

Bildung today, the authors argue, is often used in a highly instrumental form, meaning the re-production of stable and pre-determined knowledge through transmission. But the classic German concept of *bildung* is quite different, in particular conveying the conception that a human being is, or should be, an entity that builds or creates itself and in a way that is not pre-ordained:

> *Bildung* is consequently something that humans do for themselves, an active business that entails an educator of ability who increases the individual's possibility of freedom...One of the Enlightenment project's basic ideas was faith in humans' reasoning ability to free humans socially, politically and culturally. This emancipatory way of thinking came from the idea that all humans have the possibility to actively create knowledge and the courage to think for themselves.

But this concept of *bildung* was not an exercise in individualism: '*bildung's* most important subject was people as a whole and not, as one can be led to believe, the individual himself', its concern being with how people participate in society. The concern with how humans participate both in the construction of knowledge and in society was also a feature of progressive education. This theme of relationships in education is also supported by the philosophy of dialogue:

> The acquiring of knowledge must be understood as a process that assumes an active interaction with other people and phenomena in the environment...The dialogical principle – the dialogical way of think-ing – is involved in a long philosophical tradition with its origins in Plato-Socratic dialogues...During the 1900s Martin Buber developed and clearly formulated in his main work, I and Thou *[Ich und Du]*, the idea that individual existence can only be developed in the presence of other people in similar circumstances...Knowledge is, for Buber, not something that individual people have or possess, but something one establishes or brings about through relationships to the world...This interactionist view of *bildung* is also alive in Elsa Köhler's[8] theory of culture. Köhler meant that cultural traditions cannot be passively taken over by a new generation, without being tested, redefined, rejected and newly developed by them via the subject's activity in relationship with his surroundings...
>
> In modern scientific philosophy, there is also support for similar ideas. Cybernetrician and biologist Gregory Bateson has, through his studies, found that teaching is not a simple transfer of a finished unit of *bildung*, but that the essence of learning and evolution is explo-ration and change. He says: 'In the transfer of human culture, people try to always copy and transfer to the next generation the skills and values of the parent generation, but the attempt always fails. This is unavoidable because the transfer of culture is connected with learning, not with DNA'.

What is being proposed here as the basis for a successful meeting place is finding a balance between discontinuity and continuity. On the one hand, it is about breaking up 'truth regimes', the dominant discourses that govern what we think and do and lead to the unthinking acceptance of certain constructions and pedagogical practices and to the dismissal of others. But on the other hand, the meeting place

> must build on that which is good and then go on, and not let there be a self-fulfilling prophecy, but instead a continual critical examination and reflection. When the child comes in through the door at the pre-school and the school, it should not be like entering a closed circle of tradition and institutionalised practices.

Apart from the common heritage of ideas that can facilitate the work of the meeting place, there are other reasons for being hopeful. The vision of a possible meeting place builds not only on a common heritage of ideas, but also on 'the vision of potentially equal communicative negotiations, social relationships, and insights about the importance of solidarity between people, as well as between society,...and the individual'. Pedagogical activities in both ECE and CSE are connected, or should be, to the same critical – or, as Mouffe would term it, political – question: 'what do we want for our children here and now and in the future – a question we must ask ourselves in every historical epoch.' Similarly we need a value-based discussion about another question, what do we want from our societal institutions?

Last but not least, ECE and CSE face the common challenge of responding to changing social conditions, which bring about altered relationships between children and adults, students and teachers, and recognising that learning is not confined to institutions:

> The gap between what adults know because they are adults and what the child and youth know becomes increasingly less important in our quickly changing society. It can even be the case that children and youth can understand and handle the modern society better than adults. This is especially clear when one views the way children and youth have handled the new channels of communication and media. In view of this, it is extra important that the pre-school and school strive towards a pedagogical philosophy which sees the child and starts from the child and their experiences and knowledge, which many times are inter-woven outside the pre-school and school. It is this knowledge and experience that the children take with them which must be used as a starting point for the continued learning.

What happened next

The paper by Dahlberg and Lenz-Taguchi aroused much interest in Sweden, addressing an issue of widespread concern and doing so in a way that many found creative and sympathetic. Some efforts were made subsequently to develop closer relationships not only between ECE and CSE, but also with free-time services which, as already noted, were moved into the education system at the same time as ECE and had been brought into schools along with their workforce of free-time pedagogues. A senior Swedish civil servant notes that:

> Initiatives taken since [the integration of ECE and free-time services into the education system] have sought to build closer links between pre-school, free-time services and school, treating all as equal parts of the education system. Development work is focusing on the integration of pre-school pedagogy into primary schools and creating pedagogical 'meeting places' between all three services.
>
> (Korpi, 2005, p. 10)

The extent, nature and consequences of this development work – what 'meeting places' were created and how they worked – has neither been documented nor evaluated on a national level. However, a national evaluation of pre-schools was conducted in 2008 by Skolverket (the National Agency for Education) to mark ten years since the pre-school received its own curriculum and became the first step for children into the overall education system, one consequence of the 1996 transfer of ECE into that system. This evaluation gives some indication of the changing relationship between ECE and CSE in Sweden since that major reform.

The evaluation notes that an 'underlying motive for the transfer to the educational system and the [pre-school] curriculum's introduction was to strengthen the pre-school's pedagogical assignment at the same time that pre-school pedagogy would have an increased impact in school' (Skolverket, 2008, p. 8). This is, perhaps, closer to the exchange model in the 'strong and equal partnership' relationship, with each side benefiting from the other's strengths. There is no reference to the idea of a 'meeting place', the report framing its discussion in terms of unidirectional influence, intended or otherwise. For one of the conclusions of the evaluation is that, rather than ECE having more impact on CSE, schoolification of ECE has been occurring, with the school having increased its impact on pre-schools, not the other way round:

> The pre-school has gained increased importance as a preparation for school, and the assignment has become narrower with a larger focus on language development. Children's development, performance and

proficiencies are being identified and assessed to an increasing extent. This development is hardly in line with the reform's intentions.

(ibid., p. 30)

The 'larger focus on language development' is viewed by Skolverket as evidence of more attention to preparation for school, which is in contrast to the broad approach contained in the pre-school curriculum:

> a large number of [municipalities] prioritise the work with language and language development with the justification that over the long-term, this improves the achievement of goals in compulsory school. This increases the possibility to interpret the results in terms of a shifting of the pre-school's assignment to increasingly involve acting as a preparation for compulsory school. The question is whether the strong prioritisation of one area in the curriculum is being made at the expense of the assignment to promote children's all-around development? International studies have brought attention to such developments in other countries where 'narrowing the curriculum' has become a more common pattern in pre-school and school.

(ibid., p. 29)

Skolverket relate their assessment to the distinction made in the two OECD *Starting Strong* reports between a 'pre-primary' and 'social pedagogy' approach to early childhood provision (see p. 11 above), noting that the recent development they observe in Sweden towards preparation for school is not only out of keeping with the intention behind ECE reforms but

> is in opposition to the curriculum tradition, which in an OECD context, is designated as the Nordic [i.e. social pedagogic] model and where Sweden is used as a good example. Consequently, the evaluation shows a complex and somewhat contradictory image where the educare [sic] model lives on and is being developed at the same time as the Swedish pre-school, in certain regards, is moving closer to another curriculum concept.

(ibid., p. 30)

So rather than the emergence of a pedagogical meeting place between pre-school and school, the Skolverket evaluation suggests a creeping advance of a 'readiness for school' relationship, with an accompanying 'schoolification' of the ECE system – though such change is neither universal nor officially sanctioned and the overall relationship remains very different from the USA or France.

But there is another way in which relationships between ECE and CSE can be gauged, that is in the continuing development of team working *within* schools, especially with children from 6 (when they enter non-compulsory 'pre-school classes') to around 10 or 11 years of age. The focus here is not on the relationship between ECE and CSE (except to the extent that attendance by 6-year-olds in pre-school classes in schools, before compulsory school age, might be termed part of ECE), but on the relationships that have developed in schools among pre-school teachers, school teachers and free-time pedagogues working together in teams. The development of team working may provide further insight into the feasibility of a 'meeting place' approach, given that one intention of team working has been for children and schools to benefit from a coming together of three professions, each with their own traditions, identities and competencies.

The reformed Swedish school – with its extended day and team working – has not received systematic national evaluation, as has the reformed pre-school; we are reliant, therefore, on patchier evidence from local studies (for a fuller discussion of the re-formed Swedish school, see Johansson and Moss, 2012). Most research has focused on organisation, for example the physical setting, leadership, time schedules and planning, and co-operation, in particular inter-professional working in schools, including the multi-professional team, and the relationship between pre-school classes, free-time services and the schools they are situated in (Persson, 2008). Within these teams, school teachers are most influential; they take the lead in planning and undertaking collaborative work. They are themselves aware of this leadership role and the other members agree with this way of working. But the teachers report being influenced by the team: they say they now work in a more flexible and child-centred way, and that they experience support from the team, especially the free-time pedagogues. Greater knowledge of other professionals has made them more aware of the whole day in school, including the free-time periods, as being a common responsibility and that using all of the team's competencies is necessary to achieve good results in teaching.

Teamworking, however, has not affected teachers' basic role: to be responsible for children's learning and choice of structured didactic tasks. Indeed, working in a team has made the teachers more conscious of their own professional competence as teachers; there is a clear division of pedagogical responsibilities between the teachers and the free-time pedagogues in the daily work. Nor has it affected their working schedules. Most school teachers still confine their presence in the team to 'school hours' (8 am to 2 pm), leaving the periods before and after to pre-school teachers and free-time pedagogues (who, consequently, are most likely to meet and know parents). In part, this reflects a continuing difference in employment conditions within the team: school teachers earn rather more than pre-school teachers and free-time pedagogues and are not required to spend more than school hours with children.

The free-time pedagogues agree with the teachers' accounts. They regard their focus as the social development of the child. They see their role as to support children's co-operation in a group and to try to establish a good balance between the more structured activity in the school during the morning and the freer and more child-centred activity in the afternoon. They consider children's free-time as important for informal learning and developing social competencies, including peer-group relations, values and norms. When they work together with a teacher in the classroom during school hours, there is a clear division of labour and responsibility between them: the teacher is accepted as the leader, in charge of classroom-based learning. The free-time pedagogue assists the teacher by, for example, working with pre-planned activities in a sub-group of pupils.

Research findings show that the active participation of the school principal is essential for developing a good climate for co-operation in which teams experience an atmosphere of openness to new solutions to old problems (Johansson, 2006). A number of other principles for successful team working have also been identified: common goals; team members feeling confident that they are allowed to develop their own work and to test new ideas in their daily practice; team members recognising that co-operation is the best way to undertake their respective tasks; co-operation proving rewarding for all team members; consensus about when and how co-operation should take place; and co-operation being recognised as a condition for collective learning processes (Ohlsson, 2004)

Pre-school classes for six-year-olds in school have also received some research attention. They were introduced to support a smooth transition between pre-school and school and, as we have seen, with the expectation that they would bring the influence of the pre-school into the school. But studies of the content of the pre-school class point to the same trend recorded earlier in Norway: the risk of 'schoolification', with the school culture and more traditional educational approaches tending to dominate the pre-school class so that it becomes, in reality, the first school year for the children (Karlsson *et al.*, 2006).

What is missing here is research into the processes of team formation and working, documenting what happens in the everyday school life at the meeting of these different professionals. We have no way of knowing how this complex relationship, between educators from three different traditions (pre-school, school and free-time), is enacted or evolves over time. So we do not know in any detailed way what types of relationships are emerging. How many work teams can be said to adopt a school-focused approach, with pre-school teachers and free-time pedagogues making few inroads and being subjected instead to 'schoolification' of their identities and practices? How many can be said to work with a 'strong and equal partnership', where the strengths and distinctive contribution of each profession are recognised and accommodated within the team? How many have adopted a 'pedagogical meeting place' approach, where all concerned have worked together to create new understandings and practices, albeit with some room for specialist inputs? And how many have assumed another form of relationship altogether? Furthermore, we do not know how far and in what way the complex process of team working has been supported; the role of the principal, noted above, indicates one potential source of support, but there could be many others.

Sweden, perhaps more than any other country, has confronted the relationship between ECE and CSE, as well as between CSE and free-time services. It has recognised the relationship to be complex and contentious, and discussed different forms it might take. There is acknowledgement, for example in the Skolverket evaluation of pre-school reforms, that implementation of reforms not only takes time – '[i]n the school area it often takes 10–15 years or more before you see the results of established reforms' – but that it can also 'lead to other results than those intended' for a variety of reasons:

> [the reasons can be] that the reforms have insufficient support, that they have not been clarified or have inner contradictions, that there are poor conditions in regard to the implementation, or that the reforms are not sufficiently strong enough in relation to existing traditions and established systems.
>
> (Skolverket, 2008, p. 18)

It is possible that there are instances of the successful re-formation of relationships – between pre-schools and schools and among team members working in schools – that have demonstrated the possibility of a 'strong and equal partnership' or creating a pedagogical 'meeting place'. If so, they have not been systematically documented. But the Skolverket study suggests a tendency, widespread enough to be picked up in a national evaluation, towards more unequal relationships, in which schools and school teachers are dominant partners and readiness for CSE is increasingly on the agenda of ECE.

Concluding reflections

> Criticism is a matter of flushing out that thought [which is present and operative in everyday behaviour, in the institutions we take for granted] and trying to change it; to show that things are not as self-evident as once believed, to see that what is accepted as self-evident will no longer be accepted as such ...
>
> In these circumstances, criticism (and radical criticism) is absolutely indispensable for any transformation. A transformation that remains within the same mode of thought, a transformation that is only a way of adjusting the same thought more closely to the reality of things can merely be a superficial transformation.

> On the other hand, as soon as one can no longer think things as one formerly thought them, transformation becomes both very urgent, very difficult, and quite possible.
>
> (Foucault, 1988, p. 155)

This chapter has considered three relationships that have been proposed between ECE and CSE: readiness for school; a strong and equal partnership; and the vision of a meeting place. The first, I have argued, has become the dominant discourse, understood as a relationship of ECE readying or preparing the child for CSE. It is very problematic. It is conservative, taking the school's understanding or social construction of the child, education, learning and knowledge for granted; it is hierarchical, assuming the 'lower' educational level, ECE, must serve the needs of the 'higher', CSE, and in the process 'grasping' the otherness or alterity of ECE, so making the Other into the Same; it is simple and linear, assuming the child and her learning follow predetermined, sequential and predictable stages; and it is monologic, with one-way communication from higher to lower. It is, in short, inscribed with a very particular set of understandings or constructions, in particular of the child and learning, though these are invariably implicit and taken-for-granted, neither made explicit nor offered as one possible and, therefore, contestable alternative.

We do not, however, need to go further than the authors who have contributed to other books in the series *Contesting Early Childhood* to see that very different understandings of the child and learning are not only available but have also informed some pedagogical practice. A recurring theme in the series, though by no means restricted to it, is that children are learners from birth, not needing to be readied to learn, but inherently capable and avid to do so. For example, this has been understood for many years in the early childhood education in Reggio Emilia. This understanding emerges from Reggio's answer to one of the critical – or political – questions they have asked as the basis for their educational project: 'What is our image of the child?' There is, of course, no correct answer to such a critical political question, only alternative possibilities, and from these Reggio has made a collective and political choice. Carlina Rinaldi, in her book in this series *In Dialogue with Reggio Emilia*, describes their choice, their construction or image of the child:

> There are many images of the child, and many images of childhood. We need only think of psychoanalysis or the various branches of psychology and sociology. Though these theories are quite different, they tend to have one recurring aspect in common: the deterministic identification of the child as a weak subject, a person with needs rather than rights.
>
> These positions have probably gained widespread approval because they work well for certain images of motherhood, women, and the

family, images that are more 'convenient' and accommodating. They are certainly easier to manage than the image that is part of our theory, *which views children as strong, powerful, and rich in potential and resources, right from the moment of birth.* In this sense, we share the values and meaning of the constructivist and social constructivist approaches. We see a child who is driven by the enormous energy potential of a hundred billion neurons, by the strength of wanting to grow and taking the job of growing seriously, by the incredible curiosity that makes children search for the reasons for everything. A child who knows how to wait and who has high expectations. A child who wants to show that he or she knows things and knows how to do things, and who has all the strength and potential that comes from children's ability to wonder and to be amazed. *A child who is powerful from the moment of birth because he is open to the world and capable of constructing his own knowledge.* A child who is seen in his wholeness, who possesses his own directions and the desire for knowledge and for life. A competent child!

Competent in relating and interacting, with a deep respect for others and accepting of conflict and error. A child who is competent in constructing, in constructing himself while he constructs his world and is, in turn, constructed by the world. *Competent in constructing theories to interpret reality and in formulating hypotheses and metaphors as possibilities for understanding reality.*

(Rinaldi, 2006, p. 123; emphases added)

It is clear from this extended quotation how the image of the child and the understanding of learning are interwoven. The child is rich and competent from the moment of birth because he or she is capable from birth of learning understood as theory building and meaning making, i.e. constructing knowledge and identity.

An important part of Reggio Emilia's image or construction of the 'rich child', 'powerful from the moment of birth', is the theory of the hundred languages of childhood, a theory that emerged early on in this municipal project, during debates about the privileged position given in traditional education to just two languages, speech and writing, which 'supported the power, not only of certain knowledges, but also of certain classes' (Rinaldi, 2006, p. 193). The 'hundred languages', a theory full of democracy and a metaphor for the extraordinary potential of children, refers 'to the different ways children (human beings) represent, communicate and express their thinking in different media and symbolic systems; languages therefore are the many fonts or geneses of knowledge' (Vecchi, 2010, p. 9). These many linguistic possibilities range from mathematical and scientific languages to the poetic languages, 'forms of expression strongly characterised by expressive or aesthetic aspects such as music, song, dance or photography' (ibid.). The choice of a hundred does not denote a precise count, but is intended to be 'very provocative, to claim for all these languages not only the same dignity, but the right to expression and to communicate with each other' (Rinaldi, 2006, p. 193).

Loris Malaguzzi, the first director of ECE in Reggio Emilia and one of the leading pedagogical thinkers and practitioners of the twentieth century, not only insisted on the hundred languages being a potential from birth, but also feared that most children lost many languages, not least through the baleful influence of the conservative school. The issue for him was not getting young children ready for school, but the very real danger of schools depriving young children of their potential and competence. Childhood was not, therefore, necessarily a period of progress; it could rather be a period of retreat and loss. He chose to write poetically about this danger:

> The child has a hundred languages
> (and a hundred hundred hundred more)
> but they steal ninety-nine
> the school and the culture
> separate the head from the body...

Developing this theme of loss, at least in some educational regimes, Vea Vecchi, one of the first *atelieristas* – an educator with an arts background working in a pre-school – in Reggio Emilia's 'municipal schools', criticises a form of traditional education that again has the capacity to destroy important qualities that children bring into the world:

> When we are born we are whole, and the whole of our senses strain to relate with the world around us in order to understand it. Very quickly, however, we find ourselves 'cut into slices', a phrase used by Loris Malaguzzi to define the state of separation in our culture which forces us to pursue knowledge on separate paths...We need to reflect seriously on how much individual and social damage is being caused by education and culture which prefer to separate than to work on connections...How much does a school which works with decontextualised objects and situations lead to thinking in separate fragments and mistaking information for knowledge, which is only obtained by organising and placing parts in relation to each other? How much does ignoring the fact that emotions are an integral part of learning and educational processes distort the global process of knowledge building? We could continue this type of questioning, *highlighting how hierarchical and discriminatory is our school culture when dealing with different languages, with teaching/learning processes and with children's general approach to exploration, understanding and construction of reality.*
> (Vecchi, 2004, pp. 18–19: emphasis added)

Vecchi returns to this critique of the compulsory school system in her book for this series *Art and Creativity in Reggio Emilia*.

> I fear that as in the past, *the real problem is that artificially and super-ficially separating disciplines is part of school and that in the education of both pupils and teachers, an aesthetic dimension is not considered in the least important* ...We need to truly reflect on how much this has diminished the thinking and formation of younger generations...It is important to society that schools and we as teachers are clearly aware · how much space we leave children for original thinking, without rush-ing to restrict it with predetermined schemes that define what is *correct* according to a school culture. How much do we support children to have ideas different from those of other people and how do we accus-tom them to arguing and discussing their ideas with their classmates? I am quite convinced that greater attention to processes, rather than only the final product, would help us to feel greater respect for the inde-pendent thinking and strategies of children and teenagers.
>
> (Vecchi, 2010, p. 138: emphases added)

In short, compulsory schooling has pedagogical choices to make and schools need, therefore, 'to consciously take a position on *which know-ledge* they intend to promote' (2010, p. 28, original emphasis). They can pursue an idea of teaching that chooses 'to transmit circumscribed "truths" in various "disciplines"'; or they can choose 'to stand by children's sides together constructing contexts in which they can explore their own ideas and hypotheses individually or in groups and discuss them with friends or teachers' (ibid.).

The ideas of learning and knowledge that have flourished in Reggio Emilia place great value on the unexpected, on the creation of new theo-ries and concepts, on respectful listening and questioning to which the answers are not already known. Hence learning is understood as a process of meaning making or theory building, in relationship with others who are called on to listen to the theories. Hence, too, Loris Malaguzzi's image of knowledge as a tangle of spaghetti, similar to the image of knowledge as a rhizome, developed by the French philosophers Gilles Deleuze and Felix Guattari (1999, see also Deleuze and Parnet, 1987). In a rhizome there is no hierarchy of root, trunk and branch. It is not like a staircase, where you have to take the first step before you move onto the next one, which is also similar to the tree metaphor of knowledge that remains so prominent in education. The *rhizome* is something that shoots in all directions with no beginning and no end, but always *in between*, and with openings towards other directions and places. It is a *multiplicity* functioning by means of connections and heterogeneity, a multiplicity which is not given but constructed. Learning, then, is a matter of experimentation and problematisation – *a line of flight* and an exploration of *becoming*, echoed in Rinaldi's observation that 'the process of "becoming" is the basis of true education' (2006, p. 80).

These ideas of learning and knowledge – so different to the linear, sequential, predictable notions that underpin the readiness for school discourse – are productive of pedagogical practice, in particular the impor-tance Reggio Emilia attaches to project work, which

> is sensitive to the rhythms of communication and incorporates the significance and timing of children's investigation and research. The duration of a project can thus be short, medium, or long, continuous or discontinuous, with pauses, suspensions, and restarts. The statement of a hypothesis on how the project might proceed is valid only to the extent that it is seen precisely as a hypothesis and not as a 'must', as one of a thousand hypotheses on the direction that might be taken. Above all, making hypotheses is a way to increase the expectations, excitement, and the possibilities for being and interacting, for welcom-ing the unexpected as a fundamental resource... [Project work] is a way of thinking, a strategy for creating relations and bringing in the element of chance, by which we mean 'the space of the others'; i.e. that undefined space of the self that is completed by the thoughts of others within the relational process.
>
> (ibid., pp. 132–133)

Similar ideas and practices are explored by Liselott Mariett Olsson in her book in this series *Movement and Experimentation in Young Children's Learning*, drawing on work in Swedish pre-schools influenced by Reggio Emilia and Deleuze and Guattari. She develops a strong critique of goal or standards-based education, with its intense valuing of prescribed and predictable outcomes, arguing that it puts much effort

> into taming subjectivities as well as learning processes: predicting, controlling, supervising and evaluating according to predetermined standards. This is very much what haunts all subjectivity and learning today; movement in subjectivity and learning becomes automatic and forgotten and experimentation becomes tamed, lifeless and predictable... Learning processes seem very often to be judged and evaluated from an already set outcome, from the point of view of the content of knowledge to be attained...
>
> [L]earning must be treated as impossible to predict, plan, supervise or evaluate according to predefined standards. This presents a real challenge today, as we have seen throughout this study how much importance is put on the achievement of predetermined goals.
>
> (Olsson, 2009, pp. 6, 117)

I could continue – but I hope the point is made. What might be termed the mainstream discourse about the relationship between ECE and CSE, with school readiness at its heart, is situated in a particular positivistic paradigm and informed by particular images or understandings of children, learning, knowledge and education. From other paradigmatic positions and working with other images and understandings, this dominant discourse of readying children – to learn, to enter school, to achieve predetermined outcomes, to progress sequentially – is no longer self-evident, indeed is highly contestable. It ignores the potential with which children are born, being ready to learn from day one of life; indeed it threatens to waste this capability. It applies a reductionist, fragmented and narrow approach, which is more about taming, controlling and predicting than creating learning based on movement, experimentation and meaning making.

Educators who contest the dominant discourse, such as those in Reggio Emilia, do not dismiss literacy or other icons of school readiness. Rather, they place them into a wider context of multiple languages, which together contribute to rich learning by a rich child; and argue that literacy and numeracy call for 'theoretical perspectives and didactical tools that align themselves and are closer to children's own strategies for engaging' with these particular languages (Olsson, forthcoming). Similarly, we need not dismiss all predetermined outcomes; rather, it is important to keep open a space where movement and experimentation, lines of flight and unexpected directions can thrive, a space for outcomes that are not predetermined, that are unexpected, that provoke surprise and wonder. This is and/also, not either/or, thinking, though not without a continuous and inescapable tension between closure and openness and over the scope of contestation.

The dominant 'school readiness' discourse puts ECE at issue, judging it against the taken-for-granted and therefore uncontested regime and purposes of CSE. By contrast, the strong and equal partnership and the vision of a meeting place contest both ECE *and* CSE, putting the meaning and practice of *all* education and *all* educational institutions at issue. Both of them, but particularly the meeting place relationship, are potentially transformative, inviting and welcoming critical thinking about existing understandings and practices, both in ECE and CSE; both are egalitarian, assuming all sectors of education to be of equal value, with their own identity and contribution to make to the whole, and with each sector respecting the alterity of other sectors and open to learning with them; both are open to complexity, non-linear ideas about learning and the rhizomatic image of knowledge; and both are dialogic, implying not only exchange and listening but also, again in Rinaldi's words, 'a process of transformation where you lose absolutely the possibility of controlling the final result'.

But there are, perhaps, some differences of emphasis and presumption. The 'partnership' relationship, to the extent it is elaborated in the *Starting*

Strong reports, appears to place emphasis on each party learning about and adopting some of the existing strengths of the other, CSE for example taking on parental involvement and social development, both well-established features of ECE. It presumes a process of exchange between what already exists. The 'meeting place' relationship emphasises both parties working together to create *new* underpinning understandings on which base new shared ways of working can be developed, such as documentation. It presumes a process of co-construction, bringing something new into being. That process, though, does not start with a *tabula rasa*. It, too, assumes both parties bringing something of themselves to the meeting place; but not so much for purposes of exchange, but as materials to be used in processes of co-construction.

One of the striking features of the discussion by Dahlberg and Lenz-Taguchi of the meeting place relationship is the importance it attaches to the search for a 'common heritage of ideas in the pre-school and school tradition' – acknowledging the existence of difference but also the possibility of finding some common ground. Importance is attached to the adoption of a historical perspective by contemporary ECE and CSE, through which both may recall past thought and experience, which may have become lost in current discourses but which reclaimed may provide that 'common heritage of ideas.' History always contains complex and multiple narratives, providing a relativist challenge to all essentialist claims. So taking a historical perspective entails recognition of an educational pluralism that is rich in diverse theories, concepts, understandings and practices. The historical process – excavating past strata to explore this plurality in search of strands of common heritage – can thus contribute to the present-day construction of shared understandings and practices; and, equally important, through highlighting alternatives it can contribute to restoring the primacy of politics and ethics to education, rescuing it from the current dominance of technical and managerial practice.

I noted earlier that for Dahlberg and Lenz-Taguchi the meeting place could encompass relationships across 'all forms of education and lifelong learning', and it is important not to lose sight of this possibility. Through the meeting place relationship, it is possible to envisage the whole field of education for children, young people and adults – ECE, CSE and beyond – co-constructing and working with:

- shared images of the child, the teacher, the school itself – for example, the child and teacher as co-constructors of knowledge, values and identities; the school as a place of encounter and collaborative workshop capable of producing many projects;
- shared understandings of learning, knowledge and education itself – for example, learning as meaning making, rhizomatic knowledge, and education in its broadest sense;

- shared values – for example, democracy and experimentation as fundamental values;
- shared ethics – for example, an ethics of care and an ethics of an encounter;
- shared curricular goals, built round broad aims and thematic areas;
- shared pedagogical approaches – for example, a pedagogy of relationships and listening;
- shared practices – for example, project or thematic work that strives for connectedness, the use of ateliers and atelieristas, a central role for pedagogical documentation.

What emerges here is a common idea of education that flows across the years and through different types of schools and other educational institutions, rather than a disjointed set of different educational 'enclosures', each providing for arbitrarily defined age groups, each with its own understandings, goals and practices, each tasked (and struggling with) readying students for the next level up, and requiring a series of 'transitions' from one educational enclosure to another. What this common flow might look like is suggested in the writings of Carlina Rinaldi in her book for this series (Rinaldi, 2006), when she talks about 'schools': for though she is referring to the 'municipal schools' for ECE in Reggio Emilia, she could as easily be talking about any type of school. As the three instances cited below illustrate, her use of 'school' seems a deliberate attempt to reclaim a generic concept of 'school', turning away from its frequent association today as a place of transmission and reproduction and foregrounding instead a place of democracy and relationships, creativity and research.

> In schools, creativity should have the opportunity to be expressed in every place and in every moment. What we hope for is creative learning and creative teachers, not simply a 'creativity hour'. This is why the *atelier* must support and ensure all the creative processes that can take place anywhere in the school, at home, and in the society. We should remember that there is no creativity in the child if there is no creativity in the adult: the competent and creative child exists if there is a competent and creative adult.
>
> (p. 120)

The metaphor that might best represent our image of the school is that of a construction site, or a permanent laboratory, in which children's and teachers' research processes are strongly intertwined and constantly evolving. Here, teachers build an awareness of knowledge and the processes of its construction through a progressive understanding of the structure and skills being developed by each child and the group of children, as well as of their individual and group identities. The question of 'knowledge of knowledge' leads to another fundamental point of our philosophy: one of the primary tasks of the teacher, and thus of the school, is to help the child and the group of children learn how to learn, fostering their natural predisposition toward relationships and the consequent co-construction of knowledge.

(p. 126)

These reflections lead to another value that is part of our experience, and that is, the value of democracy, which is intrinsic to the concept of participation: participation of the families, but also of the children and teachers in the school project. This extremely important issue deserves at least a brief mention, because we must not forget how closely the school is connected to the society in which it is situated. There is the recurring question of whether the school is limited to transmitting culture or can be, as we in Reggio aspire to, a place where culture is constructed and democracy is lived. School and democracy, a theme that was dear to Dewey, is an important commitment for all of us: school as a place of democracy, in which we can all live democracy.

(pp. 140–1)

This approach to education – as a lifecourse project inscribed with common understandings, values, goals and practices – opens up the possibility of a truly dialogic relationship between different areas of education, a relationship in which, for example, teachers working with 16-month-olds and with 16-year-olds would be able to dialogue and document together as equal partners in a relationship of mutual learning. Not just able, but wanting to do so. This is perhaps, too, the vision of the school of the future hinted at in *Starting Strong II*, in which inter-disciplinary knowledge 'will be constructed through personal investigation, exchange and discussion with many sources, and co-constructed in communities of learning characterised by team teaching' (OECD, 2006, p. 222).

The vision of the meeting place opens up other possibilities for cross-sectoral dialogue, not only for constructing new shared understandings, values, ethics and practices. One such possibility is for a meeting place to provide space for interested educators drawn from different sectors of the educational spectrum to collaboratively explore particular theoretical perspectives of common interest. At present there seems little evidence of such cross-sectoral collaboration, reflecting the fragmented and hierarchical nature of the education system. Yet step back a bit to see the broader picture, and it is apparent that educators in different sectors are interested in similar theoretical perspectives: they just fail to notice or meet those in other sectors, let alone border cross into them. This book series, for instance, provides a forum where authors from the ECE field explore their interests in theoretical perspectives that, at present, find no recognition in the mainstream positivist discourse, in particular perspectives that might broadly be labelled post-foundational, including post-modernism, post-structuralism, post-colonialism and so on; a cursory glance at the literature shows similar interests in CSE. But there is no meeting place for inter-change on shared theoretical interests.

The concept of an educational meeting place opens up, therefore, the possibility of border crossing between ECE and CSE, by both educators and researchers, to realise more fully the potential of particular theoretical perspectives. Imagine those in the field of ECE who are interested in the thinking of Michel Foucault and Gilles Deleuze, and who (as this series demonstrates) are going beyond interest to applying this thinking in the pre-school – 'doing Foucault' (the title of Glenda MacNaughton's book in the series) or 'doing Deleuze' – in a meeting place with counterparts from primary, secondary or higher education. That could create, to draw on Deleuzian language, new assemblages that might work with movement and experimentation to generate new vitality and intensity, new desires, new lines of flight, new thought.

The vision of a meeting place has further potentialities. It can help to realise the proposition that Gunilla Dahlberg and myself made in an earlier book in this series *Ethics and Politics in Early Childhood Education* (2005): that early childhood institutions (and, by implication, all forms of educa-tional institution) should be, first and foremost, places for political and ethical practice, rather than, as now, places primarily of technical practice. Politically, the 'meeting place', with its close affinity to the forum or the agora, a place of encounter for citizens, children and adults alike, has strong democratic connotations. The meeting place creates a new *space* for participatory democratic practice, inviting the inclusion not only of educa-tors but of all concerned with education as a public and community project – potentially everyone. It provides opportunities not only for democratically co-constructing new understandings – of the child, the educator, the school, learning and knowledge – but also for addressing other political questions, such as: What is the state we are in and what future do we hope for? What do we want for our children? What is the purpose of education? What are the fundamental values of education and what ethics does education work with? Through deliberating and contesting such questions, and through using the space for working with documentation, the meeting place can contribute to the democratic political idea of a transparent education and transparent (pre) school that can, as Malaguzzi hoped, generate 'legitimacy for education and the institutions of the pre-school and school'.

Ethically, the concept of a meeting place can evoke the concept of the ethics of an encounter, also an important theme in *Ethics and Politics in Early Childhood Education*. A central theme of this ethical approach to rela-tionships is the importance of relating to the Other in a way that respects the Other's alterity and avoids the process of grasping to make the Other into the Same. The desire to classify children into pre-made categories, so prevalent in education today, is one example of grasping; pursuing a 'readiness for school' relationship that leads to 'schoolification' of ECE can be seen as another. Dahlberg (2003) summarises the consequences in both cases:

> Putting everything which one encounters into pre-made categories implies we make the other into the Same, as everything which does not fit into these categories, which is unfamiliar has to be overcome. Hence, alterity disappears. This betrays the complexity in children's lives...[Working with the ethics of an encounter] [t]o think another whom I cannot grasp is an important shift and it challenges the whole scene of pedagogy.
>
> (p. 270)

A pedagogical meeting place could provide one opportunity for taking up that challenge, respecting and welcoming alterity and complexity and creating new thinking from the provocation of an encounter with difference.

Overall, as will be apparent by now, the 'vision of a meeting place' provides for me the most satisfying account of a future relationship between CSE and ECE, from which might emerge one form of a 'strong and equal partnership': indeed, it seems to me that a meeting place is one way of expressing and constructing a 'strong and equal partnership', taking us beyond the concept into the realm of implementation. To that extent these two relationships are not necessarily distinct. But it is no universal blueprint, a 'meeting place programme' to be taken off the shelf and applied anywhere. Dahlberg and Lenz-Taguchi's text, with its analysis and ideas, draws on Swedish educational history and discourses and is the product of a particular context, 1990s Sweden, a time and place marked by a strong, distinctive and articulate ECE, widely available, fully integrated and with widespread public support, a context in which a dialogue with CSE was possible to envisage and explore. Moreover, even with so much going for it, it appears that implementing a 'meeting place' in Sweden has been neither straightforward nor successful.

But to say that *Förskola och skola – om två skilda traditioner och om visionen om en mötesplats* cannot supply us with a proven blueprint, exportable to anywhere at any time, is to miss the point. The idea of transferable and predictable programmes or universal and stable projects can only appeal or be credible to the most unthinking positivist. I would argue that we should come, instead, to such rich texts as reminders that there are alternatives, as provocations to our own thinking, and as contributions to our own theory-building. They put (in the evocative words of Nikolas Rose) a 'stutter in the fluency of meta-narratives' (1999, p. 20), which leaves us space to take issue with them. Moreover, we can use the concepts and the processes as tools, applying them to different contexts, with different traditions, and producing different results.

In any case, *Förskola och skola – om två skilda traditioner och om visionen om en mötesplats* hardly counts as a blueprint. It lacks the necessary detail to qualify. It is more a sketch of a possibility – a broad vision – than a detailed account. It remains a work in progress leaving much to be done, not only on the 'what' of formulation, but also the 'how' of realisation. At what levels might meeting places operate – national, local, institutional? What forms might these meeting places take and how might their co-constructive work be facilitated? How might they address issues around exclusion and disparities of power among potential participants? How might the outcomes of their deliberations be put to work in practice, how might new shared understandings find expression in everyday life? These are question to which Dahlberg and Lenz-Taguchi devote little space, indeed implementation is not part of their terms of reference.

So, it is one thing to set out the vision, important though that is, and another to realise it. The readiness for school approach, at least in its most conservative forms, is simple in theory and simple in implementation. It requires applying certain types of human technology to steer ECE towards greater conformity to the needs and demands of CSE, expressed in certain predefined norms and standards. These technologies include: pre-school curricula, 'training' pre-school educators, setting new goals, establishing new modes of assessment of performance, introducing incentives and sanctions. It is essentially about applying a new regime to a particular sector (ECE) to enhance the performance of the regime in another sector (CSE). Moreover the returns from the new regime, even if banal, are likely to be observable and relatively quickly too; school performance as defined by the traditional CSE regime is likely to improve somewhat if ECE is re-engineered to prepare children for that regime. It would indeed be rather shocking if such change, applied with the full weight of modern technical practice and the full resources of the 'social investment' state, did not produce results.

But easy implementation hides the hollowness of this particular readiness relationship. The whole exercise ignores the political questions and the larger issues that they raise: the meanings of education, learning or knowledge; the images of the child, the teacher and the school; the fundamental values and ethics. It is a technical carapace, masquerading as the whole body.

Implementing the vision of a meeting place is quite another matter, especially given the complex nature of the envisaged process, the political and ethical dimensions and the many obstacles to forging the new relationship based on common understandings and practices. Yet it goes to the heart of how transformative change can be brought about, change that entails radically new ways of working inscribed with radically new ways of thinking, and which requires far more than the application of human technologies. You cannot legislate for or otherwise demand meeting places that are genuinely dialogic and productive – of new understandings of the child and teacher, learning and knowledge and of new ways of working that require democratic values, dialogic relations and interpretive abilities. This means breaking away from modernity's need for predictability and certainty, mastery and calculation, compliance and closure.

It seems to me that implementing the vision of a meeting place is immensely difficult but by no means impossible. It brings us into the important field of how to bring about transformative change in ways that are democratic and participatory, recognise complexity and context, and are responsive to reflection and changing conditions. Important as this field is, it is not the task of this chapter to go further into it (for further discussion of transformative change, see Fielding and Moss, 2011). It is simply to highlight one part of the dilemma facing those who wish for an education different from the current neoliberal juggernaut, with its fundamentalist beliefs in markets, management, competition, privatisation, standards and technical practice; who wish instead for a democratic, dialogic and emancipatory education, such as underpins *Starting Strong's* 'strong and equal partnership' and Dahlberg and Lenz-Taguchi's 'vision of a meeting place'. This is not, I would argue, a cause for despair, but a reason to renew contestation and reconceptualisation, to insist there are alternatives, and drawing on existing cases develop strategies for transformative change working at all levels from national through local to the individual pre-school and school.

I started this final section with a quotation from Michel Foucault about transformation. What he highlights is the enormous importance of thought, as a means of governing us through (to use Roberto Unger's term) 'the dictatorship of no alternative', but also as a means of transformation, a process set in motion when we realise that what we took to be self-evident and necessary is not in fact so, and that there are quite different ways of thinking available to us. Once we can think differently, once we can critique the dominant discourse and once we can envision alternatives, then 'transformation becomes both very urgent, very difficult, and quite possible'. For me, the main rationale for the series *Contesting Early Childhood* is to create a space for resisting the dominant discourse in one arena of education (ECE) and envisioning alternative discourses – and as such, provoking a desire for transformation.

This book, I hope, is in the same mould. The dominant readiness for school discourse, and the schoolification it encourages, are neither necessary nor inevitable. There are alternatives, two outlined here, but doubtless others too. Of course, some may still opt for readiness and schoolification: that is a legitimate choice. But those making such a choice should do so in the full awareness of what they are doing – making a political decision between conflicting alternatives. They should be prepared, also, to offer a rationale for that choice; assertion is no longer enough when we can no longer take it for granted. Others, I hope, will be encouraged to delve deeper into the alternatives, elaborating what is already on offer, extending the offer by adding new visions, and experimenting with the practice of implementation.

Notes

1   In preparing this chapter, I have had access to an unpublished English translation. Quotations from the paper come from this translation, with some minor editing.
2   Pedagogues are a graduate profession quite distinct from school teachers. They are qualified to work across a range of services for children and young people. For further discussion of the profession of pedagogue, see Cameron and Moss, 2011.
3   Nikolas Rose refers to 'human technologies' as technologies of government 'imbued with aspirations for the shaping of conduct in the hope of producing certain desired effects and averting certain undesired events.' These technologies include: 'forms of practical knowledge, with modes of perception, practices of calculation, vocabularies, types of authority, forms of judgement, architectural forms, human capacities, non-human objects and devices, inscription techniques and so forth' (Rose, 1999, p. 52).
4   Free-time pedagogues (*Fritidspedagog*) originally worked in separate free-time services, used by children after school hours. They followed these services into schools in the 1990s.
5   Mixed age groups might consist, for example, of 6- to 8-year-olds, including the pre-school class and first two school grades, and 9- to 11-year-olds. The team and children are together during the extended school day, though the school teachers are usually present only during those parts of the school day designated for education; pre-school teachers and free-time pedagogues are present during these periods, working alongside school teachers, as well as before and after.
6   *Starting Strong* also recognises the significance of social constructions: 'social constructions of children, families and the purposes of ECEC are reflected in how ECEC systems are envisaged and structured' (OECD, 2001, p. 43). I know of no other national or international policy documents, at least in the English language, which even refers to the social construction of childhood, let alone allots it any significance.
7   By 1994, both the authors of the paper, many pre-school teachers and even some policy makers in Sweden were inspired by the pedagogical ideas and work in Reggio Emilia, which brought 'new inspirational thinking...to the Swedish pre-school' (Korpi, 2007, p. 64). One reason for this close and important relationship between Reggio Emilia and Sweden, recognised by Malaguzzi, was shared values and understandings.
8   Elsa Köhler (1879–1940) was an Austrian psychologist and teacher whose pedagogical ideas influenced Swedish pre-schools and schools.

Part II

Authors' responses

Chapter 2

A response from the co-author of 'a strong and equal partnership'

John Bennett

> There is the recurring question of whether the school is limited to transmitting culture or can be, as we in Reggio aspire to, a place where culture is constructed and democracy is lived.
>
> (Rinaldi, 2006, p. 140)

In his introductory essay, Peter Moss outlines the recommendation contained in the *Starting Strong* reports (OECD, 2001, 2006): 'a strong and equal partnership [between early childhood education and the compulsory] education system'.[1] The features of that partnership were:

- Early childhood services should be recognised, like compulsory schooling, as a public good and an important part of the education process. All children should have a right to access quality ECE services before starting school.
- A more unified approach to learning should be adopted across both systems, recognising the contribution that the early childhood approach brings to fostering key dispositions and attitudes to learning.
- Attention should be given to transition challenges faced by young children as they enter CSE, or transit from one type of ECE service to another. There should be a greater focus on building bridges across administrative departments, staff training, regulations and curricula in both systems.
- A strong partnership with the education system should provide the opportunity to bring together the diverse perspectives and methods of both ECE and CSE, focusing on their respective strengths, such as the emphasis on parental involvement and social development in ECE and the focus on educational goals and learning in CSE.

Underlying these features were a number of personal convictions:

- That early childhood services contribute to child health, well-being, social development and education in the broad sense, that is, education as both self-actualisation and knowledge acquisition (the former being especially important in the early childhood years).

- That two widespread early childhood paradigms of that time – namely, a childcare model and an early education model – were not ideal for young children's well-being or learning. The childcare model aimed primarily to free parents to work and in so far as children's interests were taken into account, it focused on protection, health and care. Many centres did not seem to understand or prioritise the developmental needs and learning capacities of young children. At the same time, the early education model for children from three years onwards was, in many countries, an extension downward of traditional primary schooling, with a predominantly cognitive curriculum, a top-down teaching pedagogy and child:staff ratios inappropriate for young children often (and still so) in excess of 20 young children per trained adult. Neither model took sufficiently into account mainstream early childhood research, not to mention the insights of educators such as Froebel, Steiner, Montessori, Dewey or Malaguzzi.
- Primary education could benefit from the knowledge and experience of young children accumulated in the early childhood sector, and in the process help children and families negotiate the transition from ECE to CSE. Co-operation could and should be built between the sectors, keeping in mind that true partnership is based on respecting difference and not one party colonising the other.

Examples of strong and equal partnerships in Nordic countries

During the reviews of 20 or so countries, in the late 1990s and early 2000s, that constituted the OECD's *Starting Strong* project, several examples of respectful partnerships were seen, where dialogue between the ECE and CSE sectors was visible and cordial. Whereas in many countries there was an expectation – at least among many working in primary schools – that ECE should 'deliver' to the primary school children who were 'ready for learning', by which they meant able to follow the routines of the school and having some knowledge of literacy and numeracy, in the four Nordic countries reviewed, such demands were rare: most school staff had a positive opinion and understanding of ECE pedagogy and of the distinctive learning strategies of young children. It was felt that the pre-school years should be devoted to child well-being, self-actualisation, socialisation, and playful learning; playful learning included understanding and practising the uses of reading and writing, and reviewers noted – particularly in Finland – that many of the older pre-school children were already reading at the age of 5 or 6 years, while it was noticeable in all the Nordic countries that young children frequently used signs and play writing in their games. In addition, these countries had put into place a bridging or 'pre-school' class for 6 to 7-years-olds, staffed wholly or partly by early childhood pedagogues or teachers and generally located in the local school. During the pre-school class year, children participated in a mix of ECE and school-like activities, before transiting without difficulty into the first grade of CSE.

Why did this respect for ECE exist so strongly in the Nordic countries? One of the reasons, I believe, is the high profile that young children and their services have in these countries. Their parliaments regularly debate children's issues, the UN Convention on the Rights of the Child is taken seriously by public authorities, and its implementation is regularly scrutinised.

Again, a strong integrated ECE system has existed in these countries from at least the 1970s. Moreover, the sector was initially located politically and administratively not in education but in social welfare. Long before ECE was seen as the foundation stage of learning, early childhood services were considered – by governments and people alike – as an essential component of the Nordic welfare state, a strong bulwark against child poverty and against inequality of opportunity among both women and children; there was a conviction that tackling poverty and inequality called for both redistributive policies and strong early childhood services. This provided the early childhood sector with a strong identity and safeguarded it from absorption by education. An integrated ECE system developed, bringing children from 1 to 6 years together into the same services, focused on health, social inclusion and broad learning.

Another relevant factor was the support provided to the Nordic early childhood sector for many decades by a strong group of university researchers and teachers. This remains the case today; for example, an estimated 100+ PhDs are working today directly with children in Swedish pre-school centres. This highly qualified group contributed to giving ECE a separate and strongly theorised identity in precisely those areas – concepts, goals, curriculum and pedagogical practice – where early childhood sectors in other countries were found to be weak. In addition, these countries were continually learning from each other and, although having theorised the field far more than most other countries, were eager also to learn from abroad; for example, during the OECD review team's visit to Sweden, the Reggio Emilia Institute in Stockholm, founded in 1992, was conducting classes, conferences and public lectures on Reggio Emilia's pedagogical work.

All this had led in the Nordic countries to a well conceptualised, innovative early childhood system. Although some *schoolification* had taken place (Skolverket, 2004), ECE was still seen primarily as introducing children to society, fostering key social dispositions as well as attitudes to learning. Bridging the public and private spheres, it sought to reconcile the rights and wishes of children and parents with the expectations of the preschool and the local community. A holistic approach to learning was practised and great emphasis was placed on supporting children in their current developmental tasks and interests. These tasks were considered to be much wider than just preparation for school: they included developmental readiness, health and motor development, behaviour and self-regulation, learning to live together, language development with expression and communication through the hundred languages of children, learning to learn through play and the other natural learning strategies of young children.

National curriculum frameworks guided, in general terms, the pedagogical work and the content of children's learning in early childhood centres. Curriculum content was not detailed, as often happens in countries where CSE has a strong influence on ECE, but, at the same time, it oriented teachers to arouse children's interest in selected areas of knowledge, including mathematics, science and early literacy. Parents were seen as important partners and the health and well-being of children were important curriculum goals. Learning orientations were based on previous consultations with the main stakeholders, and so were not considered as instruments of normalisation but rather as points of reference to guide the life and work of the pre-school centres. In parallel, each centre was expected to formulate its own curriculum or learning plan guided by the national framework.

Although not expressed quite as clearly as in Reggio Emilia, knowledge was considered in the Nordic early childhood services as originating chiefly from relationships and from the personal interests of children. A strong administrative concern about what children were learning was not overtly present as in other countries. Teachers or pedagogues sought to respect the natural learning strategies of young children, that is, learning through play, interaction, activity, and personal investigation guided, of course, by a curriculum. The phrase 'a time for childhood' was often heard – a belief that young children should not be hurried, that the course of education was long. Co-operative project work was used to give children the experience of working together and to build up knowledge and more complex understandings of chosen themes. The belief was widespread that encouraging the initiatives and meaning-making of children strongly supported cognitive development.

In working with children, staff used a concept of pedagogy that brought together notions of care, upbringing and learning, assumed to be not separate fields needing to be joined up but inter-connected parts of the child's life. An important objective was that 'all children should develop a desire and curiosity for learning, and confidence in their own learning, rather than achieving a pre-specified level of knowledge and proficiency' (Korpi, 2005, p. 11).

At an administrative level, the importance of ECE was recognised, not only because of its contribution to gender equality and female employment, but also as the foundation of socialisation and learning. This was particularly true in Sweden where the Ministry of Education, Research and Culture, since 1996, had had responsibility for both ECE and CSE (today, ECE is in the education system in all Nordic countries). Small but expert early childhood units existed in ministries, while locally most municipalities had specialised personnel and committees looking after the interests, health and education of young children.

An idealised account?

No doubt, the above account is somewhat idealised. The fact is that exceptions to the rule can easily be found in generalisations about any national system. Thus, it was possible to find mediocrity in the Nordic countries in any of the areas mentioned, for example, in certain aspects of governance, in the importance given by some municipalities to children's issues, or the kind of pedagogy practised in certain centres. Yet, it is important to underline that all these countries were already far advanced in providing high quality, universal and affordable services for the great majority of young children, irrespective of socio-economic status or location.

The Nordic countries also showed clearly that it was possible to have an early childhood system with a strong identity, able to act independently and co-operate with compulsory education on a more or less equal basis. In Sweden, for example, childcare and early education were integrated and the early childhood centres (known as *förskola* or, literally, 'pre-school') catered comprehensively for children from 12 months to 6 years. The holistic development of children was the primary aim; but in giving responsibility for the sector to the Ministry of Education in 1996, the government sent out a strong signal that pre-school activities should be organised around early learning. Child:staff ratios were excellent (5.4 children to one trained adult) and half the staff were graduate teachers, certified in early childhood theory and pedagogical practice. A similar situation could only be to the advantage of young children in other countries where early childhood systems were much weaker in conceptualisation, organisation, coverage and quality.

A contrasting picture in other countries

At that time, in many other countries, infants from the age of 3 months were frequently placed in private childcare settings of very doubtful quality and children of 3 or 4 years of age were already enrolled in public early education characterised by school-like surroundings and over-crowded, instructional classrooms. The *Starting Strong* reports concluded this was not good either for the well-being or learning of these children, especially for children from minority and/or low-income backgrounds. Many of these children needed more personalised attention and learning support in smaller groups.

It was also clear in these cases that an equal partnership between ECE and CSE had not developed. Several reasons for this will be discussed below, but one is particularly relevant, namely, that in most OECD countries early childhood systems were split between childcare and early education. This split still remains a formidable barrier to forging a strong identity for the early childhood sector.

The Nordic countries practised a far more rational division of services than the 0–3/3–6 division found in most countries elsewhere, and focused on family well-being, infant health and social welfare from pre-natal to one year or 18 months (including well-paid parental leave), followed by an assured place in a unitary ECE service for children from 12 months or so up 6 years. The Nordic model allows:

- a stronger focus on family health and welfare during the roughly two-year peri-natal period (pre-natal to around one year), ensuring better maternal and infant well-being;
- a much higher enrolment rate for young children in early learning services by the age of two years than in other countries;
- a much stronger return to work by women than in the rest of the OECD, female employment rates in the Nordic countries being among the highest in the world. In comparison, the 'childcare for working mothers' model of services does not deliver to the same extent infant and maternal well-being, excellence in services, or outstanding female participation rates in the labour market.

The Nordic rejection of a split childcare/early education system also avoids an unnecessary duplication of administrations and the perpetuation of two different sectors with different goals, operational procedures (opening hours, fees, programmes etc.), qualification levels, salary regimes and the like. Divided auspices tend to exaggerate the weaknesses of both sectors. In general, separation of the sectors in split systems gives rise to a neglect of education and stimulation within childcare services, and a neglect of care and the social dimension of family and community in early education services. One finds many poorly qualified, even untrained staff in childcare; and many graduates trained as primary school teachers in early education. Such teachers, though admirable in many respects, are generally not trained in the family, health and social dimensions of educating young children. Early education services become organised like junior schools, with high numbers of children per teacher, insufficient care and attention to individual children, and inappropriate pedagogies. The present economic recession reinforces the tendency as few countries today are making progress in providing more effective child:staff ratios either in early education or the early classes of CSE; by 'effective' I mean ratios that would improve the quality of pedagogy and the health and well-being of young children, thereby ensuring long-term success in education.

ECE is extremely weakened by this separation of childcare and early education sectors. There is little hope of a common professional identity emerging across the whole early childhood system. Again, because the initial education of the professionals working in each sector is separate – and is often confined to 'training' or vocational colleges – there is equally little chance of common developmental theories and pedagogical practices emerging. Coming from different administrative, professional and theoretical backgrounds, early childhood professionals do not speak with a unified voice and are unable to establish an equal partnership with the education sector.

In split systems, the 'schoolification' of the ECE sector was, and remains, the most difficult issue to resolve. The relationship between ECE and CSE – partnership hardly seems the right word – is defined by the downward reach of compulsory schooling and its control of early education. In 'schoolification', early education is assimilated, both conceptually and administratively, to a traditional primary school model. School-like goals, organisation and methodologies in ECE are strengthened. Schoolified early childhood services are characterised by age segregation, with children grouped by year of birth; personnel trained as teachers using a predominantly knowledge transfer model with whole class exercises; large numbers of young children assigned to each group and insufficient attention given to the needs, talents and agency of the individual child; and often a neglect of children's play, family outreach and the social dimensions of early education. A schoolified early education sector is often matched by a childcare sector with limited educational goals and focused mainly on keeping children safe and well while parents work.

At the same time, it should be admitted that the incorporation of early education into primary school facilitates transition from one to the other. Transition to school is generally handled successfully in this model, as early education classes and the school often share the same premises, making the transition less daunting for children. In addition, as the content and classroom organisation of early education resembles that of primary schooling, a bridging curriculum going from the last grade of the former across the two first years of the latter can be put into place easily.

The trouble is that this transition curriculum is applied early, compared, for example, to the later introduction of primary school pedagogy in the Nordic pre-school class at the age of 6 years. Although an academic curriculum can make transition into school easier for children, it still remains a transition based on the extension downwards of primary schooling and does not take into account the needs, capacities and interests of young children. The goal is a compliant child, attuned to listening to the teacher and channelled toward reaching specified levels in skills deemed useful in school. Research suggests that this narrowing of content does not correspond to the psychological and developmental needs of children; there is wide agreement that young children learn best through meaningful interaction with caring adults, their peers and with real materials and experiences rather than the teaching of isolated skills (Katz, 2011; Bodrova, 2008; Elkind, 2007; Marcon, 2002). And it is a far cry from Malaguzzi's vision of the rich child, eager to use the 'hundred languages of childhood', that is the myriad ways in which thinking and emotion can be expressed.

Good pedagogical practice in many countries

All this is not to imply that everything was, or is, wrong in ECE outside the Nordic countries. There were many excellent programmes in the countries that the OECD review teams visited. Many education ministries, administrators and teachers were strong advocates of learner-centred education and active learning methods for young children. And in quite a few countries, teachers were trained in the basics of early childhood education, that is, in the practice of a relational pedagogy, respect for developmental readiness and the natural learning strategies of young children. Many countries had also a broad curriculum addressing health and motor development, self-regulation and behaviour; social skills and the emergence of values; a focus on language development with an emphasis on expression and communication; and a regular and strong contact with the parents of children.

By and large, however, ECE was held back by a labour economist vision of 'childcare for working parents' (only secondarily, for children!) and by an understanding of education that was forged in the late nineteenth century, namely, seeing education as the transmission of predetermined knowledge and values, decided by government or other adult interests. The contrast with practice in places that had strongly theorised the early childhood field was striking. In Finland, for example, the pre-school classes run by the Ministry of Education for 6-year-old children were characterised by 'concrete experimentation, children's own investigation, playful activities, imagination, interaction, drama, active participation, information acquisition, problem solving, and reflection' (Sinko, 2006). In fact, the whole Finnish primary school was marked by a socio-constructivist learning conception in which the active role of children was considered essential, and in which there was no grading or ranking of children. Likewise, the influential *Experiential Education* movement in the Flemish community in Belgium was beginning to change the focus in many *kleuterschool* (see Chapter 8), from covering the contents of the curriculum toward supporting each child's well-being and involvement in deep learning.

The influence of Reggio Emilia was also growing, particularly in settings that were open to experimentation and reflection on democratic practice in education. The Reggio schools were strongly influenced by their social and historical context and were concerned 'to maintain a vision of children who can think and act for themselves' (Dahlberg *et al.*, 2007, p. 12). Reggio opposed dominant educational discourses, such as seeing early childhood services as places to produce pre-defined outcomes that had not been discussed with staff and parents or that ignored the interests, experience and choices of young children. Its adoption of a 'pedagogy of listening' sought to respect the efforts of children to make meaning of their experience, and contested the dominant notion of ECE as being merely preparation for school (Rinaldi, 2006). At the same time, as Peter Moss indicates, Reggio Emilia has retained the name *scuola* or 'school', seeking to enhance the ideal of the public school and restore its prestige.

Is the recommendation of 'a strong and equal partnership' relevant today?

To my mind, the recommendation of 'a strong and equal partnership' between ECE and CSE remains as necessary as ever, in particular, the *equal* partnership element. Obviously, the recommendation needs better theorisation and embodiment in practice – in other words, we need a better understanding of what the notion means, what the conditions are for such a partnership to emerge, and how it might be operationalised in concrete terms. But the need to build up such a partnership remains as little progress has been made in this respect since the publication of the *Starting Strong* reports.

More governments and policy makers may advocate partnership now than in the past and, no doubt, would like to see a smooth and seamless continuum in services from childcare into early education and thence into compulsory schooling. But this continuum is seen as predominantly an operational challenge, a smoothing out of difficulties as they occur. Action may take the form of introducing more 'quality' or 'learning' into childcare services, more care and equity into early education (but without reducing child:staff ratios), and evening out the transition between early education and the primary school. Useful as these policies are, they underestimate what a real partnership between the early childhood sector and primary school could bring about.

The potential contribution of ECE

A true partnership is a relationship between equals, in which both sides have something to contribute. Communication and co-operation are important aims but partnership should not be confined to good relations. An essential element is the ongoing dialogue between the partners about the traditions, goals, concepts, contents, processes and practices of education –

all in the best interests of young children. Just now, the contribution of ECE to this dialogue could be great as it so happens that strong traditional themes in ECE – listening to the learner; supporting the child to take charge of her own learning; providing authentic learning environments and processes; encouraging creativity and freedom; learning through team projects; learning to live together – are again being discussed seriously within the wider education field. Likewise, the notion of a liberal education introducing children and students to a broad range of disciplines, activities and civic responsibilities is again attracting attention, a notion that has always been central in early childhood pedagogy with its emphasis on the *whole* child and her introduction into society.

When one reads research on twenty-first-century goals for education or more recent commentaries on findings from the OECD's Programme for International Student Assessment (see Chapter 1), one is struck by the similarities between the concepts discussed and the traditional goals and practices of ECE. For example, the Partnership for 21st Century Skills (http://www.p21.org/) in the United States speaks about the need to develop in students critical thinking and problem solving, communication and teamwork skills, and the ability to create and innovate through applying knowledge, imagination and invention. In parallel, Andreas Schleicher (2011), head of the PISA project, while defending strongly the mastery of clearly defined core content (in compulsory education), also emphasises the ability to apply knowledge creatively.

Schleicher argues that it is extremely difficult for curriculum developers to forecast now what students will need in the global economy of tomorrow. He notes that the ten professions most in demand in 2009 did not even exist in 2003. Schleicher divides work into five categories: *routine manual* (work done by hand in the same way every day); *non-routine manual* (work done by hand that requires the application of knowledge, skill and judgment); *routine cognitive* (white-collar, administrative jobs using knowledge items traditionally learnt in schools); *non-routine analytic* (the application of knowledge in new settings – a category which PISA is able to measure already); and *non-routine interactive* (the capacity to communicate, collaborate, manage and resolve conflicts – a category for which the PISA team is developing indicators). Demand for the two routine categories of worker is dropping sharply, while, demand for non-routine manual (artisan) work remains steady. But demand for the last two categories – *non-routine analytic* and especially, *non-routine interactive* – is growing sharply.

It is not an exaggeration to say that the practice of *non-routine interactive* and *non-routine analytic* skills has been a feature of early childhood theory and practice since the time of Froebel and can be found today in teacher accompanied, play-based early childhood programmes. In this regard, the approach of Reggio Emilia seems entirely contemporary, for example, its practice of respectful educational relationships with children that are sensitive to their investigative interests, and its desire for children to interact and to keep open the 'hundred languages', that is, 'the different ways children (human beings) represent, communicate and express their thinking in different media and symbolic systems' (Vecchi, 2010, p. 9). As Rinaldi (2006) writes: '[Learning takes] many directions and often leads to unexpected places', a sentiment that is echoed by Eisner (2002): 'Life is a multimedia event, and the meanings that we secure from life are not simply contained in text; they yield their content through a wide variety of forms.'

In short, the contribution of the early childhood tradition to the emerging debate in education is potentially very valuable. However, with a few notable exceptions, this contribution has not been made: ECE is often inaudible in the debate. Some of the reasons have already been mentioned, for example, the weakened state of split systems and the incorporation of the early education sector into the ambit of the primary school. This separation exacerbates the weaknesses of each sector – undermining qualifications, pedagogical practice and research in childcare and narrowing curriculum in early education toward emergent literacy and numeracy. For example, the recent federal *Early Learning Challenge* in the United States reinforces the alignment of ECE with 'kindergarten', the pre-school class for 5-year-olds in primary schools, and proposes even the use of kindergarten entry assessments.

This remaking of early education into a junior form of traditional schooling impoverishes early childhood research and undermines the specificity of the early childhood tradition. Early childhood is a brief moment in the education cycle when relationships, processes, modelling and the child's personal meaning-making are far more important than any one selected skill or content, useful as that skill may be in later schooling. Young children learn deeply through relationships, through their bodies and freedom of movement, through their personal interests and their play, through watching, listening and doing. This is a critical moment in life when children are forging a personal identity; for this reason, an important goal of the initial education of teachers must be how to conduct a nurturing pedagogical relationship with young children, to understand how young children learn, to model social behaviour and to respond to the *many* developmental tasks that are important to the child at this moment in life. To forget this is to ignore the social and affective life of the child. With a positive socio-emotional development and a broad knowledge base, children will quickly master literacy and numeracy (and other challenges).

However, under pressure from education initiatives – which may have some limited relevance in schools and colleges – ECE tends, in many countries, to limit its scope and become 'educational' in the narrowest sense. It has little to say for itself, instead applying the accepted education fashions of the moment. Curricula increasingly give precedence to preset learning objectives at specific ages over the central task of supporting the child to make sense of *her own* experiences; teachers are trained to 'deliver' lessons and to devote much time to administrative requirements and accountability measures; table-top work takes precedence over learning by doing; socio-emotional development is restricted through placing young children in large groups with little freedom of movement, where they are obliged to interact not horizontally toward each other but vertically toward a teacher.

Of course, not all practice is like this: but my recent work in European countries suggests that governments often understand ECE as primarily a preparation for school. The central goals of early childhood are seldom discussed. Instruction is favoured over a specific, relational pedagogy for young children; the family environment or services for children under 3 years are given little importance; and the impact of the social environment on learning and success in school is insufficiently researched. In sum, by becoming a satellite of the school, the early childhood sector has lost its identity and has little of originality to contribute to the education debate.

It need not be so. When it draws on its own traditions and revisits the basic goals, concepts and pedagogical approaches suitable for young children, the early childhood research community is well capable of not only organising a comprehensive and aligned early learning system for young children from 1 to 6 years of age, but also of creating unique concepts, pedagogical approaches and innovative ideas about democratic education. This is illustrated in the splendid paper by Gunilla Dahlberg and Hillevi Lenz-Taguchi, discussed at some length in the introductory essay, on which I now offer some comments.

A reflection on Dahlberg and Lenz-Taguchi (1994)

The goal of creating a new meeting place between ECE and CSE is at the heart of this paper. The paper is organised into two parts, the first dealing with traditional power relationships and the pedagogical practices of pre-school and school in Sweden. I shall focus here on the vision of a new meeting place outlined in Part II of the paper. This vision requires that both preschool and school – ECE and CSE – should create a meeting place where concepts and pedagogical practices can be reworked in common:

The meeting place

The meeting place is a space for reflection on and construction of not only values, images and ideas, but also pedagogical practice. 'With a starting point of the view of the child as a constructor of culture and knowledge', Dahlberg and Lenz-Taguchi envision a meeting place 'where both the pre-school teachers and the primary school teachers are given the possibility to develop their pedagogical practices' (Dahlberg and Lenz-Taguchi, 1994):

If one wants to reach a long-term development of the pre-school and school's pedagogical work, then a work of change, according to our way of thinking, begins with a common view of the child, learning and knowledge. Such a work of change requires a conscious effort towards reaching a true meeting place. A meeting place where pre-school and school have a similar view of the learning child, pedagogy's role, and the pedagogical work and which is built on the same value base.

(ibid.)

In sum, a productive relationship starts with co-constructing shared understandings through encounters in which the domination of one sector by the other is avoided. The dialogue could begin with discussion of the curriculum and goal documents 'which build the foundation for the pedagogical work in the pre-school and school', including values for both ECE and CSE 'which are all about children's rights to equal life opportunities and education, to develop their resources and potential' (Dahlberg and Lenz-Taguchi, p. 33), as well as highlighting democracy as a fundamental value. Through the meeting place relationship, it is possible to envisage, as Peter Moss does, a dialogue across the whole field of education: early childhood, compulsory school and beyond.

The image of the child

Dahlberg and Lenz-Taguchi emphasise that the child and childhood can be understood in different ways: 'the child is always a social construction and not the actual child' (ibid.). Their understanding is that the child is born as an eager learner, an active constructor of culture and knowledge. The pre-school needs to move away from a construction of the child as nature, that is, the assumption that the child and her learning follow predetermined, sequential and predictable stages – the view of the child favoured in developmental psychology which, in 1994, was the dominant paradigm in early childhood pedagogy.

Another dominant construction – derived from and still current in the school – is seeing the child as a reproducer of knowledge. The young child is considered 'as an empty vessel or tabula rasa . . . [needing] to be filled with knowledge, skills and dominant cultural values which are already determined, socially determined and ready to administer – a process of reproduction or transmission' (Dahlberg et al., 2007, p. 44). This dominant discourse of readying children – to learn, to enter school, to achieve predetermined outcomes – ignores the potential with which children are born, their many talents and their innate desire to make their own meanings, a potential expressed in this statement:

Our image of the child is what Loris Malaguzzi, a leading European figure in the field of services for young children, termed the 'rich' child: by which he meant not materially rich, but a child born with great potential that can be expressed in a hundred languages; an active learner, seeking the meaning of the world from birth, a co-creator of knowledge, identity, culture and values; a child that can live, learn, listen and communicate, but always in relation with others; the whole child, the child with body, mind, emotions, creativity, history and social identity; an individual, whose individuality and autonomy depend on interdependence, and who needs and wants connections with other children and adults; a citizen with a place in society, a subject of rights whom the society must respect and support.

(Children in Europe, 2004, p. 6)

Learning

Rinaldi (2006) observes in her book in the present *Contesting Early Childhood* series that 'the process of "becoming" is the basis of true education' (p. 80). Learning must be treated as impossible to predict, plan, supervise or evaluate according to predefined standards. This presents a real challenge today, as much importance is placed on the achievement of predetermined goals. In this sense, compulsory schooling has pedagogical choices to make. Schools need 'to consciously take a position on *which knowledge* they intend to promote' (Vecchi, 2010, p. 28, original emphasis). They can pursue an idea of teaching that 'chooses to transmit to children circumscribed "truths" in various "disciplines"' (ibid.); or they can choose 'to stand by children's sides together constructing contexts in which children can explore their own ideas and hypotheses individually or in groups and discuss them with friends or teachers' (ibid.). Rinaldi (2006) likewise remarks that knowledge is primarily a social practice, based on relationships.

The teacher and a new pedagogical relationship

The image of the child as an active constructor of knowledge and culture is matched by an understanding of the ECE teacher as a reflective practitioner who, through appropriate supports and practices, co-constructs learning with children. This understanding is based on the premise that the directions and outcomes of learning are not always pre-determined. The investigative child is smothered in the teacher-dominated, knowledge-transmitting model, becoming instead a passive, compliant learner. In the new understanding of teaching and learning, a pedagogy of relationships and listening is needed, not one of transmission and question-answer.

We should remember that there is no creativity in the child if there is no creativity in the adult: the competent and creative child exists if there is a competent and creative adult...one of the primary tasks of the teacher, and thus of the school, is to help the child and the group of children learn how to learn, fostering their natural predisposition toward relationships and the consequent co-construction of knowledge.

(Rinaldi, 2006, p. 120)

Co-construction does not mean that curriculum is abandoned. Open curricular frameworks can provide both guidance and freedom to the early childhood centre through announcing (after consultation) shared curricular goals built round broad thematic areas. In this way, literacy and numeracy skills can be introduced but within the wider context of communication and expression, and with respect for what Reggio Emilia calls the 'hundred languages'. Shared pedagogical approaches are also possible, based for example, on the agency of the child and thereafter on a pedagogy of relationships and listening.

Documentation

The new relationship between teacher and child and the role of reflective practitioner calls for new educational tools and processes, in particular documentation. The purpose of documentation is to record and share what has happened in order to understand better the construction of learning and knowledge. When a piece of documentation is shared collegially, it enables teachers to discuss real, concrete things – 'not just theories or words, about which it is easy to reach easy and naive agreement' (Hoyuelos, 2004, p. 7). Through documentation, teachers can create a living and critical discussion about pedagogical practice and the enabling and limiting conditions. Documentation can serve various purposes, including learning, assessment, the creation of a culture of investigation and reflection, and generate legitimacy for education, both pre-school and school. Legitimacy is created 'when documentation is shared with parents and community as a visualisation of the pedagogy practised in the pre-school and the school' (Dahlberg and Lenz-Taguchi, 1994).

A rethinking of the school

The school is often understood today not as a space of discussion and construction of knowledge but as a place where children learn prescribed subjects or 'core knowledge' and compete with each other in reproducing it. The transfer of concrete and assessable knowledge is its primary goal. Subjects are mostly decided and organised by others, and not by the children, in contrast to the 'pre-school's tradition of child-centredness, where the ideal is that the child, as much as possible, should choose the contents and forms of expression' (ibid.).

The construction of the child in the compulsory school tradition as a re-producer of predetermined knowledge is paralleled by teacher-directed learning in which teachers dominate classroom interactions. Because of these differences in tradition, it is necessary that pre-school and school search together for a common heritage of ideas about learning and knowl-edge, acknowledging the existence of difference but also the possibility of finding some common ground. As Peter Moss notes, the use of the word 'school' in Reggio Emilia's ECE 'is a deliberate attempt to reclaim a generic concept of "school", turning away from its frequent association today as a place of transmission and reproduction and foregrounding instead a place of democracy and relationships, creativity and research.'

A common values base

Pedagogical activities in both ECE and CSE are connected, or should be, to the critical questions: *what do we want for our children here and now and in the future? What do we want from our societal institutions?* These are values-based questions that cannot be answered by government alone, but need to be discussed also by parents and communities and in the institu-tions concerned. ECE and CSE must 'gather round a living pedagogical value-base and a practically applied philosophy ... which has wide support from the personnel, parents, leadership, and politicians in the municipali-ties' (ibid., p. 38). Underlying the practice of discussion and participation is respect for the value of democracy:

> These reflections lead to another value that is part of our experience, and that is, the value of democracy, which is intrinsic to the concept of participation: participation of the families, but also of the children and teachers in the school project. This extremely important issue deserves at least a brief mention, because we must not forget how closely the school is connected to the society in which it is situated. There is the recurring question of whether the school is limited to transmitting culture or can be, as we in Reggio aspire to, a place where culture is constructed and democracy is lived. School and democracy, a theme that was dear to Dewey, is an important commit-ment for all of us: school as a place of democracy, in which we can all live democracy.
>
> (Rinaldi, 2006, pp. 140–1)

Peter Moss comments that in the meeting place, ethical values are also at stake:

Ethically, the concept of a meeting place can evoke the concept of the ethics of an encounter...A central theme of this ethical approach to relationships is the importance of relating to the Other in a way that respects the Other's alterity and avoids the process of grasping to make the Other into the Same. The desire to classify children into pre-made categories, so prevalent in education today, is one example of grasping; pursuing a 'readiness for school' relationship that leads to 'schoolification' can be seen as another.

Appraising the notion of meeting place

The notion of the meeting place – and the concepts within it – is a rich one. It goes beyond the *Starting Strong* recommendation, giving the proposal a content and direction which was not made explicit in the OECD text. If taken on board, the practice of a meeting place between early childhood and the compulsory school could revolutionise pedagogical thinking in both institutions.

However, to my mind, the vision of the meeting place is insufficiently operationalised, that is, it does not yet indicate where the meeting place or discussion might take place or in what form. At first view, it would seem plausible that research journals, training colleges and university research departments are obvious spaces for such dialogue. But each has its own difficulties and obstacles to surmount, for example:

- *Research journals.* It is possible and desirable that research journals should give room to different perspectives but a review of early childhood journals suggests that relatively few explore new paradigms and concepts. To retain a wide readership, journals tend to cover several fields of research – 'evidence-based' research (RCTs, longitudinal studies, experimental research based on representative sampling, a control group, proper statistical analysis...), practitioner research, descriptions of what works, techniques to improve quality, etc. – even if this research is inscribed in the *status quo.*
- *Universities and other institutions for education and research.* In some countries, this is quite possible; for example, in Sweden, university departments educate the future early childhood teachers and conduct a wide range of research on the Swedish pre-school and its underlying concepts and values. However, in many countries, early childhood personnel are not trained at university level, but rather in training colleges that generally do not have a mandate or budget for research. Many more early childhood staff, mostly in the childcare sector, are educated through short credit courses or may not receive any training. The emphasis is often strongly practical, for example, how to carry out certain procedures of care or on practising the skills of education, such

as, class management and lesson preparation – all useful and necessary skills but restricted to a range decided by management. Teachers are 'trained' rather than educated to reflect on the interplay of theory and practice or to engage in individual and collegial reflection on the goals of education and the particular needs and capacities of specific communities and individual children.

As a result, early childhood research remains weak and the scope of national debate – in so far as it exists – can be quite limited, focusing for example on improving classroom quality through standards, rating systems, higher staff-to-child ratios, teacher retention, etc. In sum, the conceptual debate, is not heard often enough and needs to be rooted much more concretely in all parts of ECE and CSE; and this conceptual debate is necessary as nothing can change without engaging with concepts and visions of education, both as they appear now in ECE and CSE and how they might appear through a process of co-construction.

The following spaces are proposed, but in the knowledge that difficulties are present in each one of them:

a.   *To continue the discussion in the usual intellectual fora* (research jour-nals, university research seminars, media discussions, etc.), despite the difficulties mentioned above.

b.   *To focus on shared education of ECE and CSE teachers in certain matters.* This envisages that the education of both ECE and CSE teach-ers should be organised in common on certain general education topics, for example, the philosophy and history of education. The habit of CSE and ECE talking together, without hierarchy, should be formed as early as possible, complemented by a recognition of equal status through parity of pay and working conditions. This is not to say that early child-hood methodology and pedagogy should disappear, as has happened in a number of European countries where early childhood teachers have been replaced by primary school teachers in early education.

c.   *To bring school teachers into ECE and ECE teachers into the school.* As mentioned, the latter is achieved in the Nordic pre-school classes. Team work is further strengthened in these countries by the presence of free-time pedagogues (see Chapter 1) in schools, who bring a strong social care dimension to education. Primary teachers in ECE are less usual, except in countries where primary education has taken over early education, but it would be beneficial for both sectors if some means of involving primary school teachers in authentic ECE could be found. If properly organised, the transition period can offer such an opportunity. The opportunity also exists in large children's centres that include a school as well as early childhood education and care. But there are many obstacles to such an outcome. The hierarchical nature of the professions often prevents not just the shared staffing of services but even dialogue from taking place. The presence of a large private child-care sector further complicates the organisation of common training.

d.   *To concretise the meeting place at the level of administration(s).* In another essay, Peter Moss outlines in more detail his vision of the meeting place and democratic experimentalism (Moss, 2009). He describes materialising the vision at three administrative levels: the level of government (the Nordic countries are taken as an example), the regional/municipal level (Reggio Emilia is the chosen example) and at the centre level (the example is the Sheffield Children's Centre). His text throws valuable light on the responsibilities and activities that each level can offer. For example, at the local level in Italy, some municipalities take responsibility for the children and their education, not just for providing services but for how services are understood.

> The local authority becomes responsible for the image of the early childhood institution; for the purposes the early childhood services serve in that community; and for the pedagogical practice that goes on within them... What these local projects have in common is an idea of the community creating a space for democratic enquiry and dialogue from which a collective view of the child and her relationship to the community is produced and local policy, practice and knowledge develops. This in turn is always open to democratic evaluation and new thinking.

A difficulty with this vision is that it depends for execution – perhaps even for discussion – on notions of *gemeinschaft*[2] (Tönnies, 2001), citizenship and democracy that are relatively weak in urban society today. In many instances, the very idea of community, based on proximity, neighbourliness and common interest, has faded, even if revived briefly during local elections. The abiding experience of urbanised populations today is that of the individual consumer guided by rational self-interest or, if belonging to the minority poor, by expectations that the state rather than the local community will provide assistance.

If citizenship is to survive, then our education systems need to be inspired again by that ideal of the kindergarten: *learning to live together*, which finally is a far more important and complex lesson to communicate to young children than much that passes for education in current curricula. As Dewey, Freire and other great educators have emphasised: education must also occupy itself with citizenship and democracy. This is not a utopian notion; several countries in Europe (Finland, Norway, Slovenia, Sweden) make explicit reference to democracy and to the Convention on the Rights of the Child in their early childhood curricula. The first chapter of the Swedish *Curriculum for Preschool* (Swedish Ministry of Education and Science , 1998) begins as follows (a statement echoed in the 2010 revision of the curriculum):

> Democracy forms the foundation of the pre-school. For this reason all pre-school activity should be carried out in accordance with fundamental democratic values…An important task of the pre-school is to establish and help children acquire the values on which our society is based. The inviolability of human life, individual freedom and integrity, the equal value of all people, equality between the genders as well as solidarity with the weak and vulnerable are all values that the school shall actively promote in its work with children.
>
> The pre-school should take into account and develop children's ability to take responsibility and manage their social life in society so that solidarity and tolerance are established at an early stage. The pre-school should encourage and strengthen the child's compassion and empathy for others. All activities should be characterised by care for the individual and aim at developing a sense of empathy and consideration for others, as well as openness and respect for the differences in the way people think and live.

At this level also, the early childhood sector has much to contribute to the education debate.

Notes

1   Although I co-authored the two *Starting Strong* reports, major credit for the concept of a strong and equal partnership should go to Dr Michelle Neuman (now with the World Bank), with whom I had the pleasure of discussing the issue over several years at the OECD.
2   Gemeinschaft (community feeling) is a concept developed at the beginning of the twentieth century by the German sociologist, Ferdinand Tönnies. It refers to the feeling of community and solidarity which orients individuals to the common good rather than to their own self-interest. In education, the notion was strongly developed by John Dewey (1859–1952), who saw public education as the bedrock of community and democracy. Outside a handful of commentators, the ideas of this great educational philosopher are rarely mentioned in current education debates, which tend to focus on league tables, pre-defined learning standards, techniques, tool-boxes and *what works.*

Chapter 3

A dialogue with the co-author of 'the vision of a meeting place'

Gunilla Dahlberg

This chapter is based on several discussions between Gunilla Dahlberg (GD) and Peter Moss (PM) about the 1994 paper *Förskola och skola – om två skilda traditioner och om visionen om en mötesplats* (Preschool and school – two different traditions and the vision of a meeting place) (Dahlberg and Lenz-Taguchi, 1994), which features prominently in the introductory essay. It has been edited by Peter Moss.

PM: Can you explain the context of the 1994 paper you wrote with Hillevi Lenz-Taguchi?

GD: It was written for a commission – commissions are very much part of the system in Sweden – on the extended school (*Utbildnings departementets utredning förlängd skolgång*). The report of the Commission, published in 1994, was titled *Grunden för livslångt lärande, En barnmogen skola, Betänkande av utredningen om förlängd skolgång* (The foundation for lifelong learning: a school ready for children). The Commission was looking at whether to extend compulsory schooling in Sweden (which began at 7 years) from 9 to 10 years and, if so, whether by adding an extra year before or after the current compulsory school period. The Commission was related to major changes underway, including more globalisation, the emergence of the so-called knowledge society and the increasing attention being given to lifelong learning. It was asked to consider the new requirements that these changes placed on education and the consequences of its work for growth and competitiveness.

It is also important to situate our paper in the wider context of early childhood policy in Sweden. Since 1975, all 6-year-olds were entitled to a place at a pre-school or *förskolan,* our term for a centre for children from 1 to 6 years of age. In 1991, the government introduced 'flexible' school starting, giving parents the choice of placing 6-year-olds either in pre-schools or in schools. At the time we wrote our paper, most parents were pleased with pre-schools, and wanted their children to remain there. But these changes were increasing interest in the relationship between pre-school and school.

A number of working papers were commissioned by the Extended School Commission, mostly from labour force experts and economists. Hillevi and I were asked to write a paper of around 25 pages on the difference between the pre-school tradition and the school tradition. We approached the task with great trepidation, as these traditions are so complex. We actually started the paper with an English saying – 'Fools rush in where angels fear to tread' – which we got from the book *Angels Fear: Towards an Epistemology of the Sacred*, in which Catherine Bateson completes the work her father, Gregory Bateson, was working on at the time of his death, and that he had hesitated to write as it addressed new questions about his former thinking.

Like Bateson, we felt that we were wrestling with ideas that transgressed a lot of mainstream thinking, in both early childhood and compulsory school education. I remember hesitating. Did we really have the courage to question this mainstream thinking, and in such a short space?

PM: Why did the Commission ask you and Hillevi to prepare this paper on the relationship between pre-school and school?

GD: At the time, we were both at the Stockholm Institute of Education [since incorporated into Stockholm University]. Hillevi was a doctoral student in our research group. I had been a researcher in early childhood education since 1971. In the mid-1980s, I was involved in several projects researching the reform process in the Swedish ECE system, which led to several books in which we took a critical perspective.

At that time, Sweden was going through a major process of decentralisation, from central to local government. The country was also moving from what we termed a 'rule-governed' to a 'goal-governed' system. But there was, as we saw it, a paradox in this process: the paradox of decentralisation. In the new decentralised state, evaluation came in as a new system of governing, a new means of exercising power and control. We problematised this in a book I wrote with Ulf Lundgren, then a professor at the Stockholm Institute of Education, and Gunnar Åsén, then a doctoral student and now a professor in our department. The book – *Att utvärdera barnomsorg: Att utvärdera barnomsorg. Om decentralisering, målstyrning och utvärdering av barnomsorgen och dess pedagogiska verksamhet* (To evaluate childcare: on decentralisation, goal governing and evaluation of the childcare system and its pedagogical activities) – was published in 1991. The work that led to the book was funded by the Ministry of Social Affairs [at that time responsible for ECE], who asked us to develop our thoughts on evaluation; and the senior civil servant in the Ministry wrote a preface to the book saying it was of great interest to all those engaged in discussions about the public sector and especially those engaged in the new debates in the field of ECE.

The book was written in a new economic and political context for Sweden; the fast post-war growth had lost momentum and our economy was not so good. This brought the relationship between the state and society back onto the agenda. People were asking not only about ECE, but more generally: Are we using our money effectively? Is the early childhood system productive? Do we need increased choice, based on more competition, proliferation of services and greater cost-effectiveness? Should we allow stronger marketisation? How much should we deregulate? In the late 1980s I was giving a lot of talks and lectures on these issues, offering a critical analysis of economistic concepts like 'human capital', 'effectiveness' and 'productivity'.

We argued in the book that evaluation is the most important question we have to deal with, as if we are not careful, the instruments of evaluation, not the goals, will govern practice (see also Dahlberg and Åsén, 1994). We pointed out that to legitimise ECE it was necessary to discuss issues of effectiveness and productivity from an economic perspective – but that this was only one element of legitimation. More important was how to construct an environment for children's development and learning.

Both the pre-school and compulsory school systems had previously been seen in Sweden as a common good, a public space, for which we as citizens should take responsibility. Following on, the argument we put forward was that ECE is not just a commodity, like a factory selling goods on a market. It's a cultural and symbolic activity related to the reproduction of society and civilisation, but also to constructing new knowledge, values and identities and, therefore, to change and innovation.

PM: It sounds as if this book influenced the 1994 paper. Can you say more about how?

GD: Some of the analyses and arguments in the 1994 paper are closely related to our book on evaluation. It formed, if you like, the *gestalt* that Hillevi and I had when we agreed to produce the paper. Let me give some examples.

In one chapter of the book – 'Paradoxes in the knowledge society: on the schoolification of pre-school children's lives' – we referred to studies in the United States and to the 1983 US Commission on Excellence in Education, which had explored the failure of the American school system. We observed how this discussion of the low achievement of American school children was related to fears of not being able to keep up with and compete economically with Japan in an increasingly globalised world. There had been similar fears in the 1950s, the so-called 'Sputnik psychosis', that time focused on the Soviet Union. The difference was that then the school system could be extended upwards in age; while in the 1980s the focus had to turn towards pre-school ages, as it did not seem possible to further extend the compulsory school system upwards.

In the book we described how this new climate of competition bred a whole industry of evaluation in the United States resulting in huge investments in different programmes to evaluate if pre-school programmes such as Head Start, Follow Through and High Scope were effective. This development had started a debate in the United States around 'the super baby syndrome' and arguments such as 50 per cent of children's intelligence is reached by a specific age were common, resulting in an intensified search for a 'magic period' in the pre-school years. Brain researchers became involved in the United States and all this spread to other countries. In Sweden, for example, David Ingvar said that the period between 3 and 6 years was the 'one chance for the brain'; while another neuro-scientist, Matti Bergström, argued that this supported a narrow-minded view of training children. He called instead for play and creativity during these years and he even wrote a book with the provocative title *The Child: The Last Slave*. In this context, the book *The Hurried Child*, by American psychologist David Elkind, made many researchers as well as parents concerned, as it painted a picture of more and more children being rushed and drilled, with symptoms of stress becoming visible at younger and younger ages in all classes in society.

In our book, we wrote that we must be careful not to sort children out at ever earlier ages using institutional definitions of what is good and not good, normal and not normal. Such definitions would govern children from ever earlier ages and too readily took children's failures and inadequate skills as a starting point, placing problems within the children and ignoring children's meaning-making and pedagogical activities that can support their development, learning and well-being. For many children, we argued, this would be very distressing, feeling from an earlier and earlier age that they could not handle the requirements that the pre-school placed on them: they would learn that they could not learn.

We also warned, like some other researchers, of the risk of just pushing the compulsory school curriculum and its requirements further down in age – schoolification. We referred to Daniel J. Walsh's research, in which he had examined this development in the United States and commented on the narrow ideas about knowledge and children's learning that were being expressed: to sit still, be attentive, recognise and write letters and numbers. As Michael Apple and others had shown, one consequence of this approach was that the content of education was increasingly governed by the products of commercial companies.

In another chapter in our book – 'The test in the centre' – we described how evaluation had become synonymous with studying the effects of different programmes on the individual. Consequently, education was coming to be seen as a simplified matter of being able to perform well on tests of state mandated standards. We argued that such forms of evaluation tell teachers little about how to change pedagogical practice, being for control and not for change. We were apprehensive, too, that extensive testing would take a lot of time away from really following children's learning strategies and learning processes; it would take the place of making both content and pedagogical practice meaningful for children.

The comprehensive goals of the educational system are difficult to evaluate with simple tests. To make real change happen, other types of data are required. So, here we flagged up what by then was called the 'black-box problem', by proposing that to understand and explain why a pedagogical activity functions in a specific way it is not enough to compare goals and results. One has to study the whole learning chain and all its components: the goals and results, but also the pedagogical process – and the frame factors.

Ulf Lundgren's frame factor theory was important for our thinking (Lundgren, 1977). Through extensive empirical studies, the theory tried to answer what the 'frames of possibility' were for enabling or constraining certain kinds of processes. It did this by an understanding of teaching as constrained and governed to a great extent by events and determinants outside the teaching process, such as time, space and allocation of resources. Its focus was the political steering and control of education from the perspective of the state. I think one could say that, in its broadest sense, the theory was worked out by Ulf from a concern for equality and democracy, both within education and through education.

A third example of how the book was important as a form of 'door opener' for the 1994 paper was a chapter titled 'Evaluation of early childhood education: some basic principles and a model'. We tried to sketch some principles for evaluation, at both national and local levels, using a kind of interactive and participatory perspective and the idea of *agoras* for the exchange of experience between politicians, professionals and parents. In our own circle, this had already been practised by Harold Göthson (1989) for a couple of years and we found it very promising. In this chapter, we also critiqued the routine collection of data from pre-schools and parents, data that were seldom fed back to the pre-schools, data that seemed to us both ineffective and very time-consuming.

In that context, with inspiration from the pre-schools in Reggio Emilia, we brought in the idea of continuous documentation, which would give teachers possibilities to reflect and discuss children's meaning-making and learning, covering all the components in the chain – the goals, the frames, the processes, the results – and with an emphasis on processes: something which Hillevi and I came back to in the 1994 paper. We hoped that such pedagogical documentation would introduce new knowledge as a basis for evaluations at the national level that might be more in line with the visions and goals of our pre-school system, visions and goals that respect equality and social justice. I am here saying 'hoped', because of our understanding of the complexity of pedagogical documentation; we realised it would require a lot of deconstructive work when it came to the image of the child, knowledge and learning as well as the whole organisation of the pre-school environment.

PM: Your 1994 paper places great emphasis on the social construction of the child. How did that come into your thinking?

GD: In the 1980s, at the same time as my work on reforms in the early childhood sector, I lectured a lot on the social construction of the child and in particular about three constructions: the child as nature, as knowledge and culture reproducer, and as knowledge and culture constructor. Inspiration for these lectures came both from my 1985 doctoral thesis – 'Context and the child's orientation to meaning' – and from the work of Michel Foucault on dominant discourses and from other post-structural thinkers.

In my thesis I problematised the discipline of developmental psychology. I observed that the discourse of developmental psychology was regarded within the Swedish ECE system almost as an omnipotent God for the construction of what a child is, can be and should be. It was an essentialist discourse, which had resulted in a de-contextualised child. To contest developmental psychology I used Basil Bernstein's very important and impressive research on children's orientation to meaning and its relationship with social class. In the thesis, pedagogic discourse was analysed as an act of normalisation, intended to produce homogeneity. I related this to Pierre Bourdieu, who by that time was close to us in our research group. He had said that the prevailing situation was characterised by a form of cultural inertia: it makes us see the ideology of the school as a liberating force and as a means of increasing mobility, although it is actually normalising.

I also referred to Foucault (1977), who had drawn our attention to a paradox: of homogeneity and individualisation. At the same time as pedagogic discourse produces homogeneity, it also becomes a means of exercising power through individualisation, as its methods of control make it possible to assess each child's development and, hence, also the distance between children. Subsequently I have taken this problematic further in a couple of articles about a change in the constitution of the self: a self that is constructed as autonomous rather than social and that has to take care of its own individual risks; and a self that is constructed as a consumer who must calculate the 'best buy' when it comes to a choice of pre-school and school (Dahlberg, 2000, 2003).

Also I should mention two books that were very important in my thinking. There was *Changing the Subject: Psychology, Social Regulation and Subjectivity*, by Julian Henriques and others (1984), and especially Valerie Walkerdine's contribution, 'Developmental psychology and the child-centred pedagogy: the insertion of Piaget into early childhood education'. And the book by Nikolas Rose (1989), *Governing the Soul: Shaping of the Private Self*, in which with inspiration from Foucault's thinking he presented a new way of understanding and analysing the links between expertise, subjectivity and political power. His argument that the proliferation of the 'psy' disciplines was intrinsically linked with transformations in governmentality, for example in the rationalities and technologies of political power in advanced liberal democracies, together with Valerie Walkerdine's thinking, gave me courage in the 1994 paper: to deconstruct both the idea of the 'innocent and spontaneous child' and the stage theory perspective of developmental psychology, and the associated image of the 'child as nature' so prevalent in the ECE field by then. An image we had begun to understand as quite often resulting in processes of normalisation.

Foucault's examinations of the ontological constructions of what it means to be human during specific historical period was of great value here. He had drawn our attention to the fact that as a condition of being human in our own historical period, we have to confess our hidden secrets to improve ourselves. Such therapeutic perspectives, which we had found and analysed in a research project on aesthetic learning processes, meant that instead of viewing these processes from a perspective of learning we usually had seen art and music, even play, in terms of their therapeutic value, as a way to know yourself (see Nordin-Hultman, 2004; Lind, 2010).

PM: How did Reggio Emilia enter into your thinking for the 1994 paper?
GD: The work of these theorists and philosophers combined with the everyday work that I met in the municipal schools [for 0- to 6-year-olds] in Reggio Emilia in Italy to open a new direction for my research. I first met the pedagogical work of Reggio Emilia when their exhibition – the 'Hundred Languages of Children' – came to Stockholm in 1981, the first time it had travelled outside Italy. Some years later, in 1988, I joined a small Working Group for the Study of Reggio Emilia, which met monthly to read into Reggio Emilia with the help of Anna Barsotti, a Swedish colleague who together with her husband Carlo Barsotti, a theatre producer, had been visiting Reggio for many years and become close friends with Loris Malaguzzi [the first director of Reggio Emilia's municipal schools for early childhood education]. In the Working Group we read Malaguzzi's speeches, and anything else we could find from Reggio.

We decided that talking about Reggio Emilia was not enough. We had to visit, which we did in 1989 for a week, including three days talking to Loris Malaguzzi. Some of us in the Swedish group had started to try to understand the new public management theories with their stress on leadership, which by then were becoming so prominent in Sweden, and it was this concern that got us government funding for the project. But when we asked Malaguzzi about the role of leadership in Reggio's pre-schools, his reply was clear and revelatory. Leadership, for him and Reggio, was not a question to start with: their starting point and focus was always the child. At a time when management and leadership seemed to dominate discussion of the Swedish pre-school, here was a clear voice questioning this priority and calling instead for prioritising the child and what goes on in the pre-schools – listening, relationships and learning processes.

The visit made me hopeful and gave me courage to think change is possible. I saw how in Reggio Emilia they worked with important theoretical perspectives, such as Dewey, Vygotsky, Bruner, Bateson, Maturana and Varela, Morin and many others, but without losing a focus on children's actual learning processes and creativity and on how to construct a challenging learning environment. What Reggio offered was the example of actually doing pedagogical work in a transformative and experimental way. The encounter with Reggio Emilia was a provocation and an inspiration that gave those of us involved with the Swedish pre-school hope, a belief in the world and the desire to act – to begin to construct a laboratory of alternative futures.

As I've said, before going to Reggio, I had been lecturing about the social construction of the child. But Reggio Emilia gave me the courage to believe that these theoretical and deconstructional analyses could be put to work. The first time I went to Reggio I remember coming home and thinking they are like us in Sweden, they work in the same way, but they've gone further. But on the second visit I saw they had another construction of the child, a construction tied to theoretical understandings. I could also see how they moved all the time in between the 'arena of formulation' and the 'arena of realisation' (see below), concepts from Ulf Lundgren's curriculum theory that we also brought into the 1994 paper.

One other important influence of Reggio on my thinking, apparent in the 1994 paper, is documentation. While working in an expert group on a pedagogical programme for the Swedish pre-school (1982–1987), I got excited by this way of working. In Reggio's use of pedagogical documentation, I saw a practice that followed processes and challenged children's learning. I could relate it, also, to the critical analysis of evaluation and the ideas about how to evaluate in the 1991 book. Other experts in the group asked me why I used the term 'pedagogical documentation', not just 'documentation' as in Reggio. My explanation related back to experiences in an earlier research group [see below] and Ulf Lundgren's important perspectives on curriculum theory and evaluation. Reggio's ideas of documentation did not refer just to archiving, like in a portfolio, they included reflexivity in relation to important questions, such as those raised by Ulf about the curriculum: Why are we doing this in its broadest sense? With what content are we going to work? How should this content be organised and evaluated?

Even more important, I started to understand their way of documenting as a complex process of listening. Besides this, the experience in Reggio Emilia was a pedagogical system in a whole city. A city that saw their institutions as public spaces and in which their youngest children were seen as active citizens who required great respect and the right to learn and be listened to.

PM: You said you had been researching early childhood education for many years before you were invited to write the working paper. What professional involvement had you had in the field of compulsory education?

GD: Although my field was early childhood education, by the time I came to write the 1994 paper, I'd had many opportunities to work with inspiring people and important ideas from the field of compulsory education. Moreover, because my work in ECE has been theoretically and philosophically oriented, I have always found it relevant when working outside my field.

My first research in 1971 was about children's co-operative play. But the second project I took part in was actually about the relation between pre-school and school, which led to a co-authored paper, 'Are the pre-school and school good developmental environments for children?' That project responded to other projects that had shown that integrating pre-school with school often ended up just as organisational integration, with no real impact on contents or working methods.

Then in 1977 I was privileged to be part of a new research group at the Stockholm Institute of Education called *Curriculum Theory and Cultural Reproduction.* From the beginning I was the only researcher in the group from early childhood education. The research group continued its research and discussions for 15 years. In that group, led by Ulf Lundgren, I got a strong theoretical grounding, one seldom present in early childhood. In the same year, I first met Basil Bernstein [Professor of the Sociology of Education at the Institute of Education University of London]. I had been following and writing about his work since 1973, and this led to my doctoral thesis. In the late 1970s, I also met with Tom Popkewitz [Professor at the University of Wisconsin-Madison] and his work on the political sociology of educational reform. So although ECE has remained my field, I have had important working relationships with academic colleagues from other educational fields.

PM: The English translation I have of the 1994 paper refers in the title and throughout to 'meeting place' – for example 'pre-school and school – two different traditions and the vision of a meeting place'. Is 'meeting place' a good translation?

GD: I would choose to use 'encounter'. In the 1994 paper we refer to Martin Buber and his thinking, which was related to the work of Emmanuel Levinas and 'the ethics of an encounter', discussed at length in the book you and I wrote together, *Ethics and Politics in Early Childhood Education* (Dahlberg and Moss, 2005). At the time Hillevi and I wrote the paper, I knew of Levinas and realised the connection with him, but I had not worked enough with his thinking to bring it into the paper. I only got that opportunity the next year, when I studied at the University of Wisconsin-Madison.

The idea at the heart of Levinas's thinking – that the ethics of an encounter is about respecting the alterity of the Other, not grasping the Other and making the Other into the Same – was at the back of my mind when proposing a vision of an encounter in between pre-school and school. The paper is also influenced by Foucault and the post-structuralists, and their work on processes of normalisation, how we are constructed and construct ourselves through dominant discourses. Work that Hillevi and other doctoral students have later taken further.

PM: What are the main ideas in the working paper from your perspective?

GD: The paper starts from the idea that pre-schools and schools and the traditions with which they are inscribed are historical and social constructions – they carry or bear ideas about education and its purposes and values produced in particular historical and social conditions. These traditions are very important. They contribute to what Ulf Lundgren calls 'curriculum codes', which operate as dominant discourses, placing boundaries about what theories and what concepts we use, and informing how we talk about and understand pedagogy. These curriculum codes produce concepts and practices that remain active, even after the conditions in which they were produced have disappeared. When change is sought, we often ignore these codes and the traditions of which they are part.

Ulf made us aware that we talk a lot about what we plan to do – *the arena of formulation* – but pay far too little attention to how we can bring that change about – *the arena of realisation*. If we want to bring change about, then we need to work in both arenas, otherwise it is just so many words! This is actually what has impressed me so much throughout my contact with Reggio Emilia. They do not only talk and write about pedagogy; they are working with and researching pedagogy, in its widest cultural and social sense, in its making.

There had been a debate in which it was proposed that CSE could learn from ECE, that pre-school pedagogy should go upwards into school – the reverse of schoolification. Others said you should take and mix the best of both pre-school and school. But we said that we have to start out from analyses of dominant discourses and common traditions, deconstruct them – and then construct something totally new together, what we named a vision of an encounter.

In the 1994 paper we analysed the different traditions of the Swedish pre-school and school, their different understandings and practices, for example the different social constructions of the child, knowledge and learning. But while doing this analysis we realised that the two traditions also had much in common: a platform for constructing a vision of a possible encounter, an encounter that we described as creating the image of the child as a constructer of knowledge and culture. The significance of this is that both pre-school and school have constructed barriers to relating to each other, and to remove those barriers, we argued, you have to start out by saying pre-school and school have a lot in common – you need this as a basis to continue the dialogue and for constructing a long-lasting development. In that context we argued that an encounter needs a common value base, a value base that has got consequences for how we understand the child, learning and knowledge and the role of the teacher in a wider societal context.

PM: What was this 'platform', this basis for continuing dialogue?
GD: We began by identifying three 'developmental lines' that the Swedish pre-school and school had both taken as a starting point: the Enlightenment, morality and self-control; scientification of the world and the human being; and community building. We argued that the common heritage of ideas between the Swedish pre-school and the school goes back to the Enlightenment's view of the human being, society and freedom. This view is best formulated in Rousseau's book Émile or On education (1762), with its attention to morality and self-control, but can also be seen in the pedagogy of Froebel and Pestalozzi.

In that context we also described how economic, cultural and other changes related to a gradual shift from external control towards inner self-control. Modern sciences have played an important role here, when it comes to governing and guiding the conduct of the child. With the growth of the social sciences in the 1930s, interest was partly directed away from moral questions towards a more pragmatic view of the human being based on scientific reasoning. It was a more rational code in which the empirical sciences, in an objective and neutral way, were supposed to direct how societal institutions should function. Hence, science instead of pedagogical philosophy was supposed to give answers to pedagogical situations.

We also argued that the emergence of crèches, the Kindergarten movement and compulsory schooling could be seen as a form of community building, a response to the moral crisis of the nineteenth century. Together they built up 'the social' to use a concept from Jacques Donzelot, or what later has been called the Swedish People's Home, a new social paradigm in which the state took responsibility for guiding life and behaviour towards a better society.

Albeit simplified, we saw these discourses as a possible way to activate a critical discussion about common ideas, acting as a base for the construction of a vision of an encounter. For us this did not mean presenting a model or a pedagogical approach or method: we more saw it as an invitation to a discussion.

PM: You make frequent mention of '*bildung*' and its potential importance for the relationship between pre-school and school. *Bildung* is originally a German concept, which has been influential in much of Continental Europe, including Sweden – but is not much used in the English-speaking world. Can you say more about the concept and its importance to your 1994 paper?

GD: Over the years, the idea of *bildung* has always been important in our research environment. In the 1994 paper we refer to two documents that we thought would be especially valuable for exploring the common heritage of ECE and CSE and envisioning a possible meeting place for the pre-school and school. One document is the 1991 commission report, connected to the curriculum for the Swedish school, *En skola för bildning* (A school for *bildung*) (SOU, 1992, p. 24).

Now '*bildung*' has many different interpretations, for example it is sometimes treated as transmission of pre-determined facts; it then gets lost in a narrow goal-governed idea of education. But the Commission reclaimed another idea of *bildung*, which views knowledge as consisting not only of facts but also meaning-making and understanding, as well as skills and a dimension that relates to the uniqueness of a situation and one's ability to value that situation. It also recognised knowledge as always contextualised and constructed, but without losing its instrumental aspects. In the 1994 paper, we drew on what Donald Broady, a researcher in our former research group, had written for the Commission about the classical German conception of *bildung*: the human being is, or should be, a being that constructs her/himself into something not decided beforehand. *Bildung* is, hence, an active undertaking, which implies an increase in the individual's possibilities for freedom. Donald related his thinking to Kant's well-known paper *What is Enlightenment?*, in which Kant encourages us to have courage to use our own reason without direction from someone else.

But by the time we wrote the 1994 paper, *bildung* was often interpreted as an elitist project as well as a narrow education. It was also often interpreted as an individualistic project. Along with others, we argued that *bildung* was, besides its strong trust in human reason, a project that had as its subject all human beings and not only the individual. As such it was an emancipatory pedagogical philosophy connecting the whole of society.

In the paper we connected this Enlightenment view of *bildung* to the progressive traditions of education, expressed by educators like John Dewey and Elsa Köhler, with their emancipatory ambitions and their image of the human being as a participatory citizen constructing meaning and knowledge. This led us to an image of the child as a constructer of knowledge and culture: a rich child; a child with a lot of potentialities; a child who is active in the construction of her/himself, presupposing a lot of respect for the child's way of making meaning in the world. The task for the teacher of this child is to be sometimes a co-traveller and sometimes a coach that can support and challenge the child on its journey of meaning-making and learning, although the journey and its direction is not always the one anticipated at the beginning. We maintained that this presupposes a reflective practitioner who, together with colleagues and through documentation, can create possibilities for a lively and critical discussion about pedagogical practice and its prerequisites. You can here see our inspiration from Reggio Emilia.

The second important document was the 1972 report of the *Barnstugeutredningen* (National Commission on Child Care) (SOU, 1972, p. 26). This proclaimed children's right to pre-school and a holistic idea of education, and also put forward the concept of 'dialogue pedagogy'. In the 1994 paper, Hillevi and I argued that dialogue pedagogy re-established the connection with the classical idea of *bildung* and the emancipatory struggles of the progressive movement. Taking the idea of dialogue meant that *Barnstugeutredningen* broke with the traditional role of the teacher, stressing instead sensitivity to the child by foregrounding the relational quality of pedagogy. We stated that gaining knowledge must be understood as a process that assumes an active interaction with other people and phenomena in the environment; the concept of dialogue helps us to view the construction of knowledge as embracing this process. It is also in this context that we referred to what we called 'dialogue philosophy', a concept that connects a constructivist and a relational perspective and that we traced back to Plato and Aristotle via Hegel, Mead and Buber, Köhler and Bateson.

Interestingly, there was a huge debate about dialogue pedagogy after the 1972 report, and it became very important in Swedish pre-schools. But many in the school field were against it as being too 'soft'. When pre-schools took it up, it did not have legitimation! But 15 to 20 years later, the idea of dialogue was back in the school.

So what we were saying is that a certain Enlightenment view of *bildung*, the progressive tradition in education and dialogue are further ingredients in a potentially common heritage of ideas, contributing to the development of a meeting place. As you point out in your introductory essay, 'despite their ontological and epistemological differences, the Swedish pre-school and school have much in common', and this includes this 'common heritage of ideas.'

PM: How was the working paper received?

GD: Very well. So many people wanted it that the university publishing company decided to publish it. It was referred to in a later Commission on 'Childcare and School.' It has also been referred to in many research projects and doctoral students have continued to develop the analysis.

In the 1990s, students found the paper difficult, but this is less so today. I think early childhood student teachers are now more familiar with the ideas. Previously, early childhood education had few people looking into theoretical perspectives of people like Bourdieu or the post-structuralists. But that has changed. Today's students know this work better; more are interested in critical perspectives.

PM: In the paper you indicate that differences in education, pay and status of pre-school and school teachers can affect the relationship between early childhood and compulsory school education. Is that still so today in Sweden?

GD: The 2001 reforms of teacher education [following the transfer in 1996 of responsibility for early childhood services from social welfare to education] integrated the education of all teachers – pre-school, compulsory school and gymnasium. Everyone shared 18 months of common education, before choosing more specialist courses. But the recent reforms have moved back to separate educations for pre-school, school and gymnasium teachers. There are still some shared courses, but not so much as before.

There is no agreement in the field about these developments and the issue of how teacher education should be organised. Personally, I am pleased that we've gone back to a separate and specific education for pre-school teachers, because we can ensure a suitable education; the distinct features of pre-school teaching were getting lost in the integrated programmes. I think an integrated approach to teacher education is good in principle – but before this can happen you have to legitimise pre-school education, which has to build a strong identity. At present CSE has more power and, therefore, legitimisation, than ECE. So we have to build up and strengthen the identity of early childhood education and teachers.

One thing happening now is that there is a huge shortage of pre-school teachers. So though school teachers still have a higher salary than pre-school teachers, the gap is reducing.

PM: Have there been examples of the kind of pedagogical meeting place you propose?

GD: There have been a couple of small projects where people tried to meet together, but not with a lot of inspiration from our perspective and they have not made much difference. However, schools and school teachers have shown some interest in work we have been doing with pre-schools. For example, the Stockholm Project [1993–1996, involving Gunilla Dahlberg and seven pre-schools establishing a 'co-constructive learning culture', with inspiration from Reggio Emilia, and paying particular attention to thematic and project work and pedagogical documentation, see Chapter 6 of Dahlberg et al., 2007]: a lot of schools wanted to connect with us, asking why we only worked with pre-schools. My answer was that we don't know yet what to do in pre-schools; we need to explore ideas in pre-schools. We can connect when we know more about learning in pre-schools.

I want to return to the issue of 'legitimation', which is crucial. As long as pre-schools have less legitimation than schools, then the pedagogical encounter will be a hierarchical encounter. For change to happen, pre-schools need to get equal legitimation. This was the problem with the reform of teacher education, which I mentioned above, and why I am happy that we have now reverted back to separate educations for pre-school and school teachers, with people who know about pre-school in charge of educating pre-school teachers. We must walk on two legs. We need to construct a pedagogical meeting place inscribed with the ethics of an encounter; but in parallel, pre-school must get a strong self-identity, enabling it to open up to change.

PM: So is the pre-school in Sweden gaining that strong self-identity?

GD: I think there is a trend that way. But the pre-school also needs to improve legitimacy by gaining recognition from parents as an institution for education, for *bildung*. Parents like pre-schools because they offer a good 'childcare' service. But the pre-school is much more. It is also much more than just a part of the education system. It can offer a transformative way of understanding education – learning and knowledge as far more than literacy and numeracy, knowing your ABC. This is why pedagogical documentation is so important. It opens up a window on pre-school learning to parents, so they can see what is going on and so they can participate. Parents have to be participants; they must be able to have their say in the documentation process.

P.M: Are there other examples of schools showing interest in pre-schools and the innovative work of you and others in pre-school?

GD: I do a lot of work with school principals. They are very interested in ideas and practices from pre-schools and after some initial doubts they now find our book 'Beyond Quality in Early Childhood Education and Care' (Dahlberg *et al.*, 2007) very important. The problem though is that they don't have or take the time to go deeper into the issues, to document and to follow children's learning strategies. It's almost impossible for them because of pressures from the performativity agenda.

There is a huge interest in Reggio Emilia among schools, and many teachers and politicians – for pre-schools and schools – go to Reggio Emilia. Schools are aware of our work and of the Reggio Emilia Institute in Stockholm [a non-profit organisation with a large national programme of activities, mainly with pre-schools]. The institute has recently begun a project on learning together with 16 schools. Here we can see the beginnings of another condition for a pedagogical meeting place: pre-schools and schools speaking the same language.

However, an abiding problem as I see it is that while pre-school researchers and teachers are quite acquainted with experiences and research carried out in schools, it seldom happens the other way round.

P.M: How would you describe the relationship between Early Childhood Education and Compulsory School Education in Sweden today?

GD: There is not a lot of talk today about the relationship – for example, compared to the 1970s, when we talked a lot and had a number of projects. I am trying to understand why this is the case. I think today there are so many other issues on the agenda, especially around globalisation and competition, for example the effects of PISA and Swedish students not doing that well on this benchmark, compared to other countries. Human capital theory is also much talked about, with the influence this gives to economists, even though it does not answer the most crucial questions about the meaning making and learning of children and teachers. These discussions lead to people asking if pre-school is effective in improving performance in compulsory education and to a return to the idea of testing 6-year-olds before they start compulsory school. This was what used to happen, I remember being tested when I was 6! So the relationship between ECE and CSE is not discussed in any depth, just in terms of effectiveness and school performance.

This preparation for school discourse, which starts in Sweden today, has led in recent years to more talk about mathematics, language, natural sciences – but again in a very simplified way. I mean the idea of learning as transmission of facts, of reproducing knowledge that is already known; rather than learning as a process of meaning making. With this simplified approach, we don't listen to and work with children's strategies for learning, how they make meaning, so we lose a great amount.

Of course, maths, language and science are important. But if we only looked and listened, we'd see, for example, that children in pre-school were using maths all the time. We prefer to test and diagnose at a distance rather than participate to better understand what children are actually doing, for example through pedagogical documentation. We then easily miss the possibility to challenge, deepen and extend children's learning processes. This is why our 1994 paper has sections on 'the investigative child and the investigative teacher' and 'documentation and the reflective teacher'.

There is a strong counter-movement in Sweden against this approach, with its simplified ideas of knowledge and learning and its desire for testing. Many teachers and educational researchers join in. So although the whole global context seems to be going down the road of readying children for school and simplified learning – towards A, B, C and 1, 2, 3 – we still have possibilities to resist and propose alternatives, partly because we have strong groups of academics and teachers.

PM: Nearly 20 years after you wrote the paper, how do you view it now? Has your thinking moved on?

GD: I think the paper is still very important. If I was re-writing it today, I would make it into a book, as I realise that the paper is very dense and the analysis could easily have been developed more fully. I would also bring in new theoretical perspectives and experiences; like the Stockholm Project, more of Deleuze and Guattari's immanent thinking, more from Reggio Emilia, and more from some recent doctoral theses written by researchers in our research group. This would enable us to go wider and deeper.

PM: Apart from strengthening the identity of the pre-school, what else could be done to help bring that relationship of a pedagogical meeting place into being?

GD: We need more work that connects researchers, teacher educators, pre-schools and schools – more opportunities for encounters. For example, after the end of the Stockholm Project in 1996 we had a two-day session for teachers in the participating pre-schools, where each told their history of participation. It became apparent there had been too little opportunity to dig into theory, so we offered a further two-day session where I and my doctoral students talked about our research work and the theoretical perspectives inspiring it. The offer was taken up, and pre-school teachers were given two- to three-hour presentations on a variety of themes: Deleuzian theory and its application to pedagogical work; pedagogical documentation from the perspective of Foucauldian and Derridean theories; the pre-school environment read from a Foucauldian perspective; post-structural theories and aesthetics. There was a mingling of ideas and perspectives, not just the educational project of Reggio Emilia, but also French philosophical theorists, which has been a feature of the Swedish experience.

It was an important seminar, stimulating and perplexing. This led to more developments and today a lot of pre-school teachers are more engaged in theoretical perspectives. We started a new project – 'Pedagogical and Theoretical Space' – where pre-school teachers, teacher educators, researchers and members of the Reggio Emilia Institute could meet regularly, three times a semester, for lectures as well as presentation and analysis of their own documentation of practice. Participants came from a number of *kommunes*, and soon topped 40, at which point we had to turn people away. This opened a dialogue between theory, research and practice, and between pre-school and university. A dialogue that has resulted in new creative experiences, both for research and for professional development and children's learning and meaning-making.

The book in our series by Liselott Mariett Olsson (2010) – *Movement and Experimentation in Early Childhood Education* – shows pre-school teachers and Liselott working with inspiration both from Reggio Emilia and from the theories of Deleuze and Guattari, as part of professional development work undertaken with the Stockholm Institute of Education. This book was based on Liselott's doctoral studies, but before that she had worked for a decade as a pre-school teacher and manager during which time, through activities like the 'Pedagogical and Theoretical Space', she was herself introduced to new theoretical perspectives. She writes how

> teachers, teacher students, teacher educators and researchers have met together to work with questioning pre-school practices and making room for them to change. The Swedish pre-schools involved in these efforts have now many years of experience of how to question and deconstruct one's own practice, and they have produced alternative ways of thinking of the child, the teacher and the pre-school's environment, content and form.
>
> (p. 7)

Here we have strong examples of encounters and also developing a strong pre-school identity – even though schools hitherto have rarely been included in this work.

So I think projects with a strong emphasis on following learning processes within different subject areas through pedagogical documentation and working with different theoretical and philosophical perspectives – like the Stockholm Project and the 'Pedagogical and Theoretical Space' – could provide pedagogical meeting places, encounters between the preschool and school sectors where we can all try to work on transformative moves in education. I want to emphasise that experimenting and bringing in pedagogical documentation is really important – as Deleuze says, with inspiration from Spinoza, 'we do not know what a body can do'.

What I can observe today is that the way we have been doing research during the last two decades has changed the encounter between preschools, pre-school teacher education and research. This becomes quite obvious in the doctoral theses and research projects that we have carried out since the 1994 paper and the Stockholm project (Dahlberg and Bloch, 2006; Halvars Franzén, 2010; Hultman, 2011; Lenz-Taguchi, 2007, 2010; Lind, 2010; Nordin-Hultman, 2004; Olsson, 2009; Palmer, 2010). It is a turn towards a participatory relationship built on what I now try to understand, with inspiration from Deleuze, as an immanent pedagogy, immanent evaluation, immanent research and immanent ethics. I hope that this relationship can extend in the future to the encounter between pre-schools and schools.

Part III

Five other responses

Chapter 4

Making a borderland of contested spaces into a meeting place

The relationship from a New Zealand perspective

Margaret Carr

In a research study of New Zealand children crossing the border between early childhood education and school (Carr *et al.*, 2010), we wrote about the multiple scripts that gave the children information about 'things to do or not to do, things to say or not to say, in relation to a "probable" upcoming future', as Pierre Bourdieu had said (1990, p. 53). We pointed out that many of these scripts 'bumped' up (Clandinin and Rosiek, 2007) against each other when the children moved from home to an early childhood education setting, and even more so when they went to school. We drew on the definition of narrativised and positional identities in Dorothy Holland, William Lachicotte, Debra Skinner and Carole Cain's *Identity and Agency in Culture Worlds*, which, they said

> have to do with the stories, acts and characters that make the world a cultural world. Positional identity, as we use the term, is a person's apprehension of her social position in a lived world: that is, depending on the others present, of her greater or lesser access to spaces, activities, genres, and through those genres, authoritative voices, or no voice at all.
>
> (1998, pp. 127–8)

When the children in our study went to school we observed the complex process as they appeared to select from, negotiate between, and orchestrate these apparently inconsistent social positions and scripts. We told stories about children learning to live together, take some authority in their lives, and imagine alternatives, and we looked for examples of educational design that assisted children with these negotiations and orchestrations.

Peter Moss writes in his introductory essay about three models of the relationship between early childhood education provision (ECE) and compulsory school education (CSE) that might describe this educational design: an ECE 'readying' children for CSE, a 'strong and equal partnership', and 'the vision of a meeting place' between ECE and CSE. In this chapter I wonder what such a meeting place might look like: where 'pre-school and school have a similar view of the learning child, pedagogy's role, and the pedagogical work which is built on the same value base' (Dahlberg and Lenz-Taguchi, 1994). I am reminded of Rosi Braidotti's (1994) notion of the 'nomadic subject': a 'hybrid and interconnected identity that occupies a variety of possible subject positions' (p. 158). Braidotti writes, she says, as a 'polyglot', and says that:

> In some respects, my polylinguilism forced upon me the need for an ethics that would survive the many shifts of language and cultural locations and make me 'true to myself', although the self in question is but a complex collection of fragments.
>
> (1994, p. 15)

I want to call on aspects of the New Zealand education story to try to get a glimpse of the nomadic subject as an inhabitant of an extended borderland between homes and ECE and CSA: someone who is ready, willing and able to work and learn in diverse and uncertain spaces where language and cultural locations shift in interesting ways, and who loves to cross boundaries. As Étienne Wenger has reminded us:

> (When) a child moves from a family to a classroom, when an immigrant moves from one culture to another, or when an employee moves from the ranks to a management position, learning involves more than appropriating new pieces of information. Learners must often deal with conflicting forms of individuality and competence as defined in different communities....I am suggesting that the maintenance of an identity across boundaries requires work and...(t)his work...is at the core of what it means to be a person.
>
> (1998 p. 160)

This work is at the core of a meeting place as well. I begin by imagining what the nomadic subject and the hybridity, in this context, might look like. Then I describe the borderland between ECE and CSE as three contested spaces; and finally I ask what might make this borderland a meeting place. I am wending my way towards some thoughts about Peter Moss's question: 'How might the preschool and the school meet?'

A hybrid and interconnected identity

> As the Vietnamese-born, French-educated, Californian film maker and feminist academic Trinh T. Minhaha shows, multiculturalism does not get us very far if it is understood as a difference between cultures. It should rather be taken as a difference within the same culture, that is to say within every self.
>
> (Braidotti, 1994, p. 13)

Here is a commentary on Aralynn, in the research project that tracked children from their early childhood centre into school.

> For Aralynn, [her love of] storying could continue into school...Her subject-based knowing – her love of, and knowledge about, gardening, which began at home with her mother and her grandparents – is also part of the valued school curriculum. The school teacher was enabling her to continue the imaginative princess stories that she had been developing at the early childhood centre, emphasising not so much the possibilities of being a princess but of being a story-teller, when she [Aralynn] is reminded that a story for an audience needs to make some sense. At the childcare centre she 'read' books to the younger children, as she had 'read' books to her mother and her grandmother, and the abilities she is developing in caring for others is a connecting strand throughout all the phases.
>
> (Carr *et al.*, 2010, p. 193)

Aralynn had been developing a range of imaginative princess stories at her pre-school, and she was adept at negotiating roles and agentic positions with three or four co-actors and co-authors – negotiation that was important if the play was to proceed. In her school classroom, this opportunity to develop imaginative play themes with others was not available. However, at 'writing time' she could dictate a complex and imaginative story to the teacher: she and the teacher negotiated aspects of the story as the teacher reminded her that a story written for an audience needs to make sense to that audience. At school, the teacher recognised and encouraged Aralynn's capacity to imagine the perspectives of others by emphasising this aspect of story-writing. They discussed together at some length whether one could say, as Aralynn did in one of her stories, that 'a queen and a princess' were 'useful'. Aralynn's love of gardening and nature, developed alongside her mother and her grandparents, also found a place at school. We commented:

> Alongside these pretend play and storying themes were a number of episodes, and comments from family and teachers, that referred to Aralynn's capacity to imagine the perspectives of others: her grandparents and the younger children at the (early childhood) centre in particular. And in phase three, at school, connections were made to Aralynn's love of gardening and nature, in her morning talks and an activity about growing beans.
>
> (p. 184)

In three places – at home, during ECE and early CSE – Aralynn was positioned with authority as an empathetic communicator, an adept story teller, and a keen gardener. Her early years provided her with opportunities for interconnection from one place to another. John Bransford and Daniel Schwartz (1999) write about a Preparation for Future Learning (PFL) perspective on transfer and learning outcomes. Perhaps Aralynn and her teachers are illustrating *Possibilities* for Future Learning, enabling places in which prior experience is not left behind and the image of the learner is aligned. In PFL, the emphasis is on learning dispositions and the ability of students to facilitate their own learning: 'The ideal assessment from a PFL perspective is to directly explore people's abilities to learn new information and relate their learning to previous experiences' (p. 69). Bransford and Schwartz write about how interpretive knowledge of situations (e.g. purposes and intentions) sharpens one's ability to recognise opportunities to learn. A field becomes something that we know *with* as well as know *about*: knowledge affects what students notice about subsequent events. They add that

> it seems wise to prepare them for change … The multiply embedded social settings within which people's lives unfold have a powerful effect on the degree to which they are supported in letting go of older ideas and practices and attempting new ones.
>
> (pp. 78, 81)

In searching for a way forward, we might argue for a borderland that notices, recognises and encourages a hybrid and interconnected learner. The borderland will also recognise that teachers, too, take on multiple positions, as Aralynn's teacher did when she alternated support and challenge, 'part co-driver, part guide or counsellor who gives information about the journey's direction and stimulus for the rest of the journey, and part driving force, even if the direction is not always the one she had thought' (Dahlberg and Lenz-Taguchi, 1994; quoted on page 25 of Chapter 1).

The next section of this chapter introduces three contested spaces inside this borderland, spaces where different scripts can find a meeting place: curriculum frameworks, valued knowledges, and community connections.

A borderland between ECE and CSE: three contested relational spaces

> In every culture, objects are embedded within various mental fields. These fields are bounded in such a way as to enable members of the culture to place an object in some meaningful context, usually that in which the object is normally found … . The fields specify and encourage acceptable, stereotyped, and restricted behavior on the part of individuals who act within the limits of the field. Some individuals, however, are able to extend these limits. The process of extending or redefining the limits of common objects is called *Boundary Pushing*.
>
> (Eisner, 2005, p. 8, original emphasis)

Elliot Eisner is describing 'boundary pushing' as one type of creativity in the visual arts. He adds that it 'is the ability to attain the possible by extending the given' (p. 9); this chapter translates this idea to refer to the educational field and to the ability of three contested spaces to extend (push out) their borders to make wider relational spaces or border*lands*. There are three borders that we might seek to stretch out if we are to develop an *educational* (in the widest sense) connection between ECE and CSE. By 'education in the widest sense' I refer to the elaboration of education as 'democratic experimentalism', by Peter Moss (2009), taking this term from the work of the Brazilian social theorist, Roberto Unger (2005). Democracy is described in Dewey's words, as 'primarily a mode of associated living embedded in the culture and social relationships of everyday life' (Dewey 1939, p. 2). 'Experimentalism' describes a way of living and relating that is, says Moss, 'open-ended (avoiding closure), open-minded (welcoming the unexpected) and open-hearted (valuing difference)' (Moss, 2009, p. 31): a way of living and learning in spaces where learners are enabled and expected to negotiate and imagine, to attain a possible meeting place by extending the given.

There are examples of initiatives towards a creative construction of an extended borderland meeting place in the recent history of early childhood and schooling in New Zealand. It is a good moment to write the story of these initiatives; it is an optimistic story, although in this second decade of the twenty-first century we have a wary eye on threatening storm clouds: emerging discourses of high stakes accountability and individualism in education at all levels.

The relational space between curriculum documents in ECE and CSE

This space is about the learning child. Early years provision in Aotearoa New Zealand has been able to do some of this border pushing. I sometimes wonder if we may have been able to do this because of our heritage as a nomadic people: the hybrid philosophy of Māori and, later, non-Māori migrants who have had to adapt to an environment different from home, seeking new possibilities and translating the known in a new context. New Zealanders often talk about the nation's 'number eight fencing wire' philosophy, referring to the inventive use of a particular gauge of fencing wire widely used on farms in the first half of the twentieth century. It became a national belief that anything can be repaired or made using basic ready-to-hand materials. There are two official national languages too, Māori and English, and an 1840 Treaty between Māori and the Crown, continually reminding us of multiple perspectives on many issues.

The New Zealand national early childhood curriculum, published in 1996, is in English with significant sections written in Māori. This curriculum is known by its guiding metaphor, *Te Whāriki* – a woven mat for all to stand on, with patterns and threads that represent different contexts for ECE, and therefore different cultural identities too. It was the product of a cross-cultural partnership with Māori, and the multiple perspectives of early childhood groups across the country (Reedy, 1995/2003; May, 2009, 2011; Nuttall, 2003).

> The development of Te Whāriki involved a broad consultative process with all the services and organisations. More specifically, the writers wanted the curriculum to reflect the Treaty partnership of Māori and Pakeha [non-Māori] as a bicultural document model grounded in the contexts of Aotearoa-New Zealand. This was a challenge. There were no New Zealand or international models for guidance. This became possible due to the collaboration with Te Kōhanga Reo National Trust and the foresight of Tamati Reedy and Tilly Reedy who developed the curriculum for Māori immersion centres. The theme of empowerment was important for Māori, and 'empowering children to learn and grow' became a foundation principle.
>
> (May, 2009, pp. 244–5)

Outcomes are summarised as 'working theories' and 'learning dispositions' (NZ Ministry of Education, 1996, pp. 44–45), constructs that signal a recognition that meaning is always in the making.

> Working theories become increasingly useful for making sense of the world, for giving the child control over what happens, for problem-solving, and for further learning. Many of these theories retain a magical and creative quality, and for many communities, theories about the world are infused with a spiritual dimension.
>
> (ibid., p. 44)

Te Whāriki emphasises the early childhood centre as a cultural world and the 'critical role of socially and culturally mediated learning and of reciprocal and responsive relationships for children with people places and things' (ibid., p. 9). It broke away from the categories of a traditional curriculum: the metaphor emphasised the context-based nature of a curriculum that responds to its community, and did not see itself as a preparation for the then subject-based school curriculum. The aspiration statement describes an education in the widest sense: for children 'to grow up as competent and confident learners and communicators, healthy in mind, body and spirit, secure in their sense of belonging and in the knowledge that they make a valued contribution to society' (ibid., p. 9).

But nor did it shy away from setting out some key principles and calling on those to describe a set of five broad aims or strands. As Helen May commented, above, 'empowerment' or *whakamana*, became a foundation principle, and the Māori title of each strand has *mana* as a stem. *Mana* can be loosely translated as 'empowerment (of)', or 'authority'. The strands are described under the headings of *mana atua* (well-being), *mana whenua* (belonging), *mana tangata* (contribution), *mana reo* (communication), and *mana aotūroa* (exploration), the English offering parallel concepts, not direct translations. Attached to each of the strands are 'indicative' (ibid., p. 44), non-prescriptive, outcomes that act as a dictionary for the learning that can be observed and enhanced. The word 'indicative' signals the situated and contextualised nature of the curriculum and the learning.

Whilst *Te Whāriki* was being written, the school curriculum was defining multiple achievement objectives for each of seven learning areas (or disciplinary subjects), following a 1993 document that set out 57 'essential skills' (in eight groupings: communication, problem-solving, work and study, social and co-operative, numeracy, information, self-management and competitive, and physical) (Brewerton, 2004). In 2002, a Ministry Stocktake Report made recommendations for the revision of that school curriculum, including:

> Item 272. The essential skills/ngā tino pukenga should be modified from the current organisation of fifty-seven essential skills/ngā tino pukenga in eight groupings to five groups of essential skills and attitudes to be consistent with Te Whāriki.
>
> (NZ Ministry of Education, 2002, p. 62)

After much debate and discussion, a revised school curriculum was developed and published in 2007. The advisory group for this process included ECE representatives, who argued vigorously for Item 272. As Table 4.1 shows, the new curriculum did, indeed, align dispositional outcomes with the strands of *Te Whāriki* (NZ Ministry of Education, 2007, p. 42). The label for these school dispositional outcomes is *key competencies*, derived from OECD's DeSeCo project, designed 'for a Successful Life and a Well-Functioning Society' (Rychen and Salganik, 2003).

Key competencies in the school curriculum are described as 'more complex than skills'; they 'draw also on knowledge, attitudes, and values in ways that lead to action' (NZ Ministry of Education, 2007, p. 42). There are alignments in the wording across the two curricular documents as well. *Te Whāriki* states that '[c]hildren learn through responsive and reciprocal relationships with people places and things'; while the new school curriculum states that key competencies

> continue to develop over time, shaped by interactions with people, places, ideas and things... Opportunities to develop the key competencies occur in social contexts. People adopt and adapt practices that

they see used and valued by those closest to them, and they make these practices part of their own identity and expertise.

(ibid., p. 12)

The new school curriculum also includes an aspiration statement: '(young people who are) confident, connected, actively involved, lifelong learners'. A letter from the Minister of Education that accompanied the 2007 school curriculum commented that this curriculum 'describes the key competencies students need in order to live, learn, work, and contribute as active members of our communities and it emphasises the importance of students being able to apply their knowledge and relate it to unfamiliar material (Maharey, 2007).

In a 2006 paper, commenting on the draft of the school curriculum, I asked three obvious questions about this new opportunity for continuity between ECE and CSE. Does an alignment of outcomes translate into an alignment of *mediational means*, assisting learners to access tools and languages that 'shape the action in essential ways' (Wertsch, 1991, p. 12)? Is this alignment of outcomes also aligned with *relational pedagogies*, creating a climate or culture in the classroom that 'systematically cultivates habits and attitudes that enable young people to face difficulty and uncertainty calmly, confidently and creatively' (Claxton, 2002, p. 3)? And does it come with *critique*?

In response to the question about *mediational means*, I proposed a table that included the resources that shape the actions. Table 4.1 is a version of this, adapted after discussions with teachers in a research project entitled *Learning Wisdom* (see Carr and Lee, 2012).

In answer to the question about *relational pedagogies*, I referred to local initiatives in which early childhood settings and schools were already beginning to develop these connections, climates and cultures. Sally Peters and I wrote a report on some of these, adding that:

New Zealand research has identified a key influence in the educational achievement of Māori students as the quality of in-class face-to-face relationships and interactions between themselves and their teachers (Bishop *et al.*, 2003). Macfarlane (2004) has also argued that relationship-based pedagogies and cultural centredness are key factors in Māori students' achievement.

(Carr and Peters, 2005, p. 22)

We have much to learn from this culturally responsive research; it extends the meeting place between schools and early childhood settings out into cultural communities.

In the same research study as Aralynn, we analysed the mediational means and pedagogies in the early childhood centre and school for another

Table 4.1 Possible alignment of resources across ECE learning dispositions and CSE key competencies

Te Whāriki strand	Learning dispositions towards	Key competencies	Mediating resources
Mana whenua / Belonging	Taking an interest Participation	Participating and contributing	Communities that connect with the learners' funds of knowledge, and exemplify possible selves and democracy
Mana atua / Well-being	Being involved Focus and flow	Managing self	Local resources and routines that can be orchestrated and adapted by teachers and learners. Time is available for focused activity
Mana aotūroa / Exploration	Persisting with uncertainty and challenge Resourcefulness	Thinking	Situations and tasks that provoke questions. Multiple ways of thinking and exploring
Mana reo / Communication	Expressing ideas and feelings Dialogue	Using language, symbols, and texts	Diverse languages, symbols and texts. Adults who negotiate and engage in extended dialogue. Learners who are expected to explain
Mana tangata / Contribution	Taking responsibility Kindness	Relating to others	Other people, in a range of roles and with different world views

Adapted from Carr (2006, p. 25)

of the case study children, Lauren. This research was before the revised curriculum was published. We introduced a chapter on 'asking questions' with a quote from Maxine Greene (1995, p. 6) who insisted that 'the educative task is to create situations in which the young are moved to begin to ask, in all the tones of voice there are, "Why?"'. At her early childhood centre, Lauren was indeed asking 'Why?': she questioned the routines, gender norms, the rules (of cricket), and appropriate social behaviour in a group, and she puzzled with the teachers about aspects of life and death. The teachers responded with respect, explanation and information, and they were often prepared to re-negotiate the rules and routines.

But after she had been at school for three months, Lauren's interactions with others or materials are much shorter, and focused on reading, writing and mathematics. Unlike Aralynn's classroom, there was little opportunity to engage in a discussion about a story: 'When you write your story about your Dad or your Grandad...make sure you've got a capital letter and a full stop. That's what I'm looking for today.' And, unlike at the early childhood centre, there was little opportunity to ask questions about the 'given' in told or written stories, and little space for Lauren's capacities for curiosity and critique. Earlier research had suggested that children who had inhabited over some time a particular dispositional milieu (of question-asking and exploring for instance) would attempt to seek out and construct familiar dispositional situations (Bereiter, 1995; Carr, 2001) and Lauren was an example of this. At school she often took a critical approach to group book readings to ask questions such as 'Is he [the Wizard] a naughty person?', 'Is a giant *really* scary?' and to introduce trouble to the story-line by suggesting, for instance, that the spider in a story might be a (poisonous) White Tail. These were strategies that, in this classroom, jeopardised the goodwill of even the most tolerant teacher as she juggled Lauren's imaginative flourishes against the demands of a set-text-based reading to 17 children.

In response to the question about *critique*, I turned to an example from the USA: Deborah Meier's account of the curriculum at the Central Park East Secondary School in New York's East Harlem. She writes about this curriculum becoming based on something similar to learning dispositions and key competencies: habits of mind. These habits of mind (posted in classrooms and appearing regularly in the weekly newsletter, and used to frame graduates' final projects and presentations) became critical questions: 'How do we know what we know?' 'Who's speaking?' 'What causes what?' 'How might things have been different?' and 'Who cares?' (Meier, 1995, pp. 49–50).

The relational space between learning dispositions and subject knowledges

This space is about the pedagogical work. The second border that must be stretched out into a borderland is the border that curriculum documents construct between subjects and learning dispositions or competencies. This interweaving was already a feature of *Te Whāriki*, although, as Anne Smith (2011) has pointed out, the unusual foregrounding of learning dispositions can overshadow the visibility of the subject contexts, and dialogue in the meeting place between the two sectors can suffer as a result. Lauren's early school experience with writing was an example of an apparently inflexible border: grammatical correctness and presentation was foregrounded, with no time for story discussions that included imagination and critique. A pedagogy that integrates learning disposition with discipline-based knowledges has been described as 'split-screen' or 'dual focus'. Guy Claxton and colleagues explain:

> Here we look more closely at the way in which teachers have learned to weave together the dual objectives of 'what' will be learned and 'how' it will be learned. There are different ways of designing a lesson on the Tudors [a dynasty of kings and queens in 16th century England]. With the same content – the nature of the Elisabethan court, say – one lesson could be designed to exercise students' skills of accurately transcribing notes and retaining information more-or-less verbatim; another lesson could stretch students' ability to appraise someone else's knowledge claims, and to put themselves in the shoes of people with very different worldviews from their own. Same content but a world apart in developing real-world learning habits.
>
> (Claxton *et al.*, p. 92)

Longitudinal data from a number of sources has informed our understanding that this combination, which includes the learner's agency and perseverance, sustains the learning over time (Cunha *et al.*, 2005; Wylie and Hogben, 2011).

> Earlier work in the [New Zealand longitudinal] Competent Learners study showed how important it was to provide learning that gave children and young people 'two sides of the coin' experiences, weaving together the learning of reading, writing and mathematics with development of attitudes such as perseverance, communication and self-management. *The New Zealand Curriculum*, which schools now use to frame their programmes, encourages this productive interweaving.
>
> (Wylie, 2011, p. 4)

Since the school curriculum introduced key competencies, schools in New Zealand have been exploring the opportunities to integrate knowledge and disposition, and to embed the key competencies in the Learning Areas (Cowie, Hipkins, Boyd *et al.*, 2009; Hipkins *et al.*, 2011; Hipkins and Boyd, 2011; Carr *et al.*, 2008). Rosemary Hipkins, writing about the intention of the key competencies in the New Zealand Curriculum to foster lifelong learning, pointed out that '[i]t won't be possible to achieve this holistic/ integrated approach unless and until curriculum, pedagogy, and assessment are all closely aligned' (2005, p. 36). Documentation, the reification of the learning and the educational opportunities that surround it, is a central aspect of this. Wendy Lee and I (Carr and Lee, 2012) write about the ways that pedagogical and assessment practices in early childhood centres and schools are combining stores of knowledge with stores of learning disposition.

There is another aspect to this pedagogical relational space. The integration of the dispositional with the subject content enables the learner-with-potential focus that underlies the vision of the child in *Te Whāriki*. An influential government strategy document has elaborated on this for the schooling sector. *Ka Hikitia*, the 2009 New Zealand Ministry of Education's Māori Education Strategy, highlights the role of the education system in emphasising 'potential-focused' activities.

> 'Ka hikitia' means to 'step up', 'lift up', or 'lengthen ones stride'. In the context of Ka Hikitia – Managing for Success it means stepping up the performance of the education system to ensure Māori are enjoying education success as Māori.
>
> (NZ Ministry of Education, 2009, p. 11)

Ka Hikitia outlines what it calls a Potential Approach and explains that '[f]or government, this means shifting the emphasis towards potential-focused activities'. It advises more focus on 'realising potential' and less focus on 'remedying deficit'; more focus on 'tailoring education to the learner' and less focus on 'targeting deficit' (ibid., p. 19).

There are threats to this borderland space in New Zealand. The emerging dual-focus development and 'realising potential' initiatives are at risk from National Standards for Literacy and Numeracy, including assessments at the end of the first year of school (at age 6), introduced for 2011. An entirely skills-based imperative that targets deficit and ignores potential across a range of multimodal languages can work to reduce the enjoyment of reading. Sally Peters' transition to school research has described teacher-created new-entrant assessments in which '[w]hen deficits were revealed, such as the inability to name more than a few letters of the alphabet, this became a major focus for intervention that overshadowed much of the child's experience' (Peters, 2010, p. 73). The consequences of this new policy, the possible narrowing of the curriculum in the early years and the threat to critique as teachers focus on measurable skills and standards, has yet to unfold.

The relational space between families and ECE/CSE

Finally, and following on from the notion of the multiple perspectives and multiple languages of a nomad, an extended borderland will be inhabited by families and the wider community. A meta-analysis of research on achievement in education concluded that parental expectations are far more powerful influences on children's learning than any other home factors:

> Parents have major effects in terms of the encouragement and expectations that they transmit to their children. Many parents, however,

struggle to comprehend the language of learning and thus are disadvantaged in the methods they use to encourage their children to attain their expectations. Across all home variables, parental aspirations and expectations for children's educational achievement have the strongest relationship with achievement.

(Hattie, 2009, p. 70)

Research on learning across the sectors in the UK has affirmed this too. Children who were succeeding 'against the odds' were getting support from a wide range of family members, with families' potential-focused aspirations (to go on to higher education, for instance) often mirrored by the children (Siraj-Blatchford, 2010, p. 469).

Here, from the same research project as Aralynn and Lauren, is a comment from Yasin's story as he transitioned from early childhood to school. Yasin's conversations with teachers at his kindergarten set out the contexts of a cultural self: the country outside New Zealand, India, where his nana and extended family live, and his family in New Zealand who were widening his perceptions of self as a global citizen by introducing him to new languages – Spanish, Arabic and Mandarin – and new skills – art, music, tennis and soccer. It refers to three phases of the research: one and two at 18 months to 2 years of ECE; three to observations during the first year of school, at age 5.

> Yasin's lengthy storying discussions in the figured worlds of home and kindergarten were welcome, and while in phase one he introduced his family to almost every conversation, by phase two he is introducing home information in response to the topic at hand rather than 'out of the blue'. At school, however, he appears to recognise that spontaneous storying about himself does not have the same public and legitimate space. He seized the chance in a technology lesson to introduce his knowledge from home of the fabrics that his mother sews, but his extra-curricular lessons may have taught him to 'read' a diversity of educational environments, to recognise a figured world in which one follows directions, gets on with the set tasks, and does not try to engage the teacher in discussions about self and family.
>
> (Carr *et al.*, 2010, p. 192)

Unlike Aralynn's early experiences at school, where opportunities to make extended connections with home events and interests were transparent and available, when Yasin was scripting a self as a school pupil his cultural self was left behind, at home, except for a brief moment of connection when he displayed considerable knowledge about fabrics (although his mother – who taught him this knowledge – was not mentioned). Stuart McNaughton (2002) has concluded from his New Zealand research on literacy that schools are risky places for children whose expertise from home does not fit with the expertise recognised by their school. In the UK, research by Liz Brooker (2002) on 16 4-year-old children from low-income households concluded that the school ethos, and the pedagogic discourse of the classroom, worked to position them as unable. In her study, the rich social and cultural capital that children had available to them from home and family on entry to school was useful knowledge only when the inclusion of that capital was negotiated into the classroom. Often this negotiation had to be facilitated by the children's families.

On the whole, the curriculum in ECE is more permeable, enabling the inclusion of a cultural self and the social and cultural capital that it brings. As Yasin's experience indicated, ECE teachers could seize opportunities to enter a dialogue with him, to hear his stories in a relaxed schedule, and to allow these stories to become part of the fabric of the kindergarten as a hybrid cultural place.

A borderland of three contested spaces: what might make it a meeting place?

> Before we let ourselves joyfully celebrate our internationalism, therefore, let us ask ourselves: are we sufficiently present as citizens in our own country to start thinking seriously about being citizens of the world?
>
> (Braidotti, 1994, p. 253)

Braidotti invites us to reflect seriously about our own 'belonging to, involvement in, and implication with our culture' before we reflect more widely. We can zoom in further, to add the question: 'and are we sufficiently present as citizens *in our local school classroom and contributing early childhood setting?*' This is not a task for the meeting place alone. However, there *are* tasks for the relational borderland between ECE and CSE in which a 'shared repertoire of cultural patterns is constructed and jointly reconfigured' (Vandenbroeck *et al.*, 2009, p. 209). What policies and practices will do the work of construction and joint refiguring? Or, as Peter Moss asks 'How might the pre-school and the school meet?' As an educational construction zone, a meeting place is 'a magic place where minds meet, where things are not the same to all who see them, where meanings are fluid, and where one person's construal may pre-empt another's' (Newman *et al.*, 1989, p. ix). It is a place for dialogue.

In this section, drawing on the New Zealand experience, I outline three domains of policy and practice that can play key roles in developing, sustaining and deepening this dialogue: teachers as researchers, a permeable curriculum on either side of the border, and documentation as boundary object. I write about a vision of the possible, occasionally attained, and always at risk, as shifting political and economic forces position themselves to invade what might be called a fledgling model of democratic experimentalism (Moss, 2009) across the sectors.

Teacher researchers

Some of this borderland territory work belongs with the image of teachers. Writing about the statistics that indicate that countries with highly stratified income disparity have much greater difficulty creating a level playing field for achievement, Allan Luke (2011) writes of four features of two high-quality/high-equity systems, Finland and Ontario: highly qualified teacher education candidates and graduates, extensive investment in in-service and ongoing teacher development, low-definition or less-prescriptive curriculum, and low to moderate emphasis on standardised testing. Teachers are recognised as professionals, supported with on-going professional development, and enabled to make culturally and socially responsive curriculum decisions.

The history of ECE in New Zealand has been told by Helen May (2009, 2011). Almost 80 per cent of all early childhood teachers and all school teachers are qualified with the equivalent of a three-year undergraduate or a one-year postgraduate university degree. Early childhood and primary teachers belong to the same teachers' union. Equivalent salaries for teachers across the sectors, although fragile, have been negotiated, and both sectors are overseen by the same Ministry of Education. *Te Whāriki* was supported by generous Ministry-funded professional development and resources, and the Ministry of Education also provided professional development for schools (though both programmes have been severely pruned in the last three years). Although hampered by sector-based professional development funding, a number of cross sector initiatives have enabled sustained meeting places (Wright and Molloy, 2005).

An imaginative feature of the Ministry-funded educational landscape has been two programmes of action research projects in which teachers and the academy collaborate and co-construct potentially transformative forays into all three of the borderland spaces that were described in this chapter. The Teaching and Learning Research Initiative (TLRI) programme funds projects of from one- to three-years' duration; they must be based on a partnership with schools or early childhood centres, and publish their findings. These projects are available to ECE and CSE and tertiary teachers, and a number of projects have included cross-sector teams. From 2003–2009, the Centres of Innovation (COI) programme funded 20 early childhood centres for three-year projects; each centre – selected from applicants – was required to invite an academic advisor, to develop a research question from a range of topics, and to provide professional development for other teachers based on their research findings. A 2011 ECE Task Force Report published the following submission:

The now disestablished Centres of Innovation programme had an astonishingly powerful impact on the early childhood sector by providing research and development that filled knowledge gaps, provoking new thinking and critical debate about early childhood education teaching, stimulating services to aspire to greater heights and creating a new cohort of educational leaders in a few years.

(NZ Ministry of Education, 2011, p. 167)

In New Zealand there are publication pathways for sharing the work of teacher researchers. Peer-reviewed journals published by the New Zealand Council for Education Research (NZCER) – *Early Childhood Folio* and *SET* – are designed to take this research into the early childhood centre and the school classroom. NZCER Press also published a series, under the editorial leadership of Anne Meade, of research stories from COI teams (Meade, 2005, 2006, 2007, 2010). In addition, the COI programme funded the sharing of findings with other teachers in workshops, resources and presentations.

The topic of one of the Centres of Innovation research projects was the transition to school, now published in a book authored by the teachers and the university researchers (Hartley *et al.*, 2012). One of the chapters in that book includes a discussion of the theorising by the research team, as we dialogued together about the observations and the documentation; another is about the 'mutually interesting tasks', including an Early Childhood and Primary Schools Links Group and a joint DVD project on transition. A school teacher spoke about the former as a genuine meeting place: 'I thought, "This is good because I'm learning and we're not coming here [to visit the kindergarten] to tell". Yes we're opening up a partnership or a dialogue so I think it's going to get stronger' (Hartley *et al.*, 2012).

The authors comment on the DVD project:

> The process of making the DVD enabled an already strong relationship to become even stronger, through the collaboration and consultation that took place on this joint project. The information technology (IT) aspect also offered a new dimension to the relationship with the families of the kindergarten, who were able to utilise this visual resource in their own settings at home, facilitating further conversations about and around the transition to school. It also provided a school project within the technology curriculum and added to the school's information and communication technology [ICT] research file.

(ibid., p. 33)

A three-year TLRI project – *Key Learning Competencies across Place and Time* – seized the opportunities presented by the alignment between the outcomes across the two education sectors in the 2007 school curriculum to research in three schools and two early childhood centres. The research team (ECE and CSE teacher-researchers and university-researchers, together with research facilitators) met regularly to argue and debate together, developing working theories that explored the relationship between local episodes of learning-and-teaching and zoomed-out mid-level theories. At the end of the project one of the teachers commented:

> So I went in completely and utterly blind, having no idea what was going to be expected...Never did I imagine we'd be at this point...I always saw research as (a) way too academic for me, but (b) a sort of separate project that went alongside, something that wasn't, that wouldn't have given us this much value to this place. So, I didn't understand how much we would own it.
>
> (Carr *et al.*, 2008, p. 15)

All the teachers wrote Working Papers for the project, some published in the *Early Childhood Folio* December 2011 issue, widening the opportunities for dialogue across the borderland and border-crossing learning.

Writing in homage of Loris Malaguzzi, the first director of the Reggio municipal schools, Carlina Rinaldi (2006) says that the 'researching school' was a theme close to Malaguzzi's heart. She adds that, at the schools

> we chose to dialogue with all those people in various disciplines (psychology, human sciences, biology, neurology, art and design) who agreed to carry out research with us, constructing questions together, experiencing journeys of research together which were respectful of each person's role, without preconceived hierarchies between academic knowledge and the knowledge of educators.
>
> (pp. 172–3)

A permeable curriculum on either side of the border

This chapter has already outlined the curriculum developments in New Zealand. The early childhood curriculum document was already permeable, with the principle that *children learn through responsive and reciprocal relationships with people, places, and things.* Rosemary Hipkins and Sally Boyd point out that the school curriculum (NZC) is now flexible as well:

> As a framework curriculum, NZC provides scope for considerable variation in uptake and implementation between different schools. With the whole of the nationally mandated curriculum now outlined in one slim book, each school has to work out how to build up a more detailed local curriculum based on the framework NZC presents.
>
> (2011, p. 72)

Here is an example of permeable curriculum in the early years, responding to local initiatives (fish brought to the kindergarten by local families) and enabling on-going and collaborative meaning-making by the learners. It comes from the data from another TLRI action research project, in an early childhood centre, but schools will have many examples of just such meaning in the making. It is an excerpt from a group conversation. Four-year-olds Zeb and Anna are watching a slide show that documents the kindergarten children's exploration of fish over previous weeks. The topic of conversation has been the fish and the exploration of them. Zeb tells a story about a shark covered in ash by a volcano ('It went BANG onto a rock and all that was left in the sea was the skin and bones and they took it to a museum'). Anna commented that she had read a library book about 'extinct' volcanoes and the two children discuss whether a number of named volcanoes in New Zealand are liable to 'explode' or are extinct. The topic is not about the fish any more. The teacher (Marjan) nimbly shifts her focus from fish to volcano, affirms the new topic and repeats the name of an extinct volcano: 'OK. An extinct one. Mt Maunganui'.

> *Zeb:*   Yeah. But some volcanoes just go for one day.
> *Marjan:* For one day.
> *Z:*   Yeah, but some volcanoes go for two days and some volcanoes go for three days.
> *M:*   Mmm...[Zeb repeats and continues his previous comment, counting to ten and holding up all his fingers: 'Some volcanoes go for ten days'.]
> *Anna:*   And maybe they might go for one day.
> *Z:*   Yeah and ten days.
> *A:*   Or maybe zero days.
> [Anna and Zeb giggle]
> *Z:*   Yeah, and then and then it'll be just night. ...
> *A:*   Maybe when you're not around it explodes.
>
> (Carr, 2011 p. 267)

This was a dialogue with two perspectives. Zeb is apparently determined to talk about a volcano-eruption disaster, and Anna, also well-informed about and interested in volcanoes, appears to be keen to emphasise extinct volcanoes that erupt for zero days, or volcanoes that explode 'when you're not around'. They are sharing ideas and perspectives – including an interest in numbers and Zeb's notion that a 'day' does not include the night. Here are children engaged in a dialogue about the unexpected and the uncertain. They have provided ideas to which they and the teacher can return; they have introduced topics of interest that were not necessarily on the original agenda for the day, and they are invited to do so by the permeability and flexibility of the curriculum.

Documentation as a boundary object

Research across other educational borders has also been instructive. Three teachers and two academics have just completed a paper from a TLRI project on learning as boundary-crossing – in this case not the boundary between ECE and CSE, but the boundary between an early childhood centre and a museum (Carr *et al.*, 2012). We reflected on what assisted that learning and concluded that the support included 'boundary objects', together with sustained dialogue amongst the teachers and the children.

> We suggest that an outcome for young children of deliberate teaching in museums, with 'being curious' in mind, is a repertoire of meaning-making practices that travel across contexts. When knowledge, meaning-making practices and learning dispositions are woven together across communities or contexts, young learners can be invited to: explore what is the same and what is different between familiar and unfamiliar contexts, recognise and be curious about alternative perspectives, develop expertise and attention to relevant cues, person-alise their experience in a range of innovative ways, and enjoy dialogues in which they puzzle over and share meaning. This learning appears to be greatly assisted by boundary objects of various kinds and teachers as boundary brokers who are resourceful and skilled at dialogue and who are themselves curious and interested.
>
> (Carr *et al.*, 2012, p. 64)

These boundary objects included the portfolios of documentation constructed by the teachers and the children. Rinaldi says that '[d]ocumentation was and is still the only tool that I can see for creating crisis in terms of knowledge, professional development, identity and everything' (2006, p. 182). She links 'crisis' with the unexpected and the uncertain, and reiterates the fundamental role of documentation in the Reggio schools, making learning visible (Giudici *et al.*, 2001). Hillevi Lenz-Taguchi adds, writing about working towards a blurring of the gap between theory and practice:

> In the very 'textualizing' of practice, it is, in fact, talked and written into existence – both as practice and as theory – and in that sense made accessible and even palpable, for being rewritten, re-talked, and thereby re-performed and transformed.
>
> (2007, p. 279)

In the New Zealand early years' context documentation includes Learning Stories, written by teachers and children, taken home by families to provide a site for dialogue at home, and revisited by children in the centre or the school (Carr and Lee, 2012). Teachers in early childhood centres, supported by teachers in local schools are also beginning to develop 'transition to school' portfolios of documented learning that link to both the ECE strands and the CSE key competencies: exploring together the value for belonging, family connection and literacy of a portfolio of recent Learning Stories that foreground potential and competence, and exemplify one or more of the aligned ECE / CSE learning dispositions and key competencies. Teachers in schools frequently borrow children's ECE portfolios, revisiting and discussing the learning with the children: borderland dialogues about stories in which children have the expertise and the authorship. Here is a comment from one of the new entrant teachers in the Hartley *et al.* research project; it continues the nomadic theme.

> I guess it's like us starting a new job and moving to a new country, everything is new but if they come with this little treasure [their port-folio of learning stories from ECE], that's something that's theirs, something they can talk about, something they share…and you real-ize they are really valuable and really powerful.
>
> (Peters, 2010, p. 77)

These portfolios of stories about learning provide opportunities in the borderland for dialogue between teachers, students and families. A number of schools are writing Learning Stories as well, initiatives developed from professional development meeting places in the borderland (Smith *et al.*, 2011; O'Connor and Greenslade, 2011).

A final word

The final word can come from Rinaldi and Malaguzzi:

> Malaguzzi loved to cross boundaries, he loved to inhabit the border areas. Not boundaries that have been established once and for all, or defined a priori; but boundaries perceived as places for meeting and exchange, where knowledge and action pursue and feed each other.
>
> (Rinaldi, 2006, p. 173)

This chapter has explored some of the contested spaces in these border areas. We celebrate those learners and teachers and families who love to cross boundaries between ECE and CSE, and those aspects of educational design and curriculum that make it possible to stretch the boundaries into a borderland, often against the odds. There are a number of ways in which this relational borderland can be perceived as a place for meeting and exchange, and this chapter has described three of them. I think that these descriptions catch a glimpse of possibility, but we are all going to need to be vigilant trustees and fierce guardians if these precious borderland spaces and meeting places are to develop and flourish.

Chapter 5

From indifference to invasion

The relationship from a Norwegian perspective

Peder Haug

In his introductory essay, Peter Moss introduces three 'pure' types of relationship between early childhood education (ECE) and compulsory school education (CSE). Type I: early childhood education readying children for compulsory school; Type II: a strong and equal partnership; Type III: the vision of a meeting place. I find all of them in Norwegian developments, though not in the same order, a little more mixed and also slightly different. This will almost always be the case, in studies of realities rather than descriptions of ideals. Hybrids, combinations of different types, are very common.

Early childhood education in Norway is inextricably associated with the *barnehage* (a direct translation of the German term 'kindergarten'), which today is a fully integrated centre for children aged 1- to 5-years-old, coming under the overall responsibility of the national Ministry of Education and Research; all Norwegian children from a year upwards are entitled to a place in one of these centres. It is important to present some aspects of the history of ECE and CSE as a basis for my analysis of developments in the relationship between the *barnehage* and the compulsory school. So what I will do in this contribution is to look chronologically into the relationships between the two systems as they have developed in Norway – though space only permits inclusion of the main trends, and not all the different (and often small) attempts to break the established order.

In the book *The Evolution of Educational Thought*, there is a statement that is highly significant for my approach to the relationship between early childhood and compulsory school education: 'it is only by carefully studying the past that we can come to anticipate the future and to understand the present' (Durkheim, 1977/1938, p. 9). Fields like the one that is discussed in this book are based, to a certain extent, on a complex system of historical conditions. They are often unquestioned, historically determined and historically loaded by theories and metatheories. They are human constructions and social products of certain times and certain circumstances that influence today's thinking and practice. I also lean especially on one aspect of New Institutionalism, namely that organisations are engaged in a process of give-and-take with their immediate environments. They 'penetrate the organisation, creating the lenses through which actors view the world and the very categories of structure, action and thought' (Di Maggio and Powell, 1989, p. 13). So as ways of thinking, social values and living conditions change, this affects the relationships between the two institutions of ECE and CSE.

For the purposes of this chapter, I divide Norwegian history into three periods, each with a separate and distinct approach to the relationship between ECE and CSE. In the first and longest period (1837–1986), there is very little connection between them. None of the three types proposed by Peter Moss cover this situation, which is characterised by indifference and isolation – what I define as a Type IV relationship. In the second period (1986–2006), *barnehage* ideals are exported to school, particularly the first year of school, which was supposed to become more like the *barnehage*. Type III is most typical at this stage. In the last period (2006 onwards), school traditions and ideals are exported to early childhood education. The *barnehage* should become more like the school, and the Type I relationship seems to develop gradually as the most important, readying children for school. What all the three periods have in common is striving after a smooth transition to school, by offering an education programme whose short-term intention is to make starting school as pleasant as possible.

First period, 1837–1986: indifference and transition

The first period starts when early childhood education was introduced in Norway in 1837. There was no large-scale expansion to speak of until after 1970, when only about 3 per cent of the pre-school age population attended *barnehager*. I will concentrate here on developments from 1975, when *Stortinget* (the Norwegian Parliament) passed the first Kindergarten Act. Originally there were two kinds of institutions for children under 7 years of age. The whole-day kindergarten was seen as a necessity only for families and especially single mothers in need of social support. The alternative was a sort of pre-school offering a few hours per day especially for older children. The Kindergarten Act combined the different forms of provisions into a common and broad concept of kindergarten – the *barnehage*.

During the 1960s there were some experiments with pre-school classes for 6-year-olds, as a preparation for school. They were successful, but not continued. Nineteen-eighty-six is chosen as the end of this period because of an initiative proposed then to reduce the age of starting school from age 7 to 6 years. The *barnehage* was for the first time put under heavy pressure from interests connected to school, and with direct and extensive consequences.

Baseline

Early childhood education was for a long time not given priority in Norway, in many instances not even accepted. Interests opposed to ECE have had a strong influence, especially on family policy, almost up to the present day. There has been strong resistance to state intervention in the upbringing of young children, based on a certain philosophy of family and children, which held care and concern for younger children to be the exclusive responsibility of the family. This, it was argued, is in the child's best interest and preserves the family as society's fundamental, stabilising institution. In short, a good childhood includes the child being at home, preferably with the mother (Kjørholt, 1994).

This philosophy has brought tension and conflict in the relationship between the private family and ECE. Early childhood education was, partly unconsciously, partly symbolically, understood as a threat to the mother's role in particular and as a necessary evil for those who could not care for their own children during the day (Korsvold, 1998). A further cause or the neglect of the *barnehage* was late urbanisation in Norway; dependence upon rural primary industries lasted a long time. Development of ECE lagged behind other Nordic countries.

Within the framework of family life, children had a great deal of freedom. The ideal placed strong emphasis on free play with peers (Hoëm, 2010). This tradition of child-rearing can be traced back to what Hoëm has labelled 'the simple community', characterised by late nineteenth-century society in sparsely populated communities and based on primary industries. The space where children lived their lives was highly social, culturally and ideologically homogenous and very open, visible and safe. There was no need for adults to constantly control and supervise children individually.

For these reasons, among others, any form of organised educational activity for young children came late to Norway. For a long time, the official policy was to limit as much as possible the extent of ECE. Even pre-school teachers were critical of children attending kindergarten (Nafstad, 1976). When ECE gradually expanded during the 1970s and 1980s, the curriculum became highly child-centred.

We can also find traces of the same anti-institutional ideology in compulsory school. This reflects the notion that children should not be led too far from their own cultural and social origins, including a wide scepticism towards theoretical and school-based knowledge (Lauglo, 1993). In the 1960s, for instance, the youngest children in country villages still went to school for just three days a week. While until the end of the 1980s, compulsory schooling for children in the first grade (7-year-olds) totalled just 15 hours a week.

Norwegian society has changed since the 1970s. It has become much more urbanised, more culturally heterogeneous, more internationally oriented and, not least, values in the population have become far more varied and less shared. But the ideal of freedom for younger children still resonates. It corresponds with a certain *barnehage* ideology, which has been dominant until recently.

Growing need for early childhood care

Because of changes in both the family and employment, the need for institutional provision for pre-school children grew. This began in the 1960s, and escalated when the newly established oil industry needed a larger, more flexible workforce during the 1970s. Mostly men were recruited to that industry's offshore activities. They had to be replaced in the onshore workplaces that they left, and this was done by women. But many of them needed assistance in caring for their children during working hours. This was also connected to the women's liberation movement, which was growing fast at the time.

For these reasons, the nation had to work toward meeting the burgeoning demand for child care (Finansdepartementet, 1974). Expansion of ECE took place slowly given the extensive need, though seemingly quickly from a statistical point of view. In 1986, 29 per cent of children under 7 years of age received ECE, yet around 70 per cent of married women with children of this age worked outside the home.

Relationship to school

In 1975, the *barnehage* was an independent institution, with its own unwritten curriculum, its own educational tradition and its own ways of working. The programme was child-centred, with free play as the dominant activity both ideologically and in practice. When in that year the Kindergarten Act was discussed in the *Stortinget*, it was agreed the institution should be called '*barnehage*', kindergarten, not the alternative label of 'pre-school'. This was seen as an important declaration (Balke, 1979). The parliamentary majority also decided that 'kindergarten's main task will be to offer opportunities for play and social activities, and not teaching or transmitting of knowledge' (Innst. O. nr. 69 (1974–75), p. 4; translation by the author). The years before compulsory schooling were seen as a period with its own intrinsic value. A book commissioned by the government to assist kindergarten staff in their work sets out this view:

> Child and kindergarten are described on their own terms. Childhood is seen as a specific period in life, different from other periods, and has a value of its own. Kindergarten is defined as an independent institution, and not as a substitute for home or a narrow preparation for school.
> (Målrettet arbeid i barnehagen, 1982, pp. 7–8; translation by the author)

The *barnehage*, therefore, should take care of young children, without being bound by what was supposed to go on later in children's lives, which would have represented an unwanted pressure on institution and people alike. The official texts about the *barnehage* from this period rarely refer to preparation for school or establishing relationships with school. The arguments for the *barnehage* were exclusively based on children's needs in a fast-changing world. The view and the assertion were that children would benefit from *barnehage* programmes of high quality. This would become apparent when they started school, and research documented that children who had attended *barnehager* were better off in school compared to those with no such experience (Sjølund, 1969). But there was no need to adapt *barnehage* to school. Indeed, one of the most extensive Norwegian research projects on ECE at the time studied the relations between *barnehage*, home and local community – but did not include the relationship with school in its discussion of the local community, even though the local school is important in Norway (Balke *et al.*, 1979).

In addition, most *barnehage* workers were strongly against the school's ideology and ways of teaching. In a study of 15 different areas of *barnehage* activity, preparing for school was ranked lowest by these workers. Highest were interaction, free play, creative activities and independence (Balke, 1980). What school stood for and did was even then seen as doing violence to the children, especially the younger ones.

To make the transition between the two institutions as comfortable and free from stress and anxiety as possible for the children, *barnehager* in many places organised school preparation activities during children's final year. These concentrated on the practical aspects of being a school pupil, while subjects taught in school were not so important. The children should learn to be pupils, sit still, raise their hands, talk when asked to. Some also visited their future school to get to know the premises and possibly meet their teacher. Such transition programmes gradually became a common part of *barnehage* activity, but only for the oldest children.

At the same time, while students on courses for *førskolelærere* (*barnehage* teachers) studied aspects of school pedagogy and practice, students studying to be school teachers did not go into *barnehage* pedagogy or practice. Nor did schools take into consideration what went on in the *barnehage*. This was based on practical arguments. When only a small proportion of pre-school children attended *barnehage*, there was no need for school to co-operate or develop close relations as it would benefit only a few children. It was also ideological, given the different educational ideals of the school. So the educational programmes in ECE and CSE were quite different, and the *barnehage* and the school were two separate, independent and autonomous institutions, each with their own values.

Conclusion

The relation between the two institutions – *barnehage* and school – in this period was mainly to leave each other in peace. It was characterised by indifference, isolation, even hostility. Therefore there are reasons for suggesting that this represented a separate kind of relationship, Type IV.

To the extent that they did communicate, *barnehage* was more active towards school and school life than the other way around. It was a relationship limited to ensuring the best possible transition from *barnehage* to school, but with no intention of making children totally ready for school. The aim was to ensure that starting school should be harmonious for the children.

So I also conclude that this relationship could be seen as a variation of Type II. It is an equal partnership in the sense that the institutions accepted each other as independent and autonomous, a partnership of limited connections, which though not strong was equal. The close and strong relation of Type II, as Peter Moss describes it, did not exist. The limited relation that existed was practical and initiated by the *barnehage*. *Barnehage* and school also were organised in two different ministries, the Ministry of Consumer and Administrative Affairs (*barnehage*) and the Ministry of Education (school). The two main reasons for this state of affairs have been identified: *barnehage* was available for only a small proportion of children; and since the educational ideas behind the *barnehage* were very different, schools did not see how they could benefit from closer links.

Second period, 1986–2006: barnehage invades school

The starting age for school was a matter of controversy when the first law on school in rural areas was passed in 1739. The alternatives were 5, 6 or 7 years. With the decision for 7 years, children in Norway started school later than children in most other countries. The main reason for the decision then was the special topographic conditions in Norway, a country sparsely populated and with dangerous journeys to and from school for some children, especially during the winter.

The question of lowering the school-starting age was raised several times from the 1960s. During the 1980s there were renewed discussions, with several political initiatives to start school at 6 years. In 1986, an experiment started on how to organise education for 6- year-olds, and from 1997 this became the school starting age. It was a highly controversial reform, which is easy to understand when seen in relation to the traditions explained above. There were strong disagreements both within and outside the world of politics. The *førskolelærere* were especially against this reform. They tried to prevent it, but in vain. School teachers, by contrast, were indifferent. The central argument, making this reform politically possible, was that the new first grade in school, for 6-year-olds, should combine the best from both *barnehage* and school traditions. At the turn of the last millennium this was withdrawn, with a new school reform introduced in 2006 marking the end of the second period.

An educational experiment

The conflict about when to start school was for a time solved by introducing an educational experiment. It started in 1986 and ended in 1990. This approach was chosen because of differing views in a coalition government consisting of three parties from the political right. Each chose an experimental model that they favoured and the experiment tested their three alternatives for 6-year-olds: (1) *barnehage*; (2) joint efforts between *barnehage* and school; (3) school. The idea was that an experiment would reveal the most sensible solution. As will be clarified below, the political parties eventually compromised.

I have studied this experiment extensively, being responsible for the evaluation (this evaluation work is discussed also in the Swedish report by Gunilla Dahlberg and Hillevi Lenz-Taguchi referred to in the introductory essay). It was actually not an experiment in a scientific sense. Because of the design, it was not possible to compare the different alternatives (Haug, 1992, 1994, 2000). There were no procedures for random allocation to the different models. The criteria for comparing models were not explicit. There was a common experimental curriculum, but participating institutions were supposed to implement it according to local priorities and conditions. The variations in content and teaching *within* models were as wide as between models. It was not possible, therefore, to say which alternative was the best in the traditional experimental way. That did not matter, because the decision about when to start school was made on political grounds only, independent of what went on 'experimentally'. The experiment only postponed and legitimised the eventual decision.

In 1986 there was a change of government, shortly after the experiment had been decided on. A Social Democratic minority government came into office. Early on in their term they signalled that finding a solution to the 6-year-olds in school was a priority. But they had problems achieving a majority in the *Stortinget*, so it took time to get a final and formal decision on the matter. The experiment was to continue though, and it did.

One of the main tasks in this experiment was to develop and implement a new national curriculum for 6-year-olds. The evaluation concluded that the national curriculum did not affect the education of the 6-years-olds to any extent (Haug, 1992). One reason was that the national curriculum was vague and ambiguous, with few clear directions to be followed. The reason for this could be that the national curriculum was produced nationally, necessitating building broad national support. This was achieved by agreeing on a very broad and general plan, which accommodated several different approaches to pedagogical work with children. This also explains why the curriculum was so widely accepted.

The national curriculum was to form the basis for local curriculum plans. The experimental strategy was that each of about 150 project groups from 42 municipalities worked independently, but met at times for lectures, presentations and discussions. They were to develop the local curriculum, and from that construct a practice with the children. I also studied the planning processes and the relations between local plans and practice (Haug, 1992). The main result of the analysis was that the local plans were adopted from and adjusted to an already established practice. The plans did not to any extent change practice.

An important result from the evaluation was that there were clearly differences between *barnehage* and school when it came to ideologies and working methods. What went on with 6-year-olds was clearly affected by the institution hosting the different experimental groups, and what groups of teachers were responsible. When in *barnehage*, the activities resembled what traditionally went on in *barnehage*; when in school, activities were school-like. *Førskolelærere* in the experiment were working like pre-school teachers when they were situated in *barnehager*. But when they worked in schools, in one of the alternatives being evaluated, *førskolelærere* changed role and over-reacted, being more school-like in their work than school teachers themselves.

As Dahlberg and Lenz-Taguchi have also concluded, institutions have their own traditions that are strong and resistant to change (Dahlberg and Lenz-Taguchi, 1994; see also the essay by Peter Moss). From these results, it seemed that the alternatives involving school for the 6 year-olds, whether with *førskolelærere* or school teachers, would be much more structured than if *barnehage* was the choice. An interesting question concerns the national curriculum: if it had been more precise and less ambiguous, would this have reduced the impact of the institution? Would it have reduced the effect of locating children in *barnehage* or school? This was what happened later, as we shall see.

Lowering the age for starting school

The arguments for lowering the age for starting school are well known. New Public Management has become the dominant steering ideology, affecting education in general by an increasing interest in educational outcomes or achievements. A global and deregulated market-place has increased international competition. The economy has become more information-based, presupposing more competence in the population; a public committee concluded that '[t]he challenge for Norwegian knowledge policy is that the country does not get enough competence out of the inhabitants' talent' (NOU 1988: 28, p. 7; translation by the author). The theory of human capital (Schultz, 1961) has gone through a renaissance, becoming important yet again. Education has come to be seen as an investment, and not an expense. Social inequalities, social injustice and social reproduction have been documented to a surprising and unwelcome extent. More schooling, it is believed, is a way to meet all these challenges.

Inspired by, among others, the research of Coleman (1966) and Jencks (1972), formal and structured education at an earlier age was regarded as one way of confronting these contemporary problems (Hernes and Knudsen, 1976). This could compensate for differing levels of learning capacity and aspirations arising from unequal social backgrounds. Both *barnehage* and school were obvious alternative choices for providing this compensatory education. But in contrast to a voluntary ECE programme, the compulsory school would reach every child.

The proposal to lower the school starting age became a hot issue professionally, politically and in public debates. There had been and still were disagreements about accepting the *barnehage* as an alternative to family. Now there was pressure, too, from school to expand downwards. Many thought that 6-year-olds were too young to be taught in a traditional first grade.

Gradually, through compromise, a political majority in the *Stortinget* was reached based on the principle that 6-year-olds in school should get a totally different programme compared to what had commonly been the case for first graders. An acceptable solution to the conflict was to construct a new pedagogy based on the best from each of the two educational traditions, *barnehage* and school. This was implemented with a new national curriculum, as a part of Reform 97 of the compulsory school.

In other words, the elementary school, covering the first four grades of compulsory school, was to be changed in a pedagogically radical way. First of all, a part of the 'new' education was to be a child-centred, activity-oriented pedagogy, which contained a rather direct critique of the established school pedagogy. It was based on the notion that the established school was too 'schoolish'; it was too structured, staid, programmed, fact-oriented and, at the same time, not sufficiently challenging and developmentally-oriented in creative areas. It gave too little consideration to children and their qualities and needs.

The reform also represented a political perspective that struggled against the contemporary rhetoric in educational policy and pedagogy, with its focus on efficiency, subjects and performance. It marked a victory for the progressive and *barnehage*-oriented counter-movement in Norway. But it did not last for very long.

The best of both worlds

The curriculum formulation was that school should offer the new first-graders the very best from both the *barnehage* and the school traditions. This meant that some aspects of *barnehage* ideology and practice should be exported to school; while school should only keep the best from its own tradition and let the rest go. The national curriculum for school stated that the first year at school should be clearly influenced by *barnehage*: 'Teaching at lower primary level shall be characterised by the traditions of both *barnehage* and school, and be a comfortable transition from *barnehage* to school' (Det kongelige kirke-, utdannings- og forskningsdepartement, 1996, p. 73; translation by the author).

There were many questions. For instance, it seemed necessary to begin by discussing the traditions of the two institutions, and identify the best in each of them. I went into these issues at the time (Haug, 1992). The conclusion was that *barnehage* and school have originated from quite different needs, have different functions in society, are differently regulated, have established different educational content, methods and practice, and have different curriculum codes and curricula. The *barnehage* presents itself as a unified pedagogical alternative based on free activity, project work and, not least, daily routines associated with meals, dressing, etc. It is the relationship between these three elements that defines and constitutes the particular identity of *barnehage* pedagogy. The orientation, too, is about the present and centred round the children, a hidden and unwritten tradition.

School tradition, by contrast, is highly text-oriented, learning subject content being of the utmost importance. Pupils are supposed to learn what others have decided. It is also future-oriented. Many of the arguments for school lie in the benefit it bestows in later life, both individually and collectively. It is a visible tradition because of all the texts that exist about it.

These relatively complex descriptions of traditions were greatly simplified during the political processes. The best of the *barnehage* was said to be related, in particular, to free play. The best of the school had to do with structured and systematic subject-oriented teaching. During the first grade in school, *barnehage* tradition was meant to dominate. This meant lots of free play. Children should not learn to read and write during their first year in school; this was postponed until second grade, when an objective of the syllabus was that children should gradually acquire these skills (Det kongelige kirke-, utdannings- og forskningsdepartement, 1996, p. 118).

Førskolelærere were allowed to teach from first through to fourth grade in school, providing they took a further year of teacher education. These additional courses dealt with teaching in school, especially how to introduce reading, writing and mathematics. In the national curriculum a defined number of lessons were allocated to free activities for the first four grades. In these respects, *barnehage* tradition could formally reach as far as fourth grade.

What happened was that the *barnehage* tradition invaded compulsory school. There is little research about how far up it actually reached, though there are reasons to believe that it dominated in the first grade (Vatne, 2006). The reform was implemented as intended. But this was no long-term success; there were retreats and changes of intent, and these appeared after a relatively short time. At least one issue was of special importance for these reactions: low pupil achievements in school. Several national and international tests revealed that Norwegian pupils did not score as highly as expected. The PIRLS study from 2001 indicated that too many fifth graders did not read well enough, though the average scores were acceptable (Solheim and Tønnessen, 2003). PISA results in 2001 showed that compared to other nations, Norway was a little below average and variations between pupils were high, especially at the lower end of the range (Lie *et al.*, 2001). These results came as a shock, as they did in several other countries in Europe.

The evaluation of Reform 97 concluded that the concentration on learning in school was too weak and there ought to be more pressure to learn (Haug, 2003). Studies, too, found that social reproduction in Norwegian schools had changed, but in the wrong direction; pupils' test scores and exam results were highly correlated to parents' cultural capital (Opheim, 2004). These results were not politically acceptable, and the work to improve performance became intense. Though not scientifically documented, a common suggestion was that the *barnehage* tradition during the first grade in school had contributed to these results in two ways. First, children had to wait until grade 2 to learn how to read and write. A headline in a national newspaper illustrates a widespread view: 'Too much play and too little learning' (*Aftenposten*, 18 August, 2002). Second, with the *barnehage* tradition as the ideal from day one in school, pupils were not accustomed to working to high academic standards. They got the impression that school was play, a perception that could not continue. Therefore, changes were introduced.

Conclusion

To make 6-year-olds attend school, *barnehage* education was exported to school to compensate for school's lack of child-centredness. The concept of taking the best from each tradition makes this a combination of Type II and III relationships. School became the meeting arena for both alternatives on equal terms. What I find of most interest in this situation is the ambition that it is possible to 'take' the best from different traditions and just mix them together. From a technical or instrumental perspective this could be done, just like baking a cake. You take a bit of this and that and stir it together, and a new type of 'education' grows out of it.

According to my analysis, this was what the authorities meant. They had no sense that many saw these two approaches to education as quite different, even incompatible. Educational traditions are strongly linked to institutional and environmental factors (March and Olsen, 1989). This implies that each of the two traditions not only stands for different values, ideas and practices. They have also been developed under different conditions with respect to buildings, materials, rules, norms and expectations, representing different conditions in practice.

The basic question is whether different educational traditions can be practised independently of the conditions under which they have developed. The experiences from the earlier experiment indicated that to practise the best from two traditions was extremely difficult, and that institutional frameworks would strongly affect what went on. This was recognised when the 6-year-olds were sent to school in 1997, creating a real meeting place. *Førskolelærere* were invited in, to assist school teachers to implement the best from the *barnehage* tradition. They had to qualify though, by taking courses to become school teachers. The national curriculum clearly stated that the *barnehage* tradition had a legitimate place in school. School buildings, classrooms and outdoor play areas were rebuilt to be more like *barnehage* environments. Staffing for the first four years of schooling varied. In some schools *førskolelærere* dominated, in some school teachers, and in other cases they taught together.

Third period, 2006 onwards: school invades the *barnehage*

Since the start of the new millennium, we can trace developments going in two directions. One is a new reform in school: the Knowledge Promotion Reform, 2006. Not unexpectedly, this reform formulated high ambitions for school achievements. The reasons behind this policy were identical with those from the period before: internationalisation, global competition, etc. The introductory statement in the White Paper about this reform says that: 'the ability and desire to learn must be improved' (Det kongelige utdannings- og kunnskapsdepartement, 2004, p. 3; translation by the author). In this spirit a new national curriculum for school was introduced. At almost the same time, a national quality assurance system was implemented, including compulsory national tests. The goal of introducing the *barnehage* tradition into school was given up. School was to become 'schoolish' again. Guidance about when to learn to read was set aside. First graders were supposed to be introduced to reading and writing from when they first started school. The intention that first grade should be like *barnehage* was weakened. Free play sessions in school were abolished, to be replaced by time for teaching basic skills like reading and writing. After a while, *førskolelærere* could no longer take courses to qualify to teach in school.

Developments in barnehage

The other aspect of importance, which I will concentrate on here, is the parallel developments in *barnehage*, also strongly affected by the general trend in education policy described above. The result is that the *barnehage* becomes more closely connected in several ways to school and school education, but this time school 'invades' the *barnehage*.

From the final years of the 1990s, almost a revolution can be found in attitudes towards the *barnehage*. *Barnehager* have become today widely accepted as a provision for all children from a year upwards. This change has many causes; increased immigration, labour shortages, internationalisation and cultural diversity are all important. There was a strong need to legitimise *barnehage* as an option for all preschool children, which was done in part by arguments that high quality *barnehage* education contributes to a better school career for children, compared to staying at home or being cared for by a private child-minder. The goal that all children ought to attend *barnehage* became deeply embedded in Norwegian policy, especially since 2005 when a majority coalition government dominated by Social Democrats came into office (Kunnskapsdepartementet, 2008b), introducing an entitlement to a *barnehage* place for all children over 12 months old. As an illustration of this new thinking about the *barnehage,* at a conference arranged by the Norwegian Ministry of Education and Research in May 2011, the Minister publicly applauded a presentation about how investments in *barnehager* paid off through enhancing children's learning and development in school (Melhuish, 2011).

A new curriculum for the *barnehage* was presented in 2006 (Kunnskapsdepartementet, 2006), and revised in 2011. The paragraphs formulating the objectives of the *barnehage* and of the school were brought much more in line with each other. The curriculum maintains the need for a natural progression between *barnehage* and school, a point further emphasised in a recent White Paper (Kunnskapsdepartementet, 2009), and a booklet from the Ministry of Education gives advice about how this is to be understood (Kunnskapsdepartementet, 2008a). The close relationship between these two institutions is given several meanings. It is about the actual transition from *barnehage* to school; a child should leave *barnehage* feeling confident and looking forward to becoming a school pupil. School should welcome them. It is about the child being acquainted with school before starting at school. And it is about continuity and progression in learning content between *barnehage* and school. It is recommended that school, *barnehage* and parents have meeting places where they can discuss and inform each other.

The most common way to attend to these issues is by certain school preparation activities. They have been established in *barnehager* for ages, as described earlier. Almost all *barnehager* – 96 per cent in 2008 – now offer such transition programmes for 5-year-olds (Winsvold and Gulbrandsen, 2009). According to a national survey, the content of these activities has not changed much; they remain relatively limited. *Barnehager* take the preparation for school attendance to be about a combination of social, practical and linguistic skills, now also encouraging basic skills such as reading, writing and mathematics. Schools are involved in these activities to only a minor extent. The established meeting places for schools and *barnehager* are mainly used to exchange general information or documentation regarding individual children. Co-operation is mostly around routines to facilitate the practical transition from *barnehage* to school (Rambøll, 2010).

These school preparation activities are prioritised by *førskolelærere*. This is revealed in a recent study, which looked into the differences between the responsibilities of assistants and teachers in the *barnehage*. The reason for conducting this study is the low proportion of teachers to assistants in Norwegian *barnehager*, about a third. While generally there was little division of labour, the *førskolelærere* were more engaged than assistants in a few specific areas: that is in leadership responsibilities and in specific and narrow pedagogical activities such as teaching 5-year-olds for an hour or so once a week in preparation for school (Haug and Steinnes, 2011).

Barnehage to become more like school

In two other areas, there are much more noticeable changes in the relationship between school and *barnehage* compared to earlier. The *barnehage* is still legally independent of the school, but since 2008 both are the responsibility of the same Ministry of Education. Until then, *barnehage* and school have always been administered by different ministries. The transfer from the Ministry of Consumer and Administrative Affairs to the Ministry of Education in 2008 is deeply symbolic – just as it was in 1975, when it was decided that they should continue to belong to different ministries. It is a strong signal of a change in thinking about the purposes of the *barnehage*. The Norwegian Directorate for Education and Training, the executive agency for the Ministry of Education and Research, is now responsible for the development of both the *barnehage* and primary and secondary education, ECE and CSE. In 2012, this Directorate will assume the formal practical and administrative responsibilities for *barnehager*, which according to the Minister of Education will strengthen the connections between *barnehage* and education. Next I would expect that the *barnehage* by law will become a formal part of the education system, as has happened already in Sweden.

The new national curriculum for *barnehage* stresses systematic teaching with the aim of learning. For each category of learning content in the national curriculum for *barnehage*, there are goals to be reached in order to support children's learning and development. How to adapt curriculum content for children is a local responsibility, to be clarified in an annual plan prepared by each *barnehage*; this also goes for progression in content and activities. Compared to the first national curriculum for *barnehage* in 1995, the differences in this area are noticeable. Early childhood is still seen as a specific phase of life with intrinsic importance, as has always been the case in *barnehage* tradition. But now an additional message appears: the *barnehage* tradition must also be seen in relation to what goes on in school (Kunnskapsdepartementet, 2006). The earlier scepticism about school has been removed, or at least it is not so clearly formulated.

As a part of these changes, there is also a debate about testing of children's language in *barnehager*. The reason is first and foremost that some children start school without the necessary knowledge of and skills in the Norwegian language, with adverse effects. This applies mostly to children whose first language is not Norwegian. Language testing is seen as a solution to helping these children. Those who do not have sufficient mastery of the language will get additional help to improve their skills.

The new curriculum for *barnehage* has also been more aligned than previously with the national curriculum for school. This applies especially to learning content, which is now close to the subjects in the national curriculum for school, organised in the same categories though formulated in different words. These categories include, for instance, 'communications, language and text', 'body, movement and health', 'arts, culture and creativity', 'nature, environment and technique'. The reason for this alignment is 'to give the children a positive relation to school subjects and motivation to learn more' (Kunnskapsdepartementet, 2011, p. 68; translation by the author).

From this I conclude that the *barnehage* is in a process of getting a new role with at least partly new functions. The most specific is preparing children for school, but in another way than before. An attempt has been made to move some aspects of school tradition downwards to the younger children in *barnehage*, in particular the systematic learning of formalised subject content.

Opposition to these developments has been strong, especially the testing of language and the signals about more systematic and formal learning and the organisation of content. Recent debates have shown that many see them as a way of schoolifying early childhood education. These changes are interpreted as a break with the long-established *barnehage* tradition. It is even said that children are being encouraged to achieve better test results in school. It has also been argued that what is now happening will destroy the identity of the *barnehage* (Vatne, 2010). But what the results will actually be, we do not know as yet.

Conclusion

What has been described in the third part of the chapter is close to a Type I relationship, readying children for school, but not exactly as defined by Peter Moss. It is expected that *barnehage* should prepare children for school, the criterion for Type I. This means that ECE is supposed to take over some of the school's way of teaching and some of the school's learning content. School tradition is exported down into *barnehage*. The reason for this change is obviously to improve school achievement, with the *barnehage* tradition not deemed sufficient to support learning in school. Therefore, the changes in the third period – from school into *barnehage* – are reversing those in the preceding period. It could be said that *barnehager* are expected to adopt some of the school tradition to be able to prepare children for that institution. We are in a time of upheaval, where established *barnehage* traditions are being placed under severe pressure.

I would argue that these new ideas about the significance of *barnehage* for children's future learning have been made possible because of one single element: namely the enormous expansion of *barnehage* provision in Norway. Today it has become a place for all children. All children, aged 1 year or older, now have a right to a place in *barnehage* if their parents so wish. The goal of *barnehage* for everyone has been reached after a tremendous political effort. The number of places, the funding and the organisation are now available. The argument from the authorities is that now it is time to concentrate on the quality of the educational programme, which produces features that break with established *barnehage* traditions. Different aspects of school tradition are embraced as being of value.

The opposition is understandable, but at the same time a bit surprising because of differing signals. On the one hand, *barnehage* staff want to prepare children for school; *førskolelærere* in particular are heavily engaged in these activities. On the other hand, they do not want the school tradition to become a dominant part of *barnehage* activities. Both attitudes can be seen as consistent with the tradition of the *barnehage*. What staff are trying to do is limited to preparing the children for the transition from *barnehage* to school; children should be prepared for this move, as that is in their best interests. But to import school orientation to *barnehage* seems to be far more unwelcome. It is impossible to know what will be happen in the long term.

Discussion

I have presented the story of the relationship between ECE and CSE in Norway. I see two points especially clearly. One is that the societal context at any time is very important when it comes to defining these relationships and how they are regulated. What is seen as the best education for children varies at different times, the answer to this question being closely related to prevailing social, cultural and political conditions and understandings (Lundgren, 1991). The concept of educational quality is both a result of and part of the contemporary discourse.

The other is that how these contexts function when it comes to the relationship between *barnehager* and schools seems to be especially dependent upon the development of the *barnehage*. When the *barnehage* was only for a minority of the children in the country, there was little pressure to create close relations. Developing the institution on the basis of its own values was what counted. But when all children can attend, this almost automatically results in the *barnehage* being asked to account for its results. When a great deal of money is put into the institution, the nation demands more in return. It is no longer sufficient that the *barnehage* takes care of children; they must also educate them. The meaning of this education, just now at least, comes closer to the school's tradition.

Four different types of relations have come to the fore in this presentation of three periods in the history of the Norwegian kindergarten, one more than Peter Moss presented in his introduction. What I have also revealed is a combination of types, of hybrids rather than pure types. The type that Peter Moss has not identified is mutual indifference and even isolation, which was the starting point in my presentation. This I have defined as Type IV. From such indifference grew a notion that it could be important to prepare children for the transition from *barnehage* to school, which gradually became part of the *barnehage* tradition. It still is today, and perhaps even more strongly than at any time before. This is actually a feature of all three periods in the development of the *barnehage*.

During the second period, the *barnehage* tradition was transported into school. It was the intention that the lowest grades in school should become more like the *barnehage*. The reason was a political compromise, to allow a lowering of the school-starting age from 7 to 6 years. This move was at least partly successful, contrary to what I found in my earlier doctoral dissertation. The reasons for success are several that were not present at the time of the experiment: it had been widely accepted that 6-year-olds should go to school; *førskolelærere* who were employed to teach in school had to qualify formally; the curriculum explicitly stated that the best from the *barnehage* tradition should be a part of the school programme, together with the best from the school tradition; this was followed up in different ways, and affected both how classrooms were equipped and organised, how many children were allowed to constitute a class, and how this influenced the educational programme; and school teachers were relatively indifferent, and in many instances left it to *førskolelærere*. This, I would argue, is a combination of Peter Moss's Type II and III, strong and equal partnerships and a meeting place.

When the *barnehage* tradition was about to gain a foothold in school, a sudden change occurred. This development was not so desirable after all, because it did not contribute effectively enough to children's learning as measured by the results from national and international tests. At least that was how these results were explained. Now, instead, school tradition was to be transported to the *barnehage*, which is gradually becoming a part of the school system – not as yet formally or legally, but by joining the same ministry, by curriculum alignment and so on. Peter Moss has envisaged no type of relationship that easily fits with this kind of model. It could be a kind of model III type, a meeting place. This time the arena is in *barnehage* and not in school, and there is a notion about readying children for school (Type I).

What has happened is that *barnehage* staff seem to be clinging to the *barnehage* tradition, and are not willing to accept having elements of school tradition closely embedded in their work. The reason is that the school tradition in many ways is at odds with the core elements of the *barnehage*, and there is a view that this tradition will damage children's development and not benefit them. Instead, from the *barnehage's* perspective, the relationship with school is focused on the narrower aspect of transition.

Behind these dominating patterns, we can observe minor developments, but they are not unimportant. Neither *barnehage* nor school is untouched by the different movements of traditions. They leave something behind, as when a river floods. When traditions go back and forth like this, they affect what goes on, and both school and *barnehage* will gradually change and become more alike.

One of the most striking impressions that remains after this presentation of recent history is the weak implementation. It seems that little power has been handed over to local authorities and *barnehager* to make it possible to fulfil political intentions. The impression is that institutional reforms like these are supposed to happen by themselves, almost without any form of assistance: reform by words instead of reform by support and control.

Chapter 6

David, Goliath and the ephemeral parachute

The relationship from a United States perspective

Sharon Lynn Kagan

The provocative series, *Contesting Early Childhood*, has offered the contemporary early education and development field the opportunity to address some of its most trenchant issues. With volumes that consider diverse understandings of childhood, diverse theories of pedagogy, and diverse approaches to practice, the series stands at the threshold of ushering in new ways to think about and enact early childhood education. Such undertakings premise themselves in the traditions of leading revisionist thinkers (Ravitch, 1978), social justice theorists (Rawls, 1971) and staunch investigators of paradigmatic change (Kuhn, 1962). Reverberating through such thinking is the idea that social change will follow enhanced – and often multiple – understandings of the social context; moreover, for significant social change to be achieved, conventional and solitary historical understandings must be explicated and often re-interpreted. Consequently, revisionist reconceptualisations are indispensable to the evolution of thinking and of the social order. As such, the series makes important contributions to our ability to think and ultimately act afresh about early childhood education and development.

Perhaps on no topic is such fresh perspective-taking more necessary than around the issue of the relationship between early childhood education (ECE) and compulsory school education (CSE). Such attention is timely. With scores of nations either embarking on new commitments to young children or enhancing extant policies and programmes for the young, attention to ECE has never been greater. Armed with new data that attest to the magnitude and importance of early brain development (Shonkoff and Phillips, 2000), the effectiveness of high-quality ECE to alter children's life trajectories positively (Howes *et al.*, 1992), and the cost-effectiveness of such provision (Schweinhart *et al.*, 2005), ECE's importance and practice are soaring. And as services to young children are mounted, questions of theory, pedagogy, and delivery are evoked: What should these services do? What outcomes might they render? Who should administer them? How much will they cost (and return to) society? How do/should they comport with already existing services?

The purpose of this chapter is to examine the historical and contemporary relationships between ECE and CSE, taking into consideration diverse theories about this relationship. In addressing this topic, my goal is to suggest that although their relationship is characterised by expected and yet unresolved conflict, ECE and CSE have much to contribute to one another. Harkening to the introductory essay by Peter Moss, this chapter argues that such a partnership based on equal contributions has not been the norm, with CSE more heavily contouring ECE than the reverse. The chapter also suggests that deeply embedded structural factors contribute to a power imbalance and that any attempt to re-balance the relationship between CSE and ECE must both understand and address such power inequalities. Moreover, the chapter argues that, although discussed for decades, the relationship between ECE and CSE must be addressed now, when societies are shaping and/or expanding their ECE offerings. To avoid the discourse this volume hopes to inspire may be durably dangerous, leaving a legacy that undermines the value of ECE. By drawing examples primarily from the United States and selected other countries, the chapter offers specific strategies to engender a productive, respectful balance between ECE and CSE.

Looking at theory: the seeds of developmental continuity

For even the most neophyte student of child development and/or education, the need for continuity reverberates throughout the theoretical literature. Whether calling for the attachment of very young children to their mothers (Bowlby, 1969/1982; Ainsworth, 1989) or calling for understanding the nature of development in the familial and social context (Vygotsky, 1978; Bronfenbrenner, 1979), continuity in children's lives is necessary. Such continuity initially takes the form of the attachments needed by the infant to grow and thrive. It is further advanced by the well-acknowledged need for an individual to be knowledgeable about and grounded in the culture and context of his or her family and community.

Continuity is a core principle that transcends theoretical perspectives on development. From the biological perspective, humans develop in fairly predictable stages, characterised by an evolutionary spiral that enables the human organism to undertake increasingly complex and physically challenging tasks. Whether examining the theory of individual evolution (Darwin, 1877) or that of the adaptive evolution of entire species in the form of sociobiological studies, the continuity of development is accepted. From the psychoanalytic perspective, the continuity of development has also received considerable attention and support. Although Sigmund Freud (1856–1939), with his emphasis on inborn drives and sexual orientations, believed that development was not continuous and even, but sporadic and conditioned, he acknowledged the importance of early experience and positive parent-child relationships to foster the security of the child (Woolfolk and Perry, 2012). Heavily influenced by Freud, Erik Erikson (1902–94) understood development as continuity; that is, he regarded development as a passage through a series of eight stages, each characterised by goals, accomplishments and dangers. Importantly, Erikson understood that the accomplishments at one stage are contingent upon how conflicts are resolved in the earlier years. As such, Erikson's work not only underscored the theory of developmental continuity in childhood, but stretched this framework to incorporate life-span development (Erikson, 1963, 1980). Whether focusing on the life span as Erikson did in many of his writings, or honing in on the early years, the importance of continuity was consistently integral to ever expanding and diverse theories of development (Sameroff and Haith, 1996).

Beyond developmentalists, however, behavioural theorists also acknowledged the systematic and evolutionary patterns of development and learning. Refuting psychoanalytic rationales for development, they suggested that development can be observed through behaviour. More precisely, behaviourists contended that changes in children's cognitive, emotional and social development, and even some physical changes, were consequences of learning. They advocated the primacy of nurture over nature, suggesting that development and learning are continuous and intertwined, but that both are conditioned by experience. Social learning theorists advanced conventional behaviourist thinking by infusing socio-emotional dimensions of learning. For example, Albert Bandura (1965) distinguished between the acquisition of knowledge (learning) and observable performance based on that knowledge (behaviour), noting that both are conditioned by self-efficacy, or belief in one's capacity to influence outcomes. Whatever the specific theoretical orientation, it was accompanied by a transcendent belief in the continuity of development and learning.

Moving from the more theoretical literature to the practice of learning, developmental continuity was applied to education by its seminal architects. Johann Pestalozzi (1746–1827) and Friedrich Froebel (1782–1852) argued the importance of continuity between home and school and between parents and teachers (Green, 1969). Froebel, Pestalozzi's student, advanced the need for temporal continuity, stressing that it is 'pernicious to consider the stages of human development – infant, child, boy or girl, youth or maiden, man or woman – as distinct, and not, as life shows them, as continuous in themselves in unbroken transitions' (Froebel, 1826/1974, p. 27). Prompted by these theories, Froebel advocated a child-centred approach to pedagogy, one that would facilitate children's natural and continuous intellectual and spiritual development.

Jean Piaget (1896–1980), enunciating his fundamental developmental theory, not only explained the stages of development from infancy to adulthood, but called for the alignment of learning environments to accommodate the changing, evolving youngster. For example, Piaget's description of the preoperational child underscored the need to align the nature of the physical space to young children's changing ways of knowing and doing. Hardly unique, this orientation was shared by many learning theorists. Infusing his work with a broader sociocultural orientation, Lev Vygotsky (1896–1934) saw the challenges associated with making intellectual and social transitions and called for scaffolding youngsters as they traversed new boundaries (Vygotsky, 1978). From this perspective, transitions offered a key opportunity for learning, insofar as adults provided thoughtful scaffolding to help children adjust to new circumstances. Maria Montessori (1870–1952) emphasised the importance of predictability and routine for young children, through highly choreographed micro-routines (Lillard, 2005). Pedagogically inventive, Montessori understood the need for familiarity and repetition to strengthen children's skills and abilities so that they could more comfortably assimilate fresh knowledge and navigate new transitions.

Not intended to treat each epoch or theorist in detail, this race through developmental and applied theory suggests that never, irrespective of orientation, did learning or developmental theorists stray far from a clear endorsement of the continuity of development. Although each theorist espoused unique and variable accounts of development and learning processes, each accorded the evolutionary flow of development as a given, and each addressed the need to provide for continuity and the transitions it necessitates in children's lives. Continuity and transitions, then, may be regarded as acknowledged constants amidst an ever-changing ebb and flow of developmental and learning theory. As such, they may be well regarded as key developmental anchors that justifiably warrant the attention they have historically and consistently been accorded.

Looking at practice: the realities of developmental continuity and transition

That continuity and transitions are transcendent principles does not mean that they are automatically translated into practice. Indeed, as this analysis will show, despite their theoretical importance and multiple attempts to actualise them, bringing developmental continuity and transition to reality has been seriously inhibited by: (i) definitional and conceptual ambiguities; (ii) inconclusive research; and (iii) serious theoretical, political and structural constraints.

Before understanding these implementation inhibitors, it is important to establish that there has been no dearth of efforts to instantiate ideas of developmental continuity, transition and linkages in ECE, in the United States and globally. The importance of continuity in the lives of young children is well acknowledged and broadly accepted (Silvern, 1988). As a consequence, there have been calls for attention to be paid to diverse kinds of transitions. Some have called for *vertical* continuity, that is supporting children as they make transitions from the familiarity of the home to the centre, from the centre to school, and from grade to grade within school. Such vertical transitions seek to provide a continuity of experience for children (and often their families) as children traverse the age/grade continuum. There have also been efforts to establish continuity among the many institutions that serve children at the same time. Such so-called *horizontal* continuity (Kagan, 1991; Zigler and Kagan, 1982) attempts to create linkages among health, education, parenting and protective services, as well as other supportive institutions and settings.

Such commitments to continuity and transitions have given rise to a spate of programmes and movements, both historically and presently. Many have emanated from those committed to early education. For example, in the United States, the federal Head Start programme[1] for pre-school children has routinely shown serious interest in the form of research and demonstration programmes to foster linkages between Head Start and primary schools. Paralleling these efforts, several US-based foundations, among them W.K. Kellogg (2008), have launched major initiatives to foster transitions. Kellogg's Supporting Partnerships to Assure Ready Kids (SPARK) funded efforts in seven states and the District of Columbia to find more inventive and productive strategies to enhance children's transitions. The Foundation for Child Development (2009) spearheaded a 10-year campaign to advance the linkages from pre-K (ECE for 4-year-olds) to grade 3. Internationally, the Bernard van Leer (2009) and Aga Khan Foundations have supported interventions and examined efforts that aimed to build continuous learning experiences for young children (Bartlett *et al.*, 2010). Moreover, efforts emerging from the compulsory education community are now echoing the need to promote continuity between home and school and among the services that children need to thrive. Dubbed the whole schools approach, the community schools approach, two-generational parenting, or the Broader Bolder movement, these American efforts signal an increasing concern for linkages and transitions, going well beyond ECE. Given the bevy of continuity-transition efforts that have taken place historically and that are being attempted presently, we can now turn to a discussion regarding the challenges associated with their implantation to understand why they have been so very challenging and their results comparatively marginal.

Definitional and conceptual ambiguities

Long debated within early childhood, the definition of transition measures remains somewhat elusive. Some focus on linking various institutions that serve young children (e.g. health and child care), while others focus on linkages between ECE and CSE. Increasingly, efforts seek to achieve linkages through formal activities, for example through joint professional development for ECE and CSE teachers, formal transfers of children's records from ECE to CSE, and the development of standards, curricula and assessments that are aligned from ECE through CSE. Experiencing various degrees of success, each successive wave of innovation attempts to establish itself with a new title and a new focus. Such freshness of orientation and perspective, while inventive, does expand the transition agenda, further inhibiting the development of common definitions and understandings of transition.

Achieving a common definition of transition, one that would be serviceable for ECE and CSE, is rendered complex for several reasons. Chief among them are the inherent and different disciplinary orientations that characterise ECE and CSE. Firmly ensconced in a developmental tradition, ECE fosters an integrated approach to the social, emotional, physical, language and cognitive development of young children. ECE does not disaggregate these domains of development. In stark contrast, CSE espouses a disciplinary orientation that focuses on the discrete disciplines of language, arts, maths, science, and social studies. Such distinctions lead to fundamental differences in pedagogical approaches that render transitions very hard to implement.

Further fuelling the different orientations of ECE and CSE are the professional orientations and training levels of their respective workforces. Often, those who work with younger children have less training than their counterparts in CSE. Moreover, historically ECE and CSE teachers are prepared for their roles according to different pedagogical traditions; child-centred play is the preferred pedagogical orientation of ECE, while CSE is characterised by a more scripted and didactic approach to learning. Lacking an agreed definition and conception of pedagogy, lacking common understanding of the role of the disciplines, and lacking common training modalities and priorities, it is no wonder that ECE-CSE linkages are plagued by misunderstandings at least, and, at worst, by the misappropriation of well-known and well-regarded theories of child development.

Research inconclusiveness

With mounting calls for accountability, it is not surprising that research into the effectiveness of different interventions is being called for and, in some cases, funded. Studying transition is no exception. Welcome as research is, it is important to note that a long lineage of studies on transitions, conducted at considerable expense to the US government, has consistently yielded results that are inconclusive. Reviewed in detail elsewhere (Kagan and Neuman, 1998), transition studies date back to the Follow Through programme initiated in 1967. Follow Through was prompted by early findings that suggested a diminished effect of Head Start over time (Holmes and Holmes, 1966). To stave off 'fade out', as it came to be termed, the Follow Through and Head Start Planned Variation (HSVP) programmes sought to foster pedagogical continuity from pre-school through third grade in school. Results were disappointing, the only significant finding being that two of the models demonstrated some effect on children who were enrolled when compared with children who had some or no pre-school (Stebbins *et al.*, 1977).

Faced with these results, the US government launched Project Developmental Continuity (PDC), a demonstration programme that differed from its predecessors in that it paid explicit attention to linking Head Start with public schools across multiple dimensions (administration, management, services and pedagogy). Although armed with a laser-like focus on continuity, PDC evaluation results indicated no significant differences between PDC and non-PDC participants (Bond, 1982). Discouraged by the lack of sustained effects, the government launched the Head Start Transition Project in the mid-1980s, funding programmes to innovate new approaches to transitions. Unlike prior efforts, the Head Start Transition Project did find some positive effects on the time and effort devoted to transition; it also found that young children who participated in the programmes experienced less stress during the first few months of school than those who did not participate (Hubbell *et al.*, 1987).

However modest these findings, they propelled an investigation into the prevalence of transition arrangements in the United States through the National Transition Study. Conducted in the late 1980s, this study found that in a nationally representative sample of schools, few had formal arrangements and less than 10 per cent had had any contact with children's pre-schools or child care teachers or centres (Love *et al.*, 1992). The result of this work did help to advance a more nuanced understanding of transitions, suggesting that they needed to be adaptive to context and family. More recently, in 1990, the US Congress launched the National Head Start/Public School Early Childhood Transition Demonstration Project that sought to examine the conditions that accelerated the implementation of effective transition strategies. Difficult to evaluate because adaptive approaches to transitions were advocated, the work did identify some factors that facilitate and impede transitions (Head Start Bureau, 1996; Ramey *et al.*, 2000).

A systematic review of transition research suggests at least three major barriers to evaluation. First, in many cases, evaluations have been methodologically compromised by limited implementation of the transition practices, by a lack of suitable (and often contaminated) control groups, and by teacher and student mobility (Kagan and Neuman, 1998; Love *et al.*, 1992). In each study, serious methodological issues were reported. Second, the lack of a clear conceptual transition framework makes it difficult to discern what constitutes success. It is hard to know what precisely to implement and what to evaluate without such specification. Third, transition efforts, be it at the local or national level, are quite transitory; they come and go, attracting attention for only episodic and comparatively short-lived periods of time. Consequently, there is limited technical capacity, a particular challenge given the arduous task of implementing transitions across systems. Clearly, transitions must be better defined and conceptualised, more easily and effectively evaluated, and rendered more of a 'front and centre' issue (Kagan and Neuman, 1998; Kagan and Neville, 1996).

Theoretical, political, and structural constraints

Historically, transitions have been conceptualised as a discrete, somewhat self-contained phenomenon to be implemented. Resembling a parachute that mysteriously makes its way into the environment, transitions have had a somewhat drop-in, ephemeral quality. They land, they occupy space – but no one is quite sure what to make of them or what to do with them. Yet, transitions are more burdened and burdensome than parachutes: they carry with them the idea of somehow magically transforming the environment, of eliciting necessary social change. Often lacking strategic design and durability, transition efforts advocate monumental change: bringing continuity to highly disparate institutions whose governance, infrastructure, financing, and staffing are distinctive and diverse, often without even beginning to attend to these formative elements. Sometimes, transition efforts assume that, because ECE is framed by a strong developmental orientation, and bolstered by strong and fairly widely accepted theories, ECE should and will be accepted on a basis equivalent to the dominant institution, that is, the compulsory schools. Such assumptions, however justified, do not stand up. Like dominant genes in the genetic pool, the strong ones exert controlling influence. In the life course of transitions, then, it is not surprising that the CSE gene dominates, contouring ECE to its shape, values and prevailing customs.

Whether this is as it should be has received considerable attention. In his introductory essay, Peter Moss offers three distinct approaches to the linkages between ECE and CSE. The first, the readiness approach, contends that learning is hierarchical and that the primary function of ECE is to ready youngsters for the experience of schooling. He deals with the consequences of this approach and suggests that it has strongly contributed to the 'schoolification' of ECE. A second approach, presented as distinct, is one that conceptualises a strong and equal ECE-CSE partnership wherein the strengths of both partners are acknowledged and built upon. Such approaches would need to recognise ECE as a public good in the way that CSE is recognised. Moreover, such a partnership would need to attend to pedagogical and curricular differences, with ECE exerting an upward influence on a CSE system that often neglects, if not negates, a developmental orientation. Finally, Peter Moss, discussing the work of Dahlberg and Lenz-Taguchi (1994), offers the 'meeting place' approach, in which the traditions and cultures of ECE and CSE are taken as a starting point to developing a reality-driven approach to the linkages of these two quite disparate forms of education.

Concerned that ECE-CSE linkages might be predisposed to the downward extension of schooling, Dahlberg and Lenz-Taguchi (1994) address how each understand 'children' and 'childhood'. The authors point out significant differences in how ECE and CSE value children and how instruction is contoured by these values. For example, when regarding children merely as 're-producers' of the culture, then conventional CSE strategies (e.g. teacher-directed instruction, time usage and management strategies) may appear to be justified. If, on the other hand, young children are seen as agents of their own development, a more child-centred approach to pedagogy would likely ensue. The authors, along with Peter Moss, suggest that overcoming fissures in the ECE-CSE relationship must commence by addressing differences in values, traditions and conceptions of children and childhood, and continue on to discuss the impacts of these on pedagogy and teaching practices.

Without question, this tripartite schema is helpful. It not only makes the authors' stance clear, but provides space for contesting or embellishing it. To do so, I offer three propositions: (i) schoolification may be associated with not only the readiness stance but with others, as well; (ii) the strong and equal partnerships advocated in the second approach may be an idealised vision, that without strong provisos may exacerbate the schoolification of ECE; and (iii) however important, values and traditions do not stand alone, nor do they trump the need to address durable structures and policies if we are to achieve truly viable, respectful ECE-CSE linkages and the effective transitions for children that such linkages promote.

Schoolification

Schoolification is conventionally considered to be negative by the ECE community because, at least in the Anglophone world, it often fails to honour ECE traditions and practices, while according hegemony to the conventions of compulsory schooling, replete with structured content and prescribed (and often uninventive) pedagogical practices. Under certain and currently non-prevailing conditions, however, schoolification might not be so bad. Consider, for example, how one might feel about schoolification if schools were truly child centred and pedagogically rich and exciting places for young children and their teachers. In other words, the connotation currently ascribed to 'schoolification' is negative because the 'ECE-ification' of schools has not taken hold. Under an ideal set of circumstances, CSE would be aligned with children's developmental trajectories and would honour and respect their rights as both learners and human beings. By fostering the integrity of individual children and by honestly supporting their comprehensive development, schoolification might enjoy greater support and could be a positive influence that promotes continuity and fosters smooth transitions for young children, although clearly this is not the case today.

Given that contemporary schoolification is not ideal, it is important to consider why it imposes such a ferocious hold. What exactly empowers schools to exert a controlling force over ECE? First, schools are ubiquitous. They represent a constant in the budgets and provisions of all governments; indeed, the very word 'compulsory' underscores their universality within any given society. Across societies, schooling is regarded as both a social responsibility of the society and an enduring part of the social infrastructure. What goes on in schools and the degree to which they are fulfilling their social mission may be debated, but no society has eliminated, or talked of eliminating, its schools. As such, schools are normative and ubiquitous institutions that enjoy the general support and funding of their publics.

Second, in part because of their ubiquity, schools are known and their mission and function are generally understood by the public. Because, in many nations, most or all of the adult population have been to school, adults understand what goes on there. They may not have completed school; they may not have had positive experiences with schools; and they may not understand what precisely is taught, using what strategies. But schooling is a known reality.

Third, schools are durable. They do not have to worry if they will be in existence tomorrow and they do not exist at the behest of today's legislators. As such, they are fixtures on the social landscape.

Ubiquity, familiarity and durability all characterise CSE, but not ECE. Where CSE is universal and ubiquitous, ECE is (in many, if not all, countries) spotty, sporadic, and inconsistent. Where CSE is familiar, ECE is mysterious. Why is it necessary? How do children learn if all they do is play all day? Why should I pay for it? If it were really important, wouldn't the government support it? Where CSE is stable and durable, ECE is fragile with centres and programmes popping up and closing with regularity. In short, even in countries where schools are ubiquitous, powerful, funded social tools, ECE is often simply an after-thought. As such, schools and the ideologies they advance are entrenched, powerful forces that are no match for fledgling ECE programmes.

One could therefore conjecture that irrespective of the *intent* of the ECE-CSE linkages – readiness in Peter Moss's first option, the idealised *design* of equal partnerships as in the second option, or the *theoretical basis* for linkage as in the third option – the sheer power of CSE, as expressed in terms of ubiquity, familiarity and durability, will naturally lead to schoolification or school dominance in the CSE-ECE partnership. In other words, unless strong steps are taken, one could conjecture that neither mere intent nor collaborative design nor theoretical bases are strong enough, individually or in combination, to trump the strength of CSE. Accepting this hypothesis might not be appealing. But it might go a long way to advance our understanding of why the litany of generational efforts to create power-equal ECE-CSE linkages have enjoyed limited success.

Role equality: an idealised vision?

Given the vast disparities that exist between ECE and CSE, it is hard to imagine if and under what conditions role equality – as implied by a 'strong and equal partnership' – could be achieved. On virtually every count, CSE outpaces ECE: enrolments, expenditures, constituents. Moreover, on other measureable variables (e.g. policies, staffing), CSE exceeds ECE in influence and scope. Arguably, ECE can contribute a rich theory and a robust pedagogy, but whether these are sufficiently strong to overcome the hegemony of CSE is debatable.

Having noted the unlikelihood of attaining such role equality, one does need to question whether holding such equality as an ideal is too romanticised a vision or if it represents a worthy goal to be held, despite its limited likelihood of achievement. Adopting the David versus Goliath stance, one would hope that ECE can advance its considerable potential contributions in a way that is meaningful and useful to CSE. So it could be argued that holding on to the vision of equality is important, if not fully strategic.

Trumping conventional structures

Any vision of ECE-CSE equality will need to address formidable attitudinal, structural and operational barriers. Governments hold very different ideas about commitments to young children. In some countries, young children are seen as social progeny and hence service provision is normative. In other nations, provision for children's care is regarded as a necessary component of workforce support. And in yet other nations, the protection, care and education of young children is seen as a private responsibility, one that is sacred and not to be coveted or enacted by government: respecting the primacy and privacy of the family is sacrosanct. Attitudinally, then, young children are regarded differently from school-age children, and the governmental role in supporting them is similarly differentiated. In the United States, where the ethic of private responsibility is firmly ensconced, debate about government's role in ECE remains contested. Lacking clear support for a public role in the care and education of young children, ECE does not stand on the same footing as CSE.

Such attitudinal and value differences transcend pedagogy and constructions of childhood; rather, they are fundamentally embedded in the fabric of a nation. Because they are so deeply entrenched, these different values evoke different structures and patterns of service delivery that, at best, remain highly idiosyncratic and era specific. Historically in the United States, large-scale government intervention in the lives of young children has occurred only at times of national disasters (the Great Depression, the World Wars, the War on Poverty). With the aim of addressing a broader social concern or staving off social crises, early childhood services haphazardly emerged under the auspices of different agencies, with different goals and intentions. Although many services closed when the crises abated, the few that remain still suffer from marginal public support, exist within many different federal and state agencies, and are guided by disparate rules, regulations and mandates. Historically, programmes fought for their individual lives, never focusing on the creation of a coherent early childhood system.

Such differences are not merely conceptual; they are also structural. Consider the different ways in which ECE and CSE are governed in the United States. For CSE, nearly every state has a state board of education and every district has a district board of education. These entities are given responsibility for planning, fiscal oversight, pedagogical support and results accountability. In other words, they render cohesion to disparate local entities, called schools. In ECE, by contrast, most programmes operate as individual micro-enterprises, fending for themselves in the fiscal and policy tug of war that characterises their existence. There is no management oversight or consolidated support; ECE programmes go at it on their own.

Next, consider the ways in which the two fields are financed. CSE enjoys a constant funding stream with monies allocated from states and the federal government in routine, expected ways. As a result, schools and school boards can plan a coherent, organised approach to staffing, facilities and maintenance, just to mention a few. While funding formulae may vary at the margins and while some programmes are subjected to fiscal cuts, every single community in the United States has a place for school funding in its budget, often with schools consuming the lions' share of that budget. In contrast, the United States does not fund its commitment to young children with the same predictability or in the same amount. To the contrary, ECE programmes routinely scrounge for funds and supports.

In the area of teacher preparation, vast differences exist between ECE and CSE. CSE has an elaborated and often governmentally supported approach to preparing and certifying teachers. Mechanisms for their promotion and retention also exist. While these are not the same from state to state, great similarities exist in states' preparation and credentialing requirements. No such similarities exist in ECE. States vary dramatically over what they require of ECE teachers, how they train and support their development, and how they evaluate them. Typically, ECE teachers are less qualified and significantly less compensated than their counterparts in CSE, fuelling discrepancies and challenges to smooth, easy transitions.

Given this history of structural apartheid, ECE in the United States has faced formidable challenges in unifying itself, much less in structuring transitions with educational institutions who understand neither its challenges nor its pedagogy. Until recently, attitudinally and structurally, ECE was a world apart from CSE. Today, attempting to rectify the legacy of fragmented, episodic policies and programmes, efforts to promote collaboration among different sectors of the ECE world are taking place. Calls for collaboration are emanating from federal and state governments, business and industry, foundations, universities, and scholars and practitioners. It has become apparent that in order for ECE to assume a durable position in terms of public attitudes and funding, its value, permanence and cohesion must be advanced.

Yet, trumping these deep-seated misalignments, first within the field of ECE itself, and then between ECE and CSE, is going to take decided effort. Such strategies must be strong enough to address the enduring definitional and conceptual differences discussed above. They must override the developmental/disciplinary divide. Moreover, such efforts must be able to overcome the formidable inconclusiveness of the transitions' research base. This would be difficult at any time, but is compounded in this era of increasing results-driven accountability.

Finally, any effort to promote serious linkages between ECE and CSE must be strategic in order to overcome the political and structural boundaries repeatedly enforced by non-child inspired policies. Efforts must concern themselves not only with differences in pedagogy and philosophy and with differences in the social construction of childhood; such efforts must also reach to the core of conventional ECE and its attendant structures. Such remarkable change is going to take more than developing a series of discussions or a common meeting place, although these themselves are critically important and signal a necessary shift in the dominant discourse. Complementing such efforts, there must be a set of actionable strategies and policies that are designed expressly to promote continuity within the ECE field and between the field and CSE. In short, to overcome contemporary schoolification, the inherent inequalities between ECE and CSE, and the structural reinforcements that have perpetuated distance between the two, demands nothing short of a well-conceived, well-articulated, well-funded frontal attack on convention. Discourse is a necessary, but insufficient condition to address the magnitude of the task at hand.

Looking ahead: one approach to ECE-CSE linkages

The above discussion suggests that historic efforts to promote transition are legion – and often only marginal in their accomplishments. Based on this and on a review of global transition efforts and the challenges inherent in their implementation, a more nuanced and multi-tiered conceptualisation of transition seems warranted (Kagan and Tarrant, 2010). Like the strategies advanced by other authors in this volume, I strongly respect and support the need for discussions and agree that discussion about the nature of childhood, conceptions of children, and theoretical conceptions of pedagogy are important and necessary. But given experience and my understandings of the research, I also call for an assault on the *structures* that shape contemporary transitions for young children.

Three elements characterise the suggested approach. First, this approach advances a new way of thinking about transitions and their relationship to ECE; second, it suggests that a new and action-oriented *zeitgeist* is needed; and third, to accomplish both, it proffers a new definition of transitions. In suggesting these elements, I aim to honour the intent of this volume, notably inspiring debate and new concepts.

This new approach rejects conceptualisations of transitions as one-time events that occur as a child is leaving the familiar ECE setting, in favour of understanding them as deeply embedded beliefs, structures and systems that must be systematically altered if continuity for young children is to exist. This approach acknowledges both historical and value predispositions that have contoured decades of practice and policy efforts to redress inherent discontinuities. It suggests that the lack of effective transitions between ECE and CSE has deep roots in the structure of compulsory education and needs a 'rethink' that addresses the strategic importance of such transitions to the developing child. The need for effective transitions within ECE must also be acknowledged. To 'rethink' these transitions is not an optional add-on; rather, it is fundamental and central to the practice of education during the years from birth to age 8. Rather than regarding transitions as a weakness to be eradicated, this approach regards transitions as an opportunity to advance development across the early years, and to inculcate a more caring, child centred, developmentally appropriate and holistically integrated approach to conventional compulsory education.

In order for such a shift in thinking to be operationalised, it must be accompanied by a shift in the general *zeitgeist*, a term that refers to the 'spirit of an age' or 'the trend in thought and feeling in a period.' A new *zeitgeist* rejects transition as additive and asks ECE to regard transition as a construct as fundamental to the field as play. Such a *zeitgeist* should advance the understanding, study and application of transitions as part and parcel of early childhood theory, training and practice – understanding 'early childhood' as covering birth to 8 years of age. As such, transitions must become not simply part of the mindset, but part of the culture of early education, infiltrating its practices and policies. A change in the transition *zeitgeist* means that transitions will be generally regarded as normative.

Such a *zeitgeist* will not emerge without achieving some general consensus regarding the definition of and images associated with transition. A prevalent image of transition, noted earlier, advances transition as a vertical and horizontal construct. This work suggests another lens through which to envision and create transitions, notably through the *structures* that advance transition. It characterises transition, then, not only as having vertical and horizontal properties, but as having structural ones that are often overlooked. Avoiding discussion and reconceptualisation of these structural dimensions of transition has impeded our understanding and the implementation of transitions. More precisely, in this construction the structural lens has three distinct elements, each of which suggests the need for alignments between ECE and CSE. They are pedagogical alignment, programmatic alignment and policy alignment. Elaborated individually below, each is needed to complement the others and all are needed to accomplish vertical and horizontal continuities. Each of these structural elements is actionable and demands sustained attention as well as operational alterations.

Pedagogical alignment

The first type of alignment includes efforts targeted at: (a) how childhood is conceptualised; (b) what and how children learn; and (c) how teachers learn and teach. It deals with the *raison d'être* of ECE. Concerned with content and process, pedagogical alignment addresses the degree to which ECE and CSE hold common beliefs about childhood, children and their development and learning. Moreover, pedagogical alignment asks CSE and ECE to consider commonalities in conceptual and theoretical orientations. Practically, such alignment of beliefs and orientations influence pedagogy and practice in a number of ways: such alignment can be observed in the approach to developing and implementing standards, curricula and instructional documentation/assessments as children move from their youngest years through primary school. Pedagogical alignment refers to the way teachers conceptualise childhood and children (miniature adults vs. continually curious children); how they approach teaching (didactic vs. emergent); what they teach (subject areas vs. developmental domains); and what values they espouse (how they view parents, home culture, language). Pedagogical alignment also focuses on the linkages between our expectations for children and how and what teachers are taught in their teacher preparation programmes and in-service supports. Intimate and involving the nature of the interactions between children and the caregivers in their lives, pedagogical alignment is at the heart of transitions and has been the focus of transition work for decades.

Programmatic alignment

The second type of alignment moves beyond the child and adult in their learning settings to embrace the nature of the services that children and families experience as they move between and among child-serving settings – in the United States, for example, from home to family child care, from family to centre-based child care, from early Head Start to Head Start, from pre-kindergarten programmes to kindergarten, or from kindergarten programmes to primary school. Moreover, children experience transitions as they move among institutions and people – from the health care worker to the child-care centre director, from the auntie to the teacher, from the home visitor to the pedagogue, from the librarian to the child minder. Parents may be differentially involved in these transitions; they may offer different levels of support to their young children traversing diverse settings and contexts.

The point is that transitions to school are not the only transitions young children make and not the only ones for which adults must make provision. Effective transition demands attention to the different programmes and services children traverse. To that end, programmatic alignment addresses: (a) the degree and nature of parent engagement in their children's transitions; (b) the ways in which health, mental health, nutrition and other services are incorporated into the conceptualisation of the programmes children receive; (c) the nature of community outreach and engagement; and (d) efforts to promote a culture of respect and engagement in all programme elements. Programmatic alignment focuses on the congruence between the classroom and the programme components that take place outside the classroom. It seeks to alter the programmatic nature of the institutions that touch young children's lives, including family engagement, school climate and community supports.

Policy alignment

The third type of alignment relates to policy. Taking a systematic view of transitions, the policy dimension moves well beyond the classroom or the programme and embraces the laws and regulations that govern or impact services to young children. Transcending the direct services that young children receive, policy alignment seeks to establish a durable infrastructure where public expenditures for pre-school children will be comparable to those for primary school children, where ECE teachers will be prepared and compensated at rates similar to those of CSE teachers, where federal and state policies support continuity in the pedagogical and programmatic areas, and where the durability and fiscal authority and accountability that accompany policies for older children will be accorded those for young children. Policy alignment assumes the availability of a lasting mechanism for governing ECE and its linkages with CSE, as well as appropriate mechanisms for financing services.

Implementing ECE-CSE linkages/transitions

More than simply a conceptual framework, the above approach has found expression in practice. Many examples of structural and infrastructural approaches have been delineated in a recent review of transition efforts in majority and minority world countries (Kagan *et al.*, 2010). This review has suggested that, in some cases, programmes worked at all three levels simultaneously – pedagogical, programmatic and policy. More often than not, however, they have elected to focus on one or two of the alignment types. Sometimes their pedagogical work consisted only of vertically linking one pre-school with a primary school or creating an integrated institution. In other cases, entire state standards and curricula were revised to promote developmental continuity among domains and disciplines from birth to age 8. In some cases, one policy was altered; in other cases, many policies were changed simultaneously. Whatever the strategy, there are stunning examples, in the United States and beyond, of how each of the three alignment approaches has been achieved.

That such examples exist, however, should not daunt our efforts to advance an ECE-CSE transition agenda. Rather than being normative, the examples cited were exceptions. To render transitions more normative and to have them entwined into the educational/developmental fabric, a number of specific strategies could be implemented.

Pedagogical alignment

To promote pedagogical alignment, deep-seated conversations regarding the nature of childhood and the social construction of children are necessary starting points. Such discussions should lead to more commonly held understandings and intentions regarding the nature of childhood, early childhood pedagogy and practice and alignment. To operationalise such discourse, reviews of standards (along with fertile discussion of their intentions and use) should be advanced. Standards delineating what young children should know and be able to do not necessarily represent schoolification; the nature and content of the standards mediates this. Indeed, it is possible to have child-centred, comprehensive, developmentally sound standards.

Once standards are agreed upon, curriculum and documentation strategies could be aligned between ECE and CSE. International examples of this exist in France, for example, through the *cycles pédagogique* system, consisting of three cycles that cover children from the age of 3 to 11 years with the middle cycle (*Cycles des Apprentissages Fondamentaux*) spanning the last year of ECE and the first two of ECE. In addition to a continuous curriculum, an important element of this pedagogical alignment is assuring that teachers across instructional settings share common understandings of children and childhood and share views and strategies about how to make the educational setting come to life. A vivid example of this takes place in Denmark, where professional development efforts are systematically focused on supporting children and families as they make transitions to formal school. Such a focus on this type of pedagogical alignment is particularly important because Danish ECE pedagogues and CSE teachers come from very different disciplinary traditions and cultures (for more on Danish pedagogues as a profession in ECE, see Jensen, 2011). In addition to combined in-service professional development, professional teacher training programmes should be synchronised between ECE and CSE, as should the standards for teacher certification. Clearly, within the context of aligned professional development, differences in children's cultures, capacities and interests must be built upon as a central force in pedagogical advancement and alignment.

Programmatic alignment

To advance alignment among programmes in ECE and CSE, efforts must be made to promote the meaningful involvement of parents both in their children's own education and in ECE and CSE settings. Parents must be engaged as partners, and teachers need to understand how to maximise parents' pivotal roles in the home, centre and school. Examples of this type of alignment exist internationally, being seen for example in Israel in the Parents as Partners programme, as well as in many family support programmes.

Moreover, to foster programmatic alignment, educative settings must examine their programmes to discern if they are really ready for young children. 'Ready schools' guidance should be promulgated so as to provide continuity for young children as they transition into new settings or new groups of children. Strategies to incentivise schools to become ready for young children could be undertaken. Finally, it is incumbent on ECE and CSE to assure community engagement with the institutions that serve young children. Such linkages among child-serving agencies should and are being fostered, with examples taking hold globally. In India, for example, Balwadies, community-based early childhood programmes, provide such integrated health, education and nutrition services.

Policy alignment

The alignment of policies must target the infrastructure that has traditionally supported division. Policies can and should be generated that transcend settings and institutions. To the degree possible, policies should impact all programmes serving the young, not just some select few. Moreover, policies that support greater teacher equity in preparation, assignment and credentialing across the ECE/CSE divide should be considered. A unified approach to governance of ECE-CSE programmes could be envisioned, as could common approaches to accountability. An example of this kind of linkage can be found in Norway (see the chapter by Peder Haug in this volume), where all levels of education fall under the Ministry of Education. Finally, it is imperative that the rich research tradition associated with transitions be continued. Inventive methodologies should be advanced with the goal of discerning how ECE and CSE, with their differing traditions, cultures and regularities, can come together effectively.

In conclusion, this chapter has sought to establish that transitions and the attention accorded them have been around for a long time, and have received considerable support from the ECE community. Despite the best intentions, however, decades of transition work have had limited impact. New frameworks and new ways of understanding the phenomenon are warranted when progress is stalled. To that end, this chapter has sought to provide a new lens through which to better understand the challenges associated with ECE-CSE linkages. It proffers a structuralist approach, suggesting that a primary way for transitions to be effective is through a series of changes at the pedagogical, programmatic and policy levels. Through attention to each level's durable structures, it is conjectured that 'schoolification' as it is conventionally understood will be reduced and the priority accorded ECE enhanced. Inherent in this stance is the firm conviction that if David is to ever overcome Goliath and transitions are to be rendered more than an ephemeral parachute, attention is required to the deeply embedded pedagogical, programmatic and policy structures that breed institutional inequity between ECE and CSE.

Note

1   Head Start is a comprehensive child development programme designed to promote the academic and social competence of low-income pre-school children. Launched in 1965, Head Start now provides for over 900,000 children within centres in all 50 states.

Chapter 7

Bruno Ciari and 'educational continuity'

The relationship from an Italian perspective

Arianna Lazzari and Lucia Balduzzi

This chapter will explore the concept of *continuità educativa* (educational continuity) as a way to understand the relationship between different parts of the education system in Italy. The aim of educational continuity is to facilitate children's transitions across the system: from *nido* (for children under 3 years) to *scuola dell'infanzia* (for children from 3 to 6 years), from *scuola dell'infanzia* to *scuola primaria* (for children from 6 to 11 years) and from *scuola primaria* to *scuola secondaria di primo grado* (for children from 11 to 14 years). As this schema suggests, the structure of early childhood education is split. Not only are *nido* and *scuola dell'infanzia* separate institutions, but they are the responsibility, at national level, of different government ministries: the Ministry of Labour together with the Department of Family Affairs for services for children under 3 years, the Ministry of Education for services for children from 3 years. Services for children under 3 years are mainly provided by municipalities (local authorities), under regulations defined by regional governments. Services for children over 3 years, the *scuola dell'infanzia*, can be provided by the state, municipalities or private (mainly Catholic) organisations, but since 1968 have been recognised as part of the national education system and national government has ensured the availability of these services through the expansion of state-run schools (Balduzzi, 2011). Since the way the ECE system is structured and managed has affected certain aspects of the debate on *continuità educativa*, this concept will be explored by analysing both the relationship between these two segments of the ECE system and the relationship between ECE and compulsory school education, CSE.

In this chapter the concept of educational continuity will be explored from its origin up to the present day: we assume that adopting an historical stance can 'contribute to present day construction of shared understanding and practices', as Peter Moss rightly argues in the initial essay of this book. A particular emphasis will be placed upon the work of Bruno Ciari (1923–1970) in Bologna, which contributed greatly to the advancement of educational continuity by promoting local experimentalism in the field of ECE (*scuola dell'infanzia a nuovo indirizzo*) and CSE (*scuola a tempo pieno).* The values and conceptualisations underpinning the Bolognese experiment will be analysed in its social, cultural and political context. However, being convinced that such localised experience generated a 'common heritage of ideas' (Dahlberg and Lenz-Taguchi, 1994) for re-thinking the relationship between ECE and CSE within a dialogic paradigm, the influence of Ciari's work on the wider educational system will also be analysed in the light of more recent developments.

Educational continuity will be discussed throughout this chapter as a complex concept, involving both horizontal and vertical continuity and encompassing several dimensions – political, institutional, pedagogical and socio-cultural. It is played out, too, in different contexts: local and national policy-making; structural organisation of educational institutions; and educational work with children, parents and local communities. Indeed much attention will be given to describing the processes that have contributed over time to realising the concept of educational continuity, hoping that this will provide the reader with new interpretative categories for looking at the relationship between ECE and CSE from a critical perspective and revealing many possibilities for transformation.

1960s and 1970s: radical roots

Although the pedagogical debate on educational continuity gained increasing attention starting in the early 1980s and culminating in the 1990s, the political ideas that led to the debate on educational continuity are rooted in the pedagogical activism of the 1960s. The rapid economic growth in Italy that started in the late 1950s created an increased demand for education, which called for the restructuring of the whole compulsory school system. More than at any other time, during this period the national government was called on to meet the challenges posed by ensuring universal access to education. These challenges, however, were met by reforms that addressed only structural aspects of the compulsory education system, such as increasing public investment in school buildings and introducing *scuola media unificata* (comprehensive middle schools), for children from 11 to 14 years, and state-run *scuole dell'infanzia* for 3 to 6-year-olds (Genovesi, 1992). Although these measures increased children's access to basic education throughout the country, they proved to be inadequate to ensure equality of educational opportunities. In fact, by leaving relatively untouched the transmissive and reproductive teaching methods traditionally adopted by schools, along with the standardised assessment of pupils' achievement, the new compulsory school system ended up by excluding precisely those children it aimed to include, as shown by the high rate of early school leavers among children belonging to lower social classes. Many publications of the time (e.g. Scuola di Barbiana, 1967; Barbagli and Dei, 1969) highlighted how these methods promoted the performance of middle-class children to the detriment of others.

A school system that perpetuated inequalities was no longer acceptable in a context where compulsory education had been introduced for the social promotion of all citizens. During this time, many teachers, educators, academics and members of civil society started to contest the discriminatory educational practices in compulsory schools. A leading example was the publication of *Lettera ad una professoressa* (Letter to a teacher), a book co-authored by Don Milani and his students at the *Scuola di Barbiana*. Don Milani (1923–1967) was a priest who, when exiled for his radical ideas to a remote village in the province of Florence, started a school that welcomed those children who were 'excluded' from the compulsory school system. As Don Milani and his students wrote:

> Our first encounter [with the school system] took place through the children that were rejected [by the system]. [By welcoming them in our school] we realised that teaching became more difficult and more demanding. [...] But [we also realised that] without these children the school cannot be considered school anymore. It becomes a hospital that treats those who are healthy and rejects those who are sick. It irremediably becomes an instrument of social discrimination.
> (Scuola di Barbiana, 1967, p. 20, translation by the authors)

As in the case of the *Scuola di Barbiana*, contesting the traditional school model led to experimentation with new pedagogical approaches inspired by the principles of democracy, civic participation, solidarity and social justice. In many cases these highly innovative experiences were carried out by pioneer educators such as Don Milani, Bruno Ciari and Loris Malaguzzi (1924–1994):[1] the initiatives undertaken by these pioneers, however, did not take place in isolation. Both progressive teachers' movements[2] and civic movements reclaiming social justice contributed to create a widespread awareness of the relationship that inextricably links education to social and political issues (Genovesi, 1992). The pedagogical activism of those teachers and educators who started to contest traditional teaching methods, therefore, was deeply rooted in civic engagement and, at the same time, committed to social and political change:

> Engaging with children from low social classes and engaging in politics are part of the same commitment. It is not possible to be committed to children who are affected by unfair laws and not to advocate for better laws.
> (Scuola di Barbiana, 1967, p. 93, translation by the authors)

While the educational reforms promoted by the central government in those years remained anchored to conservative positions and, in practice, failed to fully realise the right to education for all children through compulsory schooling, innovative educational practices were being initiated at the local level, in schools run by progressive local authorities, through the commitment of educators, parents and municipal administrators. The experience of municipal early childhood services initiated by Loris Malaguzzi in Reggio Emilia and the experience of *scuola a tempo pieno* promoted by Bruno Ciari in Bologna are only two of many examples that attest to how local experimentalism made a significant contribution to the debate on educational continuity in Italy.

ECE as a driving force in shaping a new learning paradigm

Over the same period in which traditional teaching methods adopted in CSE were strongly contested, the experiment of municipal ECE institutions started to grow in the most advanced cities of Northern and Central Italy (Bologna, Reggio Emilia and Pistoia to mention a few among many). In these areas, the origins of ECE institutions were linked to social movements demanding rights: on one side there were women's movements claiming equal opportunities (e.g. the right to employment and maternity leave), while on the other there were social movements demanding a more equal society in which the right to education should be granted, especially to children belonging to low social classes (Balduzzi, 2006). In this context public early childhood institutions – *nido* and *scuola dell'infanzia* – were first created by municipal governments, their initiatives in response to the needs of their citizens preceding the provision of services by the state.[3]

It is worth noting that public early childhood services were first created by municipalities in those parts of Italy where citizens – for particular historical and cultural reasons – had developed and consolidated traditions of civic engagement and solidarity that increased their participation in the political life of their communities (Mantovani, 2007). It is no coincidence that often these experiences took place in areas where the population had played an active role in supporting anti-fascist resistance during the Second World War: the collective actions undertaken to promote children's right to education were rooted in a wider political concern for the values of democracy, equality and peace. As Malaguzzi himself stated, the commitment to the education of young children in those years was motivated by the desire to build a new society together as a reaction to fascism and to the war, through giving a new meaning to human and civil existence (Malaguzzi, 1995). It is for this reason that democratic participation – of children, parents, teachers, educators,[4] auxiliary staff and citizens – has become such a distinctive feature of education in the municipal schools in Reggio Emilia and, more generally, of ECE in the municipal schools that started life at that time. The social and political roots of municipal ECE institutions, therefore, played a crucial role in shaping their pedagogical identity (for a further discussion of the 'municipal school revolution' of the 1960s, see Catarsi, 2004; for more on the history and pedagogical identity of ECE in Reggio Emilia, see Rinaldi, 2006 and Vecchi, 2010).

Located at the very core of this pedagogical identity is an image of the child as a citizen and competent human being, a child actively engaging with the world around him/her from the first day of life. This is a child rich in potential, who competently uses many symbolic languages to make sense of the reality around him or her and to interact with adults, peers and the surrounding environment. This image of the child as an active agent implied a new understanding of learning that could not be limited to the transmission and reproduction of pre-determined knowledge. By referring to the studies of Piaget, Vygotsky and Bruner and by taking inspiration from the work of Dewey on active pedagogy, a new understanding of learning emerged. Learning started to be understood as a process of active co-construction that necessarily takes place in social interaction, where new meanings can be created, shared, confronted, questioned and negotiated. This vision nurtured a growing awareness that children's cognitive outcomes are inextricably linked to the way exploration of the environment is actively promoted and interactions among peers are intentionally sustained.

Starting from these premises, the features that came to characterise the pedagogical work carried out within municipal ECE institutions included:

- a holistic approach to education that encompasses multiple dimensions of children's development (cognitive, social, emotional, creative…);
- a project work methodology that values multiple ways of learning and multiple symbolic languages;
- the use of pedagogical documentation that, by making visible children's learning processes, allows practitioners to reflect on how to improve their practices.

Within this framework, one of the most significant innovations introduced by municipal ECE institutions was the collegial work of their staff:

> Co-presence[5] (and more broadly collegial work) was adopted from the beginning in opposition to the traditional – human and professional – isolation […] of teachers' work. […] Collegial work produced beneficial effects both at the educational and psychological level, both for children and adults. But beyond that, teachers' collegial work […] – within a wider systemic project – was the first step toward parents' participation and *gestione sociale*.[6]
>
> (Malaguzzi, 1995, p. 85, translation by the authors)

> The work in the group of adults should be based upon parity of roles, respect, reciprocal support and collegial decision-making; the same values that children should interiorise. We also think that these values should characterise the professional development of teachers all along.
> (Ciari, 1972; p. 228, translation by the authors)

From this perspective, repositioning the role of the child in relation to new understandings of learning and knowledge determined not only a new way of organising practitioners' work within institutions (collegial instead of individual) but also a new conceptualisation of professionalism. For this reason the new municipal institutions for ECE invested from the beginning in professional development:

> The educator that we would like to promote through the seminars and other cultural initiatives is a teacher who possesses a deep pedagogical and general culture, who has a methodological orientation but whose educational practices are open to creative development, to invention and to transformation.
> (Ciari, 1972, p. 227, translation by the authors)

It is in the context of this new pedagogy – which redefines the meanings of learning and the purposes of education within early childhood institutions – that the experimentation of *scuola a tempo pieno* took place in Bologna in 1968.

Bruno Ciari and the experimentation of scuola a tempo pieno in Bologna

Bruno Ciari was an important Italian *pedagogista*.[7] His pedagogical approach, strongly influenced by the work of educators and philosophers such as Dewey, Freinet and Gramsci, attached particular importance to a relationship between school and society that shapes learning as a contextually situated process. Between 1966 and 1970 Ciari worked for the Municipality of Bologna as the Director of Educational Services, which encompassed both early childhood education and after-school provision (*scuola dell'infanzia* and *doposcuola*). At this time, attendance at primary school was compulsory for 24 hours a week, with most primary schools run by the state and open for six mornings a week. In the afternoon, non-compulsory after-school services were offered by the municipality. This *doposcuola* service emphasised care and social aims; it provided lunch and was paid for by families with an income-related fee. In Bologna, the municipal teachers who worked in *doposcuola* services were required to have the same qualification as teachers in the state primary schools. By introducing these after-school care services, the municipality could offer primary school children the same hours, about eight per day, as those who attended municipal-run *scuola dell'infanzia.*

Despite the short collaboration between Bologna and Ciari, which ended with his premature death, the work he carried out became an important reference in Italy, especially for the *gestione sociale* of *scuola dell'infanzia* and for the *scuola a tempo pieno.* His experimentation was made possible because Bologna at that time directly managed almost all public *scuole dell'infanzia* and after-school services attended by children aged from 3 to 10 years. The experience of *scuola a tempo pieno* took shape from the voluntary initiative of 26 teachers (13 state primary school teachers and 13 municipal after-school teachers) who, supported by innovative school directors and by Ciari's supervision, decided to experiment with a new model for CSE: the *scuola a tempo pieno.* This removed the divide between education (provided during morning compulsory school hours) and care (provided during optional afternoon sessions), providing instead a fully educational day in the primary schools that undertook such experimenta- tion: in these schools all children attended morning and afternoon sessions on a regular basis. This work was directed towards giving an educational identity to these services – which until then were predominantly seen as providing care – through the active involvement of parents and local communities in their management.

We consider the work of Bruno Ciari to be particularly relevant to our discussion on educational continuity because his experimentation with the *scuola a tempo pieno* gave rise to a dialogic interaction between ECE and CSE. At a time when traditional CSE was highly contested for its authori- tarian and discriminatory methods, Ciari elaborated a new approach to CSE drawing on the inspiring experiences carried out in municipal ECE institu- tions. The idea underpinning the *scuola a tempo pieno,* which operates on a full-day basis for 40 hours a week, was to provide a more flexible and integrated framework for addressing children's diversified learning needs. According to Ciari, the principle of equal educational opportunities could only be fully realised if all children, particularly those from lower social classes, were actively engaged in learning through motivating experiences. In contrast to the elitist culture reproduced in traditional schools, where mornings were dedicated to transmissive teaching while after-school care (*doposcuola*) was provided mostly to assist children from lower social classes in doing their homework, Ciari proposed the model of the 'fully educational day' where the exchanges among children from different back- grounds would promote the creation of a common cultural space regardless of social backgrounds. Within the *tempo pieno* model, the divide between educational activities in the morning and after-school care in the afternoon was overcome through a more systemic approach to learning, grounded in co-operative work of students and teachers. Within an extended time framework, collective, small group and individual work of students could be organised according to the diversified learning rhythms of children, starting from their motivations and following their interests.

The collegial organisation of teachers' work became a crucial aspect of *scuola a tempo pieno,* as it allowed project work and inter-class activities to be undertaken within an interdisciplinary framework. Compulsory schools were no longer conceived as institutions isolated from society, where knowledge was decontextualised and reproduced in stereotyped forms, but rather as democratic communities that provided children with opportunities for learning that recognised the diversity present in society: they became places where cultural transformation was made possible.

> Such a project is based upon a new concept of education that overcomes its enclosure in its temples, its [elitist] selection and its inner divisions producing false culture. [The concept of education] is reformulated, reinvented within the dynamic relationship between a comprehensive time and a comprehensive space: in this way the process of learning and the process of educating [...] become at the same time the responsibility of each individual and of all individuals collectively – overcoming the rigidity of roles, the separation of institutions and the classification of individual destinies that has caused so much damage to school and education.
>
> (Malaguzzi, 1971, p. 140; translation by the authors)

From this perspective, the experimentation of *scuola a tempo pieno* opened the doors of compulsory education to the social and cultural life of local communities. According to the principle of *gestione sociale,* parents and community members (local authorities, civic associations, cultural agencies) became an integral part of the life of the school. In fact in the vision of Ciari and his teachers, CSE could become a truly emancipatory experience only if it were ultimately to promote children's understanding of the social context in which they lived and gave them the cultural tools to transform it:

> [What we advocate for] is a school in which children – all children – have the possibility to enter in contact with the most valuable elements of human culture; a school that provides a richness of suggestions, that opens new perspectives and thrilling possibilities; a school that deserves to be lived rather than being put up with, a school for free human beings.
>
> (Ciari, 1972, p. 142; translation by the authors)

The legacy of scuola tempo pieno

The local experimentation of *scuola a tempo pieno* was – in the pedagogical and political project elaborated by Bruno Ciari – the first step towards a broader reform that was planned to encompass the entire school system. At the core of Ciari's work in fact stood the idea that the whole school system – starting with the *scuola dell'infanzia*, up to the *scuola media* – should be revised in order to promote a more equal and democratic society rather than perpetrating inequalities on the basis of existing social classes (Catarsi, 1992). Ciari's project for the reform of CSE is in this sense totally comprehensive as it embraced not only the full period of children's experience in schools (from the age of 3 to the end of compulsory schooling) but also the social and cultural contexts in which children's experiences take place out of school (families, local community).

More than 40 years ago Ciari identified as the mainstay of CSE reform the concept of *life-long* and *life-wide* learning, which could be realised through *vertical* and *horizontal continuity*. In his project, therefore, the concept of educational continuity takes two directions. Vertical continuity between the different levels of the school system would contribute to reducing school drop-out through an educational continuum within which the higher school level carries on the educational path undertaken by the previous level. In this way the fragmentation of educational methods and the increasing pressure on the achievement of predetermined outcomes would be overcome through the adoption of methodological approaches that coherently sustain the full development of children's potentials throughout their years in school. Horizontal continuity between learning experiences carried out by children in school and in out-of-school settings would allow a reciprocal exchange between school and society aimed at promoting democracy, civic engagement and cultural transformation. Horizontal continuity, so understood, is played out in the collaboration with families and in the integration of local agencies, which both involve reciprocal relationships between school institutions and the local community environment of which they are part (Frabboni *et al.*, 1999). As stated by Genovesi:

> The school project elaborated by Ciari becomes truly comprehensive as it is marked by vertical [...] and horizontal [...] continuity. It is within this far-reaching educational project that Ciari looks for possible solutions to problems such as school selection, early school leaving and the integration of special needs children. At the same time his educational project aims at transforming school into the driving force of an educational community that becomes the ideal locus for the formation of democratic citizens.
>
> (Genovesi, 1992, p. 28, translation by the authors)

Unfortunately the project of CSE reform, coherently elaborated by Ciari both in its structural and pedagogical aspects, was never realised in full beyond local experiments.[9] The presence of conservative central governments, the bureaucratic management of compulsory schools, and the lack of a coherent strategy for teachers' recruitment and professional development were the main elements that hindered the full realisation of such a project. It needs to be said, however, that the legacy of Ciari's work inspired some of the most significant changes that took place in the field of CSE from the 1970s onwards. The local experiment in Bologna and the growing support[10] for such experience gave rise to a law in 1971 that instituted *scuola a tempo pieno* at the national level, the state taking responsibility for making this provision if parents called for it. With this law, the full-time school experiment that took place in Bologna through collaboration between state primary schools and municipal after-school services became a model for the organisation of full-time state schools across Italy. Today, both options – *scuola a tempo pieno* and half-day school – are usually available to primary school children, although the *tempo pieno* models tend to be more widespread in the regions of Northern and Central Italy.

The institution of full-time primary schools promoted the introduction of a more holistic approach to children's education into compulsory schooling: this allowed a broadening of the narrow focus on academic learning that characterised traditional schooling by drawing attention to the different dimensions of learning that promote the development of children's full potential. A few years later, in 1974, the law on collegial bodies (*organi collegiali*) was enacted. This law established decision-making committees formed by parents, school staff (school director, teachers, auxiliary staff) and students (only in secondary schools) in order to ensure the democratic participation of all actors in the management of state schools. This document, by describing school as a *community* that constantly interacts with the wider *social and civic community,* implicitly affirms the principle of horizontal continuity – through the introduction of *gestione sociale* – within the compulsory school system.

A further step toward a more democratic and integrated approach to children's education within compulsory schools was undertaken in 1977, when law 517 introduced the organisation of open classes in primary and junior high school: by breaking the traditional isolation of teachers' work, with one teacher per class, open class methodologies were intended to promote a laboratory approach to the construction of knowledge that would involve students from different classes in project work initiatives and teachers working together. This document not only promoted a more flexible organisation of educational work grounded in interdisciplinary approaches and group work methodologies, but also acknowledged the role played by these two elements in ensuring the full development of children. In the light of these considerations it could be rightly argued that the experimentalism undertaken by pioneer educators in the ECE field during the 1960s had produced new pedagogical paradigms that, to some extent, affected the way compulsory school education was conceived.

The pedagogical debate on educational continuity in the 1980s

Whereas over the 1960s and the 1970s the issue of educational continuity emerged from localised experimental practices, in the 1980s such issues gained increased attention – both in academic and political discussions – in the context of the debate on lifelong learning promoted by international organisations such as OECD, UNESCO and the Council of Europe. Following international trends, over the 1980s Italy witnessed the flourishing of psychological studies on children's development from a socio-cultural and interactionist perspective. These studies showed that children are competent human beings who actively engage in social relationships from birth onwards and who, through these first interactions, develop the cognitive structures that allow them to learn from interaction with peers and the surrounding environment (Shaffer, 1977; Camaioni, 1980; Bruner, 1981). Not only do these studies highlight that children's development is inextricably linked to the relational and cultural contexts within which educational experiences take place (Bateson, 1972; Bronfenbrenner, 1979; Rogoff and Lave, 1984), but they also confirm that children's development takes place in different ways that reflect both interpersonal and intra-personal variations (Gardner, 1983; Nelson, 1978). From the insights derived from these studies, it emerged that the classical theoretical models adopted until then by developmental psychology were insufficient to explain the complexity of children's development, which as shown by more recent research takes place along a continuum and across a wide range of individual variations.[11]

The findings of these studies, therefore, made an important contribution to the debate on educational continuity since they actually proved that there is no scientific evidence to justify a marked discontinuity in the transition between early childhood and compulsory school education. As one of the most influential Italian educational psychologists of the time, Clotilde Pontecorvo, stated the case:

> It is therefore unfair to demand psychology to draw a well-defined picture of children's development articulated in...chronologically precise phases so that schooling could be appropriately organised: it is precisely the notion of 'appropriateness' which is misleading... Perhaps what it is wished could be found in scientific knowledge is the legitimisation of political and educational choices that are *de facto* the result of historical and social processes.
> (Pontecorvo and Formisano, 1986, p. 49; translation by the authors)

By building on the findings of these studies that were carried out in the field of psychology, the debate on educational continuity, which arose out of social and political discussions in the 1960s and 1970s, took on a more specific pedagogical identity. In the light of new scientific insights, educational continuity started to be conceived as the interplay of elements of *continuity* and *discontinuity*, which support children's learning along the *continuum* of their personal development. The elements of continuity are represented by coherent educational methodologies, which are expressions of a unified approach to learning. The elements of discontinuity are represented by the progressive differentiation of educational activities that is realised by combining content knowledge and educational methods according to the developmental needs of children. In this perspective, educational continuity is a concept that needs to be concretely defined and negotiated within educational institutions, starting from professional exchanges between *nido* educators and *scuola dell'infanzia* teachers. In this respect, educational continuity has somewhat different implications according to the institutional contexts within which it is played out.

For municipal ECE institutions (services for children from birth to 6 years), educational continuity was mainly focused on the creation of a common *culture of childhood* grounded in the exploration of children's experiences in both *nidi* and *scuole dell'infanzia*. Such a culture contributed to shaping a well-defined pedagogical identity for 0 to 6 services, with features including: a holistic approach to children's development, a relational and systemic approach to learning, the documentation of educational work, the collaborative work of educators/teachers (collegiality), and the participation of parents in decision-making processes. Despite the fact that the overall responsibility for *nidi* (0–3 services) and *scuola dell'infanzia* (3–6 services) was divided nationally between different governmental departments, the investment of municipalities in the elaboration of a coherent approach towards the education of young children succeeded in creating a pedagogy of early childhood that is still today widely recognised (Lazzari, 2012). In this context, the key factor that contributed to the successful realisation of educational continuity between municipal *nido* and *scuola dell'infanzia* can be identified as the system of pedagogical co-ordination that systematically links ECE services at the local level. Local pedagogical co-ordinators (*pedagogisti* or *coordinatori pedagogici*[12]) have played a crucial role in providing shared professional development opportunities for educators and teachers and in sustaining reciprocal professional exchanges through pedagogical guidance (Mantovani, 1986; Bondioli, 1987).

With regards to the state-run institutions (*scuola dell'infanzia* and *scuola primaria*), educational continuity has mainly focused on curriculum experimentation. The experiences of educational continuity between ECE and CSE realised in Italy over the 1980s took place in the framework of the guidelines enacted by the Council of Europe in 1981, which encouraged continuity between pre-school and school programmes through the co-ordination of educational initiatives, the promotion of unified professional development paths for teachers' education, and integrated management of institutions (Scurati, 1986). In Italy, experimental projects in these areas were undertaken both by teachers' professional associations (e.g. FNISM and CIDI) and by collaborative networks of university researchers, schools directors and teachers.

As an example of the latter, experimentation with an integrated curriculum for the education of children aged 4 to 8 deserves to be mentioned; this was undertaken by Clotilde Pontecorvo (1989) and her staff in collaboration with teachers and school directors operating in *scuola dell'infanzia* and *scuola primaria* within the provinces of Florence and Rome. The project, funded by the Ministry of Education, aimed at the elaboration of a curriculum that would link the last two years of ECE to the first two years of CSE, within the perspective of educational continuity. The understanding of continuity underpinning this experiment had four fundamental principles:

- psychological studies show that children under school age competently use many symbolic languages that are expression of many forms of intelligence (Gardner, 1983);
- children's competent use of symbolic languages is rooted in sociocultural interaction (interaction with peers, adults, surrounding environment and cultural artefacts);
- as a consequence, teaching should be understood as a practice that actively promotes children's cognitive acquisitions by organising learning environments and by sustaining children's interaction;
- the contestation of school readiness approaches, in which the goals of ECE are subservient to CSE learning requirements, and the adoption of approaches centred on children's competence and motivation to learn, in which the goals of CSE are set starting from the knowledge and competence that children have already developed through previous experiences in ECE.[13]

Within this experimental project the curriculum was co-constructed by teachers and researchers together, through a constant process of negotiation that took the form of joint work and shared reflection. In both environments, educational activities were simultaneously carried out by pre-school and primary school teachers and organised with small groups of children. At the same time the educational experiences carried out with children were constantly analysed and revised within the group of teachers under the pedagogical guidance of academic researchers. The result of this project was the elaboration of an integrated curriculum that, by focusing on aspects such as the educational setting (organisation of time, space and didactic materials) and the relational environment (relationships within the group of children, between children and teachers and among teachers), provided a frame of reference for promoting children's cognitive acquisitions along an educational continuum that took account of their developmental needs.[14]

The findings of this project did not lead to policy initiatives aimed at the revision of pre-school and primary school curricula in an integrated manner. As noted elsewhere (Lazzari, 2011a), in Italy highly innovative educational programmes are often developed within localised settings through the continuous investment of municipal and regional administrations. But where, as in the case reported above, experimental programmes are carried out in the state school system with the support of Ministry of Education, a lack of continuous investment and the fragmentation of policy initiatives tends to undermine the beneficial potential of these programmes. The relevance of such research should then be considered in relation to its pedagogical contribution. The contribution of Pontocorvo's study was to introduce a more global approach to subject knowledge acquisition, starting from the observation of children's learning strategies in their early years. For example, it was acknowledged that children's competence in literacy could not be promoted by teaching them how to write letters and that children's competence in numeracy could not be promoted by teaching them how to count. Rather, promoting children's competence in literacy and numeracy means supporting them in developing the ability to combine systems of symbols and logical reasoning for communicating and solving problems.

In the 1980s, there was a further elaboration of the concept of *horizontal continuity* following the pedagogical activism of the previous decades. This concept was systematically consolidated through a wide range of inter-institutional collaborations and cultural exchanges taking place within local communities (Ventura, 1986), including:

- inter-agency collaboration of professionals working across different departments (e.g. health board, social welfare, education);
- networking between ECE/CSE institutions and other public institutions promoting informal learning (e.g. play-centres, libraries, ateliers);
- realisation of educational projects within schools in collaboration with external experts (e.g. cultural associations, artists).

From this perspective, horizontal continuity assumed a well defined pedagogical role by integrating, along a continuum, formal and informal learning opportunities situated within the broader socio-cultural context of children's local communities. It could also be said that the existence of vertical and horizontal links between the different components of the educational system has led, over the years, to rethinking these relationships according to a systemic rather than a hierarchical logic.

The consolidation of continuity through institutional practices

Although the perspective of educational continuity began to take shape in policy documents towards the end of the 1970s, it is only in the early 1990s that such a perspective finds official recognition within a broader legislative framework. Before then, educational continuity was affirmed only in principle within national curricular frameworks: *Programmi della Scuola Media/1979, Programmi della Scuola Elementare/1985; Orientamenti della Scuola Materna/1991* (which might be translated as 'Junior High School Curriculum', 'Primary School Curriculum' and 'Preschool Guidelines'). Although within these documents the need for a more unified approach to learning across the different grades of the school system was highlighted as a crucial element in promoting the full development of children's identity, this argument was not further developed to encompass pedagogical practices. We find here the apparent paradox of continuity being proposed – but only in documents about separate parts of the education system. It also suggests a lack of political will to seriously reconsider the structuring of the educational system in order to realise the principle of continuity in practice.

For this reason, according to many authors (e.g. Calidoni and Calidoni, 1995; Catarsi, 1992) the perspective of educational continuity begins to be taken seriously, both at policy and institutional level, only towards the beginning of the 1990s, when two laws are enacted – Law 148/1990 (art. 1 –2) and Ministerial Decree 16-11-1992. These laws not only acknowledged the equal status of the educational activities carried out in each type of school (pre-primary, primary and junior high), but also outlined the pedagogical practices to be carried out at institutional and inter-institutional level for the implementation of educational continuity (Calidoni and Calidoni, 1995). Within these documents educational continuity is conceptualised in the following terms:

> Educational continuity does not mean to standardise educational initiatives [undertaken by each school level] or to refuse change; rather it means to elaborate formative pathways within a coherent developmental logic, that values the competences previously acquired by children and that recognise [...] equal dignity for the educational initiatives undertaken at each school level.
>
> (C.M. 339/1992; translation by the authors)

Within this framework, ECE and CSE institutions preserve their own specific pedagogical identity but, at the same time, they are connected by mutual obligations which revolve around the promotion of children's full development as persons and citizens. Collegial meetings among ECE and CSE teachers play a crucial role in smoothing children's transition between the different levels of the education system. In the framework of inter-institutional collaboration, projects aimed at promoting educational continuity should be jointly planned and carried out by ECE and CSE teachers. Specifically, such projects should focus on: the exchange of documentation regarding children's experiences in ECE institutions, the exchange of information with children's parents, and the realisation of joint initiatives aimed at introducing children to new school environments.

Over the years, such projects have contributed to shaping innovative practices to improve children's transitions. An example is the 'memory suitcase' (Canevaro *et al.*, 1996). By conceiving transition as a journey, the 'memory suitcase' collects pictures, drawings and other artefacts that recall children's most significant experiences within *scuola dell'infanzia*. We consider this form of documentation to be particularly interesting because it values the richness of children's learning experiences as a whole, to encompass many symbolic means through which learning could be described or recalled by each child.

Discussing documentation within collegial meetings involving both ECE and CSE teachers is not only limited to the exchange of information about the personal history of each child;[15] it also extends to confrontations[16] on pedagogical approaches adopted within each setting. In this sense the discussion of documentation aims at promoting a common understanding of educational work between ECE and CSE teachers. It is on the basis of this common understanding that continuity initiatives should be jointly planned and carried out with the aim of facilitating children's transition. These initiatives may comprise: school visits in which newcomers are welcomed by older children, exchanging messages and other materials with primary school classes, working on common projects involving children in *scuola dell'infanzia* and *scuola primaria*. The involvement of children's parents is also considered to be essential in supporting the process of transition: for this reason meetings with parents are specifically organised with the purpose of providing information on the new school environment but also to exchange information about each child. Finally, within these policy documents (Law 148/1990 and Ministerial Decree 16-11-1992), the elaboration of continuing professional development paths involving ECE and CSE teachers are also encouraged through collaboration with training and research agencies at local level.

In the years following the enactment of these laws, the perspective of vertical continuity has been nurtured on the ground by innovative educational practices that took shape within *istituti comprensivi* (Cerini, 2000; Balduzzi, 2011b): these are school districts that encompass state-run *scuola dell'infanzia, scuola primaria* and *scuola secondaria di primo grado* under the management of a school director. The *istituti comprensivi* – established first in 1994 in order to facilitate the administration of small schools within rural areas – became quite soon a *laboratory for innovation* (Lega, 1999) due to the favourable conditions that characterised their organisational structure: the fact that teachers working in different schools were part of the same team increased reciprocal exchanges between different schools and reinforced a broad idea of collegiality. It is within this broad conceptualisation of collegiality, which values the diversity of teachers' competences and sustains professional development through joint work, that some of the most innovative experiences on educational continuity took place (Cerini, 2000).

The richness of pedagogical approaches that characterised these experiences carried out in the 1990s was, however, soon replaced by a more bureaucratic understanding of continuity practices. So while the approach of educational continuity found increasing recognition within official documents, the educational practices aimed at guaranteeing continuity between ECE and CSE settings became progressively more formalised, to the extent that today they tend to be followed more as formalities rather than as meaningful practices. The fact that educational continuity dropped out of the pedagogical debate in the last decade (Catarsi, 2011) and that school districts have not been encouraged to carry on experimental projects on this issue (Cerini, 2011) has contributed to a progressive impoverishment of pedagogical practices within school settings. Lack of continuous investment in experimental programmes and the discontinuity characterising educational policy-making at national level could be identified as the main factors that have lead toward the progressive bureaucratisation of continuity practices within school settings.

On the other hand it needs to be acknowledged that, over the same period, highly innovative continuity practices were carried out in the area of 0 to 6 services, aiming at building an integrated system for the education of young children at the local level. These experiences, promoted by regional and municipal governments (the national government not providing any services for children under 3 years), aimed to reinforce both vertical and horizontal links between ECE institutions within the broad vision of a multi-centred education system (Manini *et al.*, 2005) that supports the interplay of traditional services (such as *nidi* and *scuola dell'infanzia*) and of experimental services (such as play-centres, meeting places for children and parents, centres for families).[17]

Such experiences could certainly provide inspiration for exploring new paradigms of educational continuity between the ECE and CSE systems within local school districts (*istituti comprensivi*): this would mean establishing a framework for reciprocal dialogue and close co-operation by involving municipal, regional and state agencies at local level. For example, this could be supported by introducing co-ordination roles (*figure di sistema*) and by providing opportunities for professional encounters between teachers operating at different levels of the school district. This would set the basis for the creation of a common pedagogical ground upon which the relationship between children and adults in educational contexts could be rethought and renegotiated within the broader framework of local communities.

Recent policy developments and future critical issues

On the basis of the previous section, we can argue that the evolution of the debate on educational continuity in the last decade has been characterised by a series of missed opportunities. The enactment of laws on educational continuity in the context of increasing autonomy of school districts at the local level could have provided significant opportunities for sustaining curriculum experimentation, for supporting professional exchanges among teachers from different types of school, and for increasing schools' policy-making capacity within local communities through the involvement of families and local authorities. Instead, the lack of support from central government on one side and the very limited research produced on these issues on the other have both contributed to marginalising the issue of educational continuity in recent pedagogical and political debates. Furthermore, at the national level the progressive shift from responsive forms of policy-making based on wide political consultation to more centralised forms of political decision-making (Barbieri, 2011) has contributed over the years to bureaucratise – rather than to innovate – pedagogical practices within state institutions for ECE and CSE.

In the last decade we have also been witnessing a progressive weakening of pedagogical guidelines under the influence of neo-liberal national governments. The fact that the school curriculum has been reformed twice within a 10-year period (*Indicazioni Nazionali/2004; Indicazioni per il curricolo/2007*) and that it is presently under reform yet again attests, in the authors' view, to the weakening of a coherent pedagogical vision and its progressive replacement with instrumental purposes. In this situation, it is not surprising that even the enactment in 2007 of unified curriculum guidelines[18] for *scuola dell'infanzia, scuola primaria* and *scuola secondaria di primo grado* has had very limited effects on everyday practices regarding educational continuity (Cerini, 2011).

In very recent times critical issues have also been raised about teachers' initial professional education. Up to 2010, the bachelor's degree for preschool and primary school teachers was structured in two two-year courses, the first providing a generic preparation for both professionals and the second two specialised pathways: this flexible combination of two-year pathways within the degree was specifically designed to encourage educational continuity between *scuola dell'infanzia,* and *scuola primaria* through the promotion of a more trans-disciplinary approach (Nigris, 2007). But since September 2011, a unified master's degree has been introduced. The initial preparation of teachers for *scuola dell'infanzia and scuola primaria* has been upgraded to a five-year degree, with both following a similar course (with the exception of some specialist modules). The changes introduced by the new reform are looked upon with some apprehension by experts who fear that the length and the structure of the new qualification will increase the divide between *nido* educators and *scuola dell'infanzia* teachers, jeopardising the specific pedagogical identity of ECE. In particular, the prominence of a narrow disciplinary approach and the relative disregard of a broader pedagogical approach to learning are interpreted by the experts as potentially producing *schoolification* of early childhood education (Lazzari, 2011b). This apprehension could be further justified in the light of neo-liberal educational policies recently promoted at the national level, which tend to recognise the value of *scuola dell'infanzia* mostly in terms of preparation for compulsory school, within a quite narrow conceptualisation of learning and socialisation of young children: 'recent studies highlight that *scuola dell'infanzia* promotes the learning of fundamental behaviours and of initial knowledge which are useful for acquiring further competences and for relating with society' (Atto di Indirizzo, 2009, p. 9; translation by the authors).

We could, therefore, conclude our reflection by acknowledging that at present the issue of educational continuity is at the centre of multiple tensions and needs to be re-conceptualised, starting from a debate on the pedagogical values of education and schooling. This debate should involve not only teachers, school directors and academics but also parents, pedagogical co-ordinators, local policy makers and, more broadly, members of local communities. The fact that, at the time of writing, the issue of educational continuity has again started to gain attention both within the pedagogical and the political debate (Catarsi, 2011; Cerini, 2011; CORE, forthcoming) certainly reflects the urgency of re-defining the relationship between ECE and CSE in the light of the new challenges faced by educational institutions in contemporary times.

Concluding remarks

The analysis carried out in this chapter reveals how, in Italy, the relationship between ECE and CSE has taken on different forms and different meanings over time. In this context, the evolution of the concept of educational continuity represents the different political choices that have been made and their underpinning values. The concept itself was forged from pedagogical activism and local experimentalism; it was then consolidated through pedagogical and psychological research and finally formalised within a well-defined institutional framework. In later years, however, a certain decline in the debate on continuity is visible, accompanied by a lack of innovation in educational practices. In the most recent period this process seems to be leading toward an understanding of educational continuity that is increasingly centred on CSE, with the consequent risk of schoolifying early childhood pedagogy.

Our analysis of the case of Italy highlights the different interpretations of the relationship between ECE and CSE that have been elaborated during the three different periods mentioned above. In the first phase – dominated by educational experimentalism – traditional CSE was highly contested because of its selective nature and the need for a more democratic approach to compulsory school education; this led to consideration being given to early childhood pedagogy as an inspiring example. Therefore, in our view, the *scuola a tempo pieno* experiment could be considered as a concrete realisation of the 'meeting place' relationship between ECE and CSE (Dahlberg and Lenz-Taguchi, 1994). In fact, the *tempo pieno* was originated by the professional encounter of state and municipal teachers and educators who were willing to initiate a new way of understanding CSE in their everyday practices: in this sense, each party offered a specific contribution to the creation of a new and co-constructed pedagogical culture.

The second phase was characterised by the consolidation of the perspective of educational continuity within an institutional framework. A unified approach to the education of children across all levels of the education system was promoted both through research and pedagogical practices carried out across different educational settings. During this period, the 1980s and 1990s, the conditions for a strong and equal partnership based on a mutually beneficial dialogue (OECD, 2001) were realised through curriculum experimentation and wide consultation on educational reforms.

Finally, in the last stage of this process of definition and re-definition of the concept of *continuità educativa* we are witnessing today the shaping of a new relationship between ECE and CSE. The decline of the debate on educational continuity in academic research, the emergence of less consultative forms of educational policy-making and the progressive disinvestment of central government in experimental programmes have all contributed to make the perspective of educational continuity very vulnerable to the pressure of recent neo-liberal trends. In this way, an understanding of educational continuity based upon a model of school readiness is becoming increasingly predominant in policy-making with the risk of irremediably impoverishing pedagogical practices in ECE and undermining a broader approach to learning in compulsory school.

This analysis of the Italian case, which has been carried out with a specific focus on local dynamics, shows that the relationship between ECE and CSE cannot be considered as given once and for all; rather it needs to be considered as a result of political processes that are historically, socially and culturally situated. The Italian experience helps to identify some features that characterise the three possibilities suggested by Peter Moss for the relationship between ECE and CSE. Although these features are highly context-specific, in our view they can offer interesting insights for the critical analysis of the relationship between ECE and CSE in other contexts. Conceptualising the relationship between ECE and CSE as a meeting place implies, for example, that political spaces are created for experimentation and research on pedagogical practices at local level by involving children, practitioners, teachers, researchers, parents and local administrations. It requires leaving room for divergent points of view and for contestation of existing practices, nurturing dialogue as a source of transformational change. It also requires a long-term political vision within which values and purposes of education are negotiated within the public sphere. Understanding the relationships between ECE and CSE in terms of a strong and equal partnership entails co-ordinated efforts at the systemic level for the creation of a common frame of reference that make possible sustainable transformational change through democratic practices within ECE and CSE institutions. This requires constant efforts in terms of policy consultations and a strong commitment to responsive policy-making.

These two kinds of relationships between ECE and CSE – the meeting place and the strong and equal partnership – seem to be complementary rather than being mutually exclusive. It is the third kind of relationship, preparation for school, that inevitably contrasts with the other two. By considering ECE as functional to CSE and in turn CSE as functional to the market, the approach of school readiness tends to be inscribed by economic necessity rather than the educational needs of children within society. Within this perspective very little space seems to be left for transformation under the agency of individuals: children in the first place, but also parents, practitioners, teachers and local communities. Instead, political choices are taken in the name of economic necessity and this may result, in our view, in the implementation of educational practices that will increase inequalities.

In this context, reflecting on the relationship existing between ECE and CSE as a contested issue can become a provocation to reflect on the issues of education and democracy within our contemporary society. Referring back to the Italian case analysed in this chapter, we can notice that at the present time, as at the time of Bruno Ciari, the possibilities of what the future of early childhood and compulsory education could be are played out: in this situation all those who are involved in education are called to make a choice, to take a stance. We believe that concluding with the words of Ciari can be an inspiration for contemporary educators:

> Our struggle in favour of a fully educational school will play a crucial role in determining the future of the compulsory school system. The management of the schools should be in the hands of those who live in the schools: teachers, children and parents who need to be aware of educational purposes, methods and needs of the school and therefore significantly contribute to it ... Children are not in the position to stand

up for this cause: teachers, parents and citizens should stand up for them. The future of society will depend on the schools that we will be able to build, aiming at the promotion of human flourishing against the conditions that are currently threatening it. This is a high pedagogical ideal to stand for: to build a world which is more equal and fair.

(Ciari, 1972, p. 196, translation by the authors)

Policy documents

Law 820/1971. *Norme sull'ordinamento della scuola elementare e sulla immissione in ruolo degli insegnanti della scuola elementare e della scuola materna statale.*

Law 517/1977. *Norme sulla valutazione degli alunni e sull'abolizione degli esami di riparazione nonché altre norme di modifica dell'ordinamento scolastico.*

D.M. 9-2-1979. *I programmi della scuola media.*

D.p. R. 104/1985. *I programmi della Scuola Elementare.*

D.M. 3-6-1991. *Orientamenti dell'attività educativa nelle scuole materne statali*

L. 148/1990 (art. 1–2) & D.M. 16-11-1992. *Riforma dell'ordinamento della scuola elementare e Decreto Attuativo della continuità educativa (Art.2)*

C.M. 339/1992. *Circolare Ministeriale sulla continuità educativa.*

D.L. 59/2004. *Definizione delle norme generali relative alla scuola dell'infanzia e al primo ciclo dell'istruzione, a norma dell'articolo 1 della legge 28 marzo 2003, n. 53.* Allegato A, B, C, D.

D. M. 31-7-2007. *Indicazioni per il curricolo.*

Atto di indirizzo, D.p. R. 89/2009. *Revisione dell'assetto ordinamentale, organizzativo e didattico della scuola dell'infanzia e del primo ciclo di istruzione ai sensi dell'articolo 64, comma 4, del decreto-legge 25 giugno 2008, n. 112, convertito, con modificazioni, dalla legge 6 agosto 2008, n. 133.* 8 settembre 2009.

MIUR Decree, 249/2010. *Regolamento concernente: 'Definizione della disciplina dei requisiti e delle modalita' della formazione iniziale degli insegnanti della scuola dell'infanzia, della scuola primaria e della scuola secondaria di primo e secondo grado, ai sensi dell'articolo 2, comma 416, della legge 24 dicembre 2007, n. 244'.*

Notes

1   The authors acknowledge that many more educators deserve to be mentioned here such as, for example, Duilio Santarini (pedagogical coordinator of Forlì's municipal early childhood services from 1970 to 1980) and Sergio Neri

(pedagogical director of Modena's services from 1974 to 1990). However, given the space available, we have had to limit our choice to those who are particularly relevant to the discussion in this chapter. Bruno Ciari was the director of the Education Department in the municipality of Bologna from 1966 to 1970 while Loris Malaguzzi was the first director of the municipal schools, for children under 6 years, in the city of Reggio Emilia, where he worked from 1964 to 1994. Both Bruno Ciari and Loris Malaguzzi started their careers as primary school teachers and then chose to commit themselves to early childhood education from a political concern for a more equal and democratic society: their innovative pedagogical ideas found in the *scuole dell'infanzia,* which were opened from the 1960s by municipalities like Bologna and Reggio Emilia, fertile ground to grow nourished by 'mutual friendship and professional exchanges' (Malaguzzi, 1995, p. 55).

2   Among teachers' movements, two in particular need to be mentioned for the important role that they played in advocating for a more democratic education. The first is CEMEA (*Centres for the Implementation of Active Education Methods),* which originated in France in 1937 and is still operating today in many countries (www.ficemea.org). The other is MCE, Movimento di Cooperazione Educativa (*Movement for Educational Cooperation),* which was funded in Italy in 1951 under the inspiration of the pedagogical ideas of Celestin Freinet and is still active (www.mce-fimem.it).

3   A law permitting the state to provide schools for children between 3 and 6 years was only passed in 1968, some years after the first schools opened by municipalities.

4   The terms 'educator' and 'teacher' are direct translations of the terms used for core practitioners working in ECE services: *educatori* for those working in *nido, insegnanti* for those working in *scuola dell'infanzia.*

5   'Co-presence' refers to the importance attached to two or more educators or teachers working as a group in a classroom.

6   Mantovani describes *gestione sociale* as 'a concept that encompass both civic engagement and its expression in organised forms of participation and control' (Mantovani, 2007, pp. 1112–1113). Specifically, *gestione sociale* refers to the involvement of parents in decision-making committees and to the educational projects aiming at projecting the life of ECE institutions out in the community and, vice versa, at bringing members of the community into the school.

7   In Italian the word *pedagogista* is used to designate not only pedagogical coordinators (see footnote 13), but also those who are broadly involved in pedagogical work; in this sense it can refer to people like Malaguzzi and Ciari who developed new pedagogical perspectives and insights.

8   In Ciari's perspective, children's right to education should start at the age of 3 – with attendance at *scuola dell'infanzia* – and extend through primary school to middle school (*scuola media),* which ran to 14 years. Therefore in his project basic public school education (*educazione di base*) should also encompass *scuola dell'infanzia,* as he envisaged that involving children in early childhood education would contribute greatly to reducing the disadvantage with which children coming from low social classes entered primary school. At that time, *nido* services for children under 3 years – first funded by the municipality of Bologna in 1969 – were considered mainly to be for the support of working mothers, rather than directed specifically to the education of young children. Nevertheless it needs to be acknowledged that, since the beginning of their existence, municipal *nidi* were given an educational as well as care function.

9   One of the best known experiments on educational continuity between primary and junior high school has been carried out for over 20 years by the Scuola-Città

Pestalozzi in the city of Florence. This is an experimental public school consisting of eight grades, organised across four two-year courses that are closely linked to the *scuola dell'infanzia* at one end and to secondary school at the other end: http://ospitiweb.indire.it/~fimm0011/english/about_us.htm.

10   Although the main advocates of *scuola a tempo pieno* were the parents of children who attended this kind of school, many university professors supported the experience of full-time school and contributed to it with their studies and original pedagogical reflections (e.g. De Bartolomeis, 1972; Codignola, 1975; Becchi, 1979).

11   From the epistemic point of view, it became increasingly clear that educational phenomena needed to be studied within a multi- and inter-disciplinary perspective. Consequently, a holistic approach to educational sciences gained increased academic attention. A growing consensus emerged around the fact that children's development and education needed be studied not only from pedagogical or psychological perspectives, but also from sociological, anthropological and political ones (Visalberghi, 1978).

12   From its origin up to now, the role of *pedagogista* underwent several changes, as a consequence of the expansion of ECE services. While at the beginning the main functions entrusted to the *pedagogista* were supporting pedagogical work by sustaining collegial work within teams of teachers and educators, at the present time this role has become more focused on the co-ordination of educational initiatives organised at local level within an integrated system of services. Hence the transition from the term *pedagogista* to the term *coordinatore pedagogico*. An important intervention made by Emilia Romagna Region has been to encourage networking among pedagogical coordinators at different levels (municipal, provincial and regional level): this has allowed a progressive shift of focus from the work carried out within each setting toward a more systemic perspective. This further change has led to the introduction of the expression *coordinamento pedagogico* to define this system of pedagogical coordination (Benedetti, 2009).

13   This approach to continuity is rooted in the learning theories developed by Vygotsky (1978) and Dewey (1913).

14   The curriculum was structured across three subject areas: creative expression (music, drama, visual art), literacy (encompassing oral and written expression), and science (maths and scientific reasoning). In addition an inter-disciplinary area was included, encompassing those activities that cannot be categorised under any specific subject area (such as cooking).

15   Although not explicitly stated in official documents, it needs to be said that the continuity of relationships among children is also encouraged. In this sense, when primary school classes are formed, children who have been in the same group in *scuola dell'infanzia* are generally kept together when possible in order to provide children with a familiar relational environment.

16   The term *confrontation* here is used as a direct translation of the Italian term *confronto*, which refers to the process of exchanging ideas and discussing divergent views on a certain issue: this process of negotiation, therefore, encompasses also the aspect of disagreement as a resource that enriches dialogue and debate.

17   Here we refer to the experience of *scambi pedagogici* (literally *pedagogical exchanges*) that involved educators, teachers and pedagogical coordinators from several provinces in Emilia-Romagna Region (Bologna, Ferrara, Piacenza, Forlì, Modena, Reggio Emilia, Parma). The aim of the programme was to facilitate the construction of a regional system of ECE services for children aged 0 to 6 on a basis of a shared pedagogical culture. During these experience

educators and teachers took part in visits to other services, in discussions on pedagogical documentation and in focus groups where reciprocal reflections were shared (Assessorato alle politiche sociali della Regione Emilia-Romagna, 2004). This experience has been described more extensively elsewhere by one of the authors of this chapter (Lazzari, 2011b).

18 Since 2007 a unitary curriculum is in force (*Indicazioni/2007*), providing a common pedagogical culture and societal values for the *scuola dell'infanzia, scuola primaria* and *scuola secondaria di primo grado*. This unitary structure organises fields of experience (*scuola dell'infanzia*) and subject areas *(scuola primaria* and *scuola secondaria di primo grado)* within a coherent framework across all the three types of school, emphasising in particular cross-disciplinary learning and progressive formalisation of knowledge.

Chapter 8

What if the rich child has poor parents?

The relationship from a Flemish perspective

Michel Vandenbroeck, Nadine De Stercke and Hildegard Gobeyn

In this chapter, we wish to critically analyse the relationship between early childhood education (ECE) and compulsory school education (CSE) with a particular focus on equity in a context of diversity. As the hierarchical relationship between ECE and CSE is dominant in most affluent countries, we will take up the point made by Peter Moss in his introductory essay, that the dominant discourse of readying children to enter school is highly contestable. The readiness paradigm has historically been, and increasingly continues to be, underpinned by a concern about equity and social justice. However, there is good reason to doubt that it keeps its promises. Rather, it seems to be that the readiness paradigm may very well result in increased inequality, excluding precisely those it wishes to include.

Our critical analysis is based on international literature, but deeply embedded in the concrete context of Flanders (the Flemish speaking part of Belgium) for several reasons. It is the region where we live and work. It is also a region with universal access to early childhood education for children from 2 and-a-half years onwards. Full day *kleuterschool* is not only universally accessible, it is also free of charge for the parents and teachers are trained to a Bachelor level (ISCED 5). In short, the Flemish *kleuterschool* meets most international standards (UNICEF Innocenti Research Centre, 2008), albeit with rather large groups of 20 to 24 children for one teacher. Yet, results from the PISA studies show that the Flemish education system is among the most unequal in the European Union: in no other European country are the school results of young people so dependent on their families' background (OECD, 2007). This makes Flanders a challenging case to examine the relationship in which ECE is considered to be preparing children for school and, therefore, contributing to 'levelling the playing field' by creating equal opportunities.

In his introductory essay, Peter Moss rightly argues that the ethical and political choice about the possible relationships between ECE and CSE is inextricably linked with the image of the child we construct. In our analysis, we will particularly focus on how constructions of the child are intertwined with constructions of the parent, as well as with constructions of the relationship between the family and the (welfare) state, hence the provocative question in the title of this chapter: what if the Rich Child has Poor Parents? We believe that this is an important elaboration, as constructions of childhood cannot be considered without examining constructions of parenthood and of citizenship (Vandenbroeck and Bouverne-De Bie, 2006). Moreover, a recent study of curricula for the initial education of early childhood educators' in 15 European countries (Urban *et al.*, 2011) showed that parents are virtually absent (with some notable exceptions such as the French *éducateur jeunes enfants*). More attention needs to be given to the relationships between parents and educational services if one wishes to explore the second relationship sketched by Peter Moss, based on the *Starting Strong* reports: a relationship of equal partnership.

By focusing on parents' points of view, we also wish to further explore the ethical and political possibilities in ECE, with particular attention for the values of democracy. This implies that we not only wish to look at *which* knowledge is important (as Vecchi (2010) advocates), but also at *what this knowledge is for*, what education in general is for and, especially, who is enabled to participate in this discussion. But acknowledging the plea made by Peter Moss to take a historical stance, we will first give a short overview of ECE and CSE traditions in Flanders.

A concise hindsight

In most European countries compulsory schooling was introduced alongside child protection laws and child care, during the first industrial revolution – for Belgium, in May 1914. Space precludes elaborating in detail the rationale for this evolution, but as we have explained elsewhere (Vandenbroeck, 2003, 2006), *kinderopvang* (child care) for the youngest had several missions. Obviously, it enabled women to go to work, providing a cheap labour force. These working-class women were not only poor, but also accused of poor parenting. Child mortality in this era was high, and was not attributed to the harsh living conditions (low wages, poor housing, lack of sanitation) but rather to the incompetence and the neglect of working-class mothers. It was the mission of the early *crèches* to take over the maternal tasks, where mothers were thought to be deficient, as well as to educate and civilise these mothers or, as Donzelot (1977) puts it, as a way of *policing the family.*

The first child protection legislation and the prohibition of child labour, at the same time as the emergence of *kinderopvang* for the youngest children, removed the actual economic role of children in the family and in society, contributing to the construction of the child as fragile and as an investment in the future. As a consequence, parents (i.e. mothers) were constructed as the guardians of these investments and the family – based on the bourgeois family model – was expected to be the cornerstone of the desired society. Failure to conform with the dominant ideal of what consti-tuted maternal attitudes was not only considered as an offence towards the child, but also towards the society (Foucault, 1977). The new child protec-tion laws allowed for far reaching interventions in the family when children (and society) were considered to be 'in danger' and gave the state the right to substitute the 'bad father' (Peters and Walgrave, 1978).

Kleuterschool followed a different path. Rapid growth of *bewaarscholen* (care schools) occurred between the 1820s and 1850s. By the late 1850s, they were not just seen as 'caring places' for the young children of work-ers, but also as providing education for their middle-class counterparts, complementing rather than replacing the education provided by mothers, and even more so as the *bewaarscholen* turned into *kindertuinen* (kinder-garten), under the influence of Froebel-inspired liberal (and to a lesser extent Catholic) initiatives (Depaepe and Simon, 2005). Due to the influ-ence of feminist figures from the bourgeoisie, such as Gatti de Gamond (1839–1905), by the late nineteenth century professional education was provided for the (female) teachers, who, unlike crèche workers, were not recruited from among the poor. The *kindertuinen*, today's *kleuterschool*, was not associated with a deficient construction of parenting and, as a consequence, spread rapidly, first in the cities, later in more rural areas.

Belgium witnessed a fierce political struggle between Catholics and Liberals about 'the soul of the child'. While the Liberals advocated state education, the Catholics did not accept interference by the state in what they framed as private matters. As a result of this on-going struggle it was decided that there would be no compulsory school (*schoolplicht*), but compulsory learning (*leerplicht*), meaning that parents need not enrol their children in primary schools if they could show that they were teaching their children according to the minimum curriculum standards. A second result of the struggle for the soul of the child was that in many municipalities across the country both state and private (but publicly funded) Catholic schools mushroomed, including *kleuterschool*.

Compulsory learning was intended to make the most of the investment in the (economic) future of the child and promised social mobility (eman-cipation). But it also served to keep the children of the working class off the streets and to civilise them in the new industrial era. As explained above, conservative circles (i.e. the Catholic Party) opposed interventions by the state in 'the freedom of the father', while progressive, liberal sections of society strove for it, pleading for the emancipatory potential of the school, as well as it being an institution for children learning their place in society. The compromise that emerged from this so-called 'school war' was that the state could only intervene when the *pater familias* was considered to neglect his duties.

In short, both *kinderopvang* for the youngest and *kleuterschool* and *lagere school* (primary education) for older children were newly emerging institutions that can be considered as both emancipative and as a bourgeois attempt to civilise the poor. It should be noted that this occurred in a liberal welfare regime, with a minimal role for the state. The state was expected only to intervene when parents were considered deficient: the so-called *État Gendarme* (Donzelot, 1977), rather than as a way of redistributing resources and optimising the (educational and other) opportunities for all. Changes to extend the period of compulsory learning have since then always gone hand in hand with changes in the labour market (i.e. rising unemployment for early school leavers).

We now turn to the late 1960s and early 1970s, important for the present-day discussion about the role of ECE, framing ECE as preparing for CSE in new ways. It was a period of concern about the underachievement of working class (black) children in schools in the United States, following the Sputnik shock: the shock that the Soviet empire could take a technological lead, amidst the Cold War. Large investments were made in compensatory programmes, focusing primarily on compulsory school age. In the early 1970s, scientists were critical and disappointed when confronted with the lack of persisting effects from these expensive compensatory programmes (e.g. Bronfenbrenner, 1974; Thirion, 1973). As a result of this disappointment, a general consensus rose among scholars that primary school was too late to begin education and investments should be made at an earlier age to prevent children from starting compulsory school with a disadvantage, thus saving the (poor) child as well as the nation through the child (Vandenbroeck, 2003).

The framing of the early years as an optimal period for prevention has been reinforced in new ways since the 1990s and even more so in the twenty-first century. Through the OECD's PISA studies (see Chapters 1 and 2), it is well documented that children from poor families do less well at school. Recently, research has shown that the brain develops most in the early years (for a concise overview see, for instance, UNICEF Innocenti Research Centre, 2008) and combining these two mainstream findings, it is now widely accepted that the early years present the best return on educational investment (Heckman, 2006). This has led to a consistent plea for access to pre-school provision and enrolment rates are now an important indicator of a nation's well-being (European Commission, 2010, 2011). Based on correlational studies, the OECD (2011) claims that attendance at ECE is significantly related to better school outcomes in adolescence.

It is no coincidence that this prevention or social investment paradigm is dominant in neo-liberal welfare states, both in the affluent world and beyond. As Christian Morabito shows in his on-going PhD research, contemporary philosophers – such as Roemer (1998), Rawls (1971) and Sen (2009) – have laid a foundation for a shift in thinking about equality. They advocate taking personal choice, individual effort and merit into account. As a result, they propose the concept of equality of opportunities, rather than equality of outcomes, be it for somewhat different reasons. Political scientists (e.g. Giddens, 2005) have interpreted this concept further, and it has now been 'translated' by politicians who refer to equal opportunities, rather than equalising outcomes, as a compromise position on equality that is supposed to be beyond the traditional left/right divide. In this new discourse, inequality of outcome is not only tolerable in meritocratic societies, it is also supposed to be a necessary condition for economic development; individual effort and merit need should be taken into account when conceptualising equality. Both contemporary philosophers and policy makers explicitly point to education in general and ECE in particular as a means of equalising opportunities in ways that are supposed to be beyond political debate. This argument has also deeply influenced international organisations, including the World Bank, UNICEF and UNESCO (Morabito, 2011).

What is consistent in this history is that ECE has continuously been framed in a *prevention paradigm*. This implies that the meaning and value of early childhood education does not reside primarily in early childhood itself, but later in life: ECE is only a transitional period for the real education that occurs in CSE. In the same way, the meaning and value of CSE does not reside in that period of education itself, but rather in the economic return it brings as a consequence of finding a place in a competitive labour market.

What is equally consistent is that education is framed as a means to solve social problems (Vandenbroeck *et al.*, 2010). Immorality and child mortality in the nineteenth century, unemployment and intergenerational poverty today are considered as important problems, but are not treated as social problems – rather as educational ones. In so doing, they also become individual problems of children and their families. The solution is, therefore, not to look again at the distribution of resources and the growing gap between rich and poor, but at education, stressing individual responsibility for the management of one's own life chances.

Paulo Freire said that '[t]his view mistakenly presupposes that themes exist, in their original, objective purity, outside me – as if themes were *things*' (Freire, 1970, p. 97). He is arguing that a 'problem' – or 'theme' – does not exist as such; it is always socially constructed. Consequently, it can always be de- and re-constructed. Freire argues that there is no such thing as an educational problem *per se*. Such problems are, according to him, nothing more (and nothing less) than specific forms of social problems. One of the main objectives of his pedagogy and of the 'cultural circles' he installed was to form collective spaces of reflection in order to reconstruct what is considered to be the problem or the 'theme'.

Another continuity is that science is viewed as informing policymakers, practitioners and parents about the truth concerning children and what needs to be done, be it medical science and eugenics in nineteenth century, developmental psychology in twentieth century or brain science and economics in the twenty-first century. We will now develop this last theme a bit further.

The democratic deficit of education

ECE has been constructed as a preparatory phase for CSE and also as early prevention. The prevention paradigm is consistent with the concept of the social investment state: a welfare state that does not compensate for failures of the market, but invests to ensure future integration in this highly competitive market (e.g. Featherstone, 2006). Consequently, social welfare became a matter of 'no rights without duties'. Investments in welfare today are also considered as a prevention of later risks, of which the risk of being dependent on the social welfare system (e.g. in the case of unemployment) is one of the more important.

The prevention paradigm and the framing of education as a means to solve potential social problems entails risks being calculated and calls upon science to inform policy makers and practitioners about what works. It is therefore quite understandable that in the neo-liberal social investment state *evidence-based* policy and practice is foregrounded, to ensure the effectiveness and efficiency of interventions. Researchers are expected to answer the question 'what works?' As Biesta (2007, p. 5) explains, this question to researchers entails an important democratic deficit:

> Evidence-based education seems to favour a technocratic model in which it is assumed that the only relevant research questions are questions about effectiveness [...] forgetting that what counts as 'effective' crucially depends on judgments about what is desirable. On the practice side, evidence-based education seems to limit severely the opportunities for educational practitioners to make such judgments in a way that is sensitive to and relevant for their own contextualized settings.

Evidence-based education presupposes that what the educator does is an activity with a specific purpose and that there is a causal relationship to establish between purpose and action. Effectiveness is supposed to be the certain relationship between the intervention and its results. Efficiency is then about the costs of this relationship. Consequently, effectiveness and efficiency do not include a judgment about *what* needs to be achieved, the only relevant question being *how* to achieve the predetermined outcomes and the investment necessary to do so.

Yet, education is a highly complex matter in which many variables interfere: context for example, but also how children and parents accept (or refuse) the intentions of the educator, making clear and consistent causal relationships between intervention and effect highly improbable. But, more important, there is the democratic question about who is entitled to establish the educational goals. What is desirable and who says so? The fundamental problem with the prevention paradigm in general and with evidence-based practice in particular is that the goals (the desired outcomes) are defined by the researchers and, therefore, not negotiated with individual families or practitioners, as the goals need to be similar for the entire cohort. These goals are then represented as natural, self-evident and 'objective'. This is what Biesta (2007) labels as the *democratic deficit* of evidence-based practice. For democratic practice means that parents and children are involved in decisions that concern them (Moss, 2007).

Education is first and foremost an ethical and political act, as it always is (and always will be) related to our vision of the world we would wish our children to live in. Education is after all about 'ways of imagining a possible future' (Biesta, 2007, p. 21). Therefore it is ultimately about how we would wish people to be and how we would wish them to relate to society. No doubt we could easily agree on some general horizons including a worldview based on equality, freedom and solidarity. Yet it is highly improbable that we would still agree when it comes to putting this possible future into practice. While some would put individual freedom first and attach much importance to rewarding effort and merit, others may value solidarity and equality more and advocate more strongly for redistributive systems. While some educators stress autonomy, free choice and self-expression as the highest values, others may wish to limit autonomy to favour inter-dependency and belonging (Tobin *et al.*, 2009). As Sen (2009) explained through the story of the children and the flute, there is no such thing as one rational truth about what is 'just'. It is precisely such disagreements and debates about and between diverging viewpoints that are at the heart of what democracy is about (Mouffe, 2005).

The case of Flanders

The unquestioned assumption that early access to education will benefit performance in CSE and that this may help reduce poverty in the future is seriously challenged by the Flemish case. Flanders has a split system in which child-care services for 0 to 3 year-olds are part of the welfare system, while *kleuterschool* (2 and-a-half to 6 years) is integrated in the education system, as is CSE. Enrolment in Flemish *kleuterschool* is among the highest in the world; 97 per cent of children between 3 and 6 years are enrolled and in the last year of *kleuterschool*, only 0.3 per cent of children are not enrolled (Gobeyn and De Stercke, 2010). Children also go to *kleuterschool* at an earlier age (2 and-a-half years) and for longer hours (about 30 hours per week) than in most countries. In addition, enrolment in *kinderopvang* (child care) for children from 0 to 3 years is relatively high (around 40 per cent) and has grown substantially over the last two decades (Kind en Gezin, 2010). Yet, school results for Flemish children are, according to the PISA study, influenced more by the socio-economic background of their family than in any other European country and child poverty has doubled in the last decade (Cantillon, 2010).

High enrolment does not necessarily mean that children attend *kleuterschool* regularly. Figures on attendance (meaning actual presence in the school, rather than administrative enrolment) are scarce, but it is estimated that absence is highest among those groups that are 'at risk' of school failure later on: children from poor families, among which ethnic minorities are over-represented (Vandenbroucke, 2007). Consequently, ethnic minority families are encouraged to send their child more often, more frequently and at an earlier age to *kleuterschool*, in order to prevent later school failure.

For a few years now, all parents from ethnic minorities and parents living in poverty have received a home visit when their child is between 30 and 36 months to convince them of the benefits of attending *kleuterschool*. Since September 2009, a new measure has been introduced by the Flemish government. A child cannot enrol in the first year of compulsory school (at age 6), unless she has attended *kleuterschool* for at least 220 half days (Smet, 2009). If she has not, she will need to do a language test and, failing that, will have to attend *kleuterschool*, regardless of having reached the primary school age. Obviously, children whose mother tongue is not Flemish will have less chance of passing the test. This new measure implies not only that *kleuterschool* is formally expected to prepare children for CSE, but also that CSE is no longer expected to be able to deal with the diversity of home languages. It also implies that enrolling in the first year of CSE is not an unconditional right anymore, but dependent on earlier attendance at pre-school; a *de facto* lowering of compulsory school age has been introduced, a measure that is likely to affect ethnic minority children in particular. Finally, parental allowances that are meant to enable the poorest parents to cope with minor school expenses can be withdrawn if their child is too often absent from *kleuterschool* (Smet, 2009).

We can consider these measures as a way of managing *illegalisms*, which according to Deleuze (1985) are not 'illegal' acts according to the law, but rather the multitude of things that are either prohibited or labelled as undesirable. According to Deleuze (1985), some illegalisms are permitted, made possible or invented as a privilege of the dominating classes; examples are various tax reductions that favour the already privileged. Some illegalisms are tolerated, as compensation for the dominated classes, such as carnivalesque manifestations in the Bakhtinian sense (Bakhtin, 1984), not only at Carnival time, but also at various public demonstrations. Finally, some illegalisms are prohibited, isolated and made objects of intervention as well as domination. An example in this case is absence from *kleuterschool*, which cannot be considered against the law as *kleuterschool* is not compulsory, but still is the object of interventions.

From an international perspective, the case of Flanders shows what may be the ultimate consequences of policies and practices that frame ECE as a preparation of CSE in a context of universal accessibility – extending compulsory attendance, *de jure* or *de facto*, to ECE. The consequence in Flanders is policing families to attend the service that 'we' have so generously developed for 'them', without 'them' being able to participate in the debate about what kind of education is to be provided, having no say in what they would wish for their children. It is indeed remarkable that the concern about equality has not led to discussions with parents about their expectations of education in general and ECE in particular. As a result, official concern about social *in*clusion, combined with the concept of a hierarchical relationship between ECE and CSE, has led to practices of coercion and *ex*clusion.

In the following sections we give a concise account of two modest attempts to involve parents in discussions about how they are constructed as parents and how education is constructed. The first example is about ECE, the second about CSE. We end by discussing how these experiences might inspire us to reconceptualise the relationship between ECE and CSE.

Listening to parents whose children are absent from ECE

The second and third authors conducted a small scale, exploratory and qualitative study about these issues for their Masters in Social Work thesis, supervised by the first author (Gobeyn and De Stercke, 2010). In this context, they interviewed 11 parents whose children were enrolled in *kleuterschool*, but were not or rarely attending: three Belgian mothers, one Roma father and one Roma mother, three mothers from Central Europe, two North African mothers and one Central African mother. One purpose of the interviews was to explore parents' perspectives about the meaning of ECE and its relationship with CSE, as well as why their children did not attend ECE, despite the dominant discourse. A first observation is that most of these parents were reluctant to speak to the researchers and often refused to have the interviews tape-recorded; they had assimilated the dominant discourse about being deviant and guilty of bad parenting, which Freire (1970) would label as the 'culture of silence'. A thematic phenomenological analysis of the parents' narratives leads to three recurrent, interrelated themes.

School readiness

One of the most cited reasons why parents do not let their children go to *kleuterschool* is that they feel their child is not 'ready' to be in the large groups in these schools. This is expressed in different ways. A major concern of several parents was that their child was not fully potty-trained and that, in their view, the teacher cannot be bothered with potty training, considering the large groups of children she has to take care of. This is consistent with the view expressed by a Flemish Minister of Education that the *kleuterschool* teacher must be able to fulfil educational tasks and that changing nappies may hinder this work. Potty training is, according to the Minister, primarily the responsibility of parents (Vandenbroucke, 2008) – and parents entirely agree.

This points, however, at an important aspect of the preschool education system, which was also highlighted in the recent CoRe study[2] on competence requirements for the early years workforce in Europe (Urban *et al.*, 2011). In many countries education is considered in a narrow sense, so that caring tasks (such as washing, toileting, meals) are not considered educative. Such tasks are left to unqualified assistants, while qualified teachers concentrate on the 'real' education, leading to a 'split' system (between education and care) even occurring where child care and early education are fully integrated into one system.

Another example in this vein, mentioned by parents during interviews, was that their child still needs to sleep after lunch and this was not possible in the *kleuterschool*. As a Belgian mother said: 'School readiness, I don't know really. I think the child will show the moment when he is...He will show if he is ready to go to school'. We see here how this mother has internalised the concept of school readiness as a quality of the child and thus asks how this child needs to be for the school, rather than how one would like the school to be for this child.

Confidence and transitions

A second recurring theme, also related with the separation of care and education, is transition and trust. Some examples from the interviews:

> When I see him in the school...I think he is so young.
>
> (Belgian mother)

> I think I need to protect him. I have always been a protective mother...If I had the money, I would hire a private teacher and make my own library. There is a lot of aggression out there.
>
> (Algerian mother)

> I cannot comfort him when he is in school and has pain or sorrows.
>
> (Congolese mother)

When they understand the language, they will know when someone is gossiping. The children feel insecure; they do not know when other children are talking badly about them. They don't know what will happen to them.

(Kosovan mother)

The dominant discourse is that parents find it hard to let their children go and that they need to trust the *kleuterschool*. However, as we have learned from child-care services, confidence is a reciprocal matter that is slowly built during a long transition period, in which parents are not just told how to behave and how to be, but are intensely listened to and 'taken care of' (Vandenbroeck *et al.*, 2009). The parents that were interviewed can hardly be confident, since their concern is about care and care is all too often considered as separate from education. In addition, many parents are discouraged from physically being in the school. They are expected either to leave their child at the gate, or to leave the classroom when the 'real' education starts. Moreover, they receive negative feedback from their child, seeing her crying when they leave her in school, or coming home with what they call 'dirty words' and finding no possibility in the *kleuterschool* to express these worries. The careful (full of care) transition is important for all parents, and probably even more so for unemployed parents, since they are less likely to have had previous experience in using child-care services.

Poverty

A third important theme for some of the parents who were interviewed is poverty. This implies many things such as not having the money to buy the necessary bus ticket, not having decent clothes or shoes (and consequently fear that the child will be bullied or not accepted), or even not having a table for doing homework and thus fearing that their child will be criticised by the teacher. And of course poverty also goes together with bad health and frequent illness.

Kleuterschool in Flanders is predominantly child-centred, based on experiential learning and attaches a lot of importance to the 'emergent curriculum' (OECD, 2006), meaning that the life experiences of children are taken as a starting point for building the curriculum. In practice this means that the teacher will attach much importance to circle times, in which she will ask children to express their experiences and develop activities on the basis of this self-expression. In the interviews, parents show that they understand this very well and they comment that the other children will talk about their outings and holidays and the like. This means, however, that their child cannot participate in these conversations and that the curriculum will not deal with their child's experiences. In this way, some parents back up the criticism of Tobin (1995) that the pedagogy of self-expression may privilege the already privileged.

Obviously, this study has shortcomings, such as the small sample, without any ambition whatsoever to be representative; the fact that several interviews were conducted with a translator, often an acquaintance of the parent, and it was not always clear if the translation was accurate; and as we said above, some of the interviews could not be tape-recorded. Nevertheless, the narratives of the parents may point to some important aspects of the discussion on the relationship between ECE and CSE. They suggest that the concept of school readiness and the subsequent narrow educational focus, albeit a policy inspired by a concern for social justice, may end up excluding precisely those it wishes to include.

The stories of the parents can also be interpreted as a strong argument for a relationship of strong partnership between ECE and CSE, such as the OECD's *Starting Strong* reports advocated. Indeed, what these parents are asking for is the integration of care within education, cherishing a holistic view of the child, with particular attention to emotional and social aspects (peer relationships) and careful transitions, in which the parents are involved. This may be precisely what child care (for children under 3 years in Flanders) has to offer to education, both *kleuterschool* and compulsory school.

The parents' narratives also suggest that parents should be involved not just in instrumental ways (e.g. to enhance school results) but are really listened to, even at the risk of challenging some of ECE's dearest assumptions (e.g. on experiential learning).

Parents as researchers

It is a recurring feature that what constitutes the problem that education is expected to solve (or who is considered to have a problem or to *be* a problem) is debated without the people concerned, reducing parents to spectators of the debate about themselves. The objective aura of science, moreover, yields the belief that educational problems are technical in nature, rather than political, and therefore can be addressed in technical ways that do not call for public debates. What is dangerous in this case is – as Dahlberg and Moss (2007) claim – not so much the presence of one dominant paradigm, but the absence of paradigmatic discussions.

What would happen if these critical remarks were to be taken seriously and questions about what needs to be studied and how to be debated with those concerned? This is the challenge that has been taken up in France after the turmoil caused by INSERM's research on the prevention of adolescent delinquency (Institut National de la Santé et de la Recherche Médicale, 2005), published just after the riots in French suburbs in Autumn 2005, and its subsequent political use (Bénisti, 2005). In their report, INSERM suggested that the riots should be considered as delinquency, rather than as a protest against inequalities, and that the origins of this delinquency were located in early childhood, and more specifically in the deficiency of parents, especially parents from ethnic minorities. The report and its political translation formed the basis of a protest movement – *Pas de zero de conduite pour les 0 à 3 ans* (No zero for behaviour for the 0 to 3 years) – that rapidly gained over 200,000 supporters from among parents, social workers, pre-school teachers and others.

In this large protest movement against how parents were depicted in research about the prevention of juvenile delinquency (Le Collectif, 2006), groups of parents and practitioners refused to leave the construction of educational problems to scientists and claimed the right to do research on parenting themselves. The French NGO *Association Collectif Enfants Parents Professionels* started a project called *Universités Populaires des Parents*, in which existing and newly formed groups of parents conducted research, assisted by academics from various universities, with the explicit ambition to use the research to debate with policy makers about educational matters. After two years, the Flemish training organisation for the early years' profession, *Vormingscentrum Opvoeding en Kinderopvang*, proposed to introduce the experiment in Flanders, in close collaboration with French colleagues.[3] Six groups of parents were formed to do research and debate their results with policy makers (for more on this project, see Roose *et al.*, forthcoming).

One of these groups, accompanied by two social workers and the first author, consisted of 14 parents, all attending the same *basisschool* (a combined *kleuterschool* and primary school) in a rather deprived area of Ghent: two Belgian mothers and a Belgian father, two mothers of Tunisian origin, one of Central African origin and eight mothers of Turkish origin. The starting point of this group was a complaint from the school that the parents were not 'involved' enough and a request from the deputy mayor for education to study the relationships between parents and school staff. The group met monthly for more than a year. Little by little the theme of the discussions changed. It started with a question about how to improve communication between teaching staff and parents. But gradually new themes emerged: 'How did we end up in this school?', 'How does one choose a school?', 'Can we please choose another school for our children?' The following scene occurred in one of the last meetings of the first year and represented a dramatic shift of focus:

> A mother of Tunisian descent explains that she will not continue to come to the meetings after the summer holidays, as her daughter will then leave the school. She will go to a school whose name the mother is rather vague about. She tries different names, hoping that one of the other parents can recognize the sound. She tries 'Oasis'. 'Is it De Oase?'

asks the Belgian mother. 'Yes', she nods, that was the name. 'But', replies the Belgian mother, 'that is a school for idiots!' Then she explains that it is a type of special education for children with intellectual disabilities. The Tunisian mother reacts: 'That, I did not know.' 'Then why do you go there?' asks a second Belgian mother. 'They told me I have to', says the Tunisian mother. I ask her if they told her why she has to. The mother looks down, stirs her coffee and shyly shakes her head, indicating that she has no idea why her daughter would need special education.

Then, the African mother explains that her daughter went to the bridging class, two years ago [a class after ECE, for children of 6 years, who are deemed to be not school ready yet]. She was very pleased then about this initiative, since she agreed that her daughter was not ready for CSE. Now her son is in the last year of *kleuterschool* and they told her that he would have to go to the bridging class too. She told the staff that she disagreed with that, since he had already learned to read and write from his sister. I ask her what she thinks will happen in September at the start of the new school year. She says she does not know. Then I ask her why she thinks that her son was advised to attend the bridging class. The mother looks up, laughs aloud and says 'Because we are Africans, of course!'

Then a Belgian mother tells her story about how her son was thrown out of class because his school bag contained a porn magazine. The next day she wanted to explain to the teacher that her son is bullied and this must have come from one of his classmates, as they never have porn magazines in their house. But the teacher refused to talk, commenting that it is always the same 'with those stepchildren'.

What happens in this meeting is that each parent tells a very personal story, but also that these stories are made *collective* and in so doing, the parents remark that it is not just about adding up personal stories. They see a common theme in their stories: the idea that the school has given up on their child, and on them as parents. One of the Turkish mothers gives a perfect résumé, saying, 'In other schools they ask you a lot of questions. Here, nobody ever asks us anything'. By the end of the meeting, the parents decide that they do not wish to work on improving the relationship with the staff anymore: their subject of concern is school choice. They wish to research why parents have 'chosen' this school, how they can find another school for their children; and what kind of information you need as a parent to make informed choices.

The project thus started with a problem about parents, who were supposed not to be involved. Then it evolved towards a shared problem of communication between parents and staff. Finally it evolved again into a problem of parents, how to choose a better school; but also into a problem of school policy, how does one inform parents about their possibilities, which was discussed with the policy makers of the city. The difficult relationship of mistrust between staff and parents was not resolved, but the Deputy Mayor wrote a letter of appreciation to the parents and discussed with his team how in the future school staff could be counselled about their relationship with parents from diverse backgrounds.

For the academics involved, the project started with the intriguing question: 'What would happen if it is not researchers but parents that define what needs to be researched?' What we found out in this group (just as in most of the other groups) is that the answer to this question is highly unpredictable. Participative action research does not follow pre-ordained steps – formulate hypotheses, gather evidence, reflect on the hypotheses. Rather it is rhizomatic, always in the middle, always becoming, and never finished.

Discussion

The dominant conception of ECE as readying children for CSE is embedded in a preventive paradigm that goes well with neo-liberal individual meritocracy. In this ideal meritocratic society, everyone ends up with the position he or she deserves based on personal effort and choices. Education in this vein is a preparation for an economically prosperous life and ECE is necessary for a head start in this educational rat race, especially when the child is 'at risk'. Being at risk means being from poor families and/or families from ethnic minorities, since 'objective' research has shown that these children fail more often at school – and thus are at risk of later dependency on the state, juvenile delinquency, drug abuse and the like and thus objects of expensive interventions. In this sense, education contributes to the myth of personal achievement and of schooling as one of the most salient pathways to upward social mobility. Sociologists (e.g. Bourdieu and Passeron, 1970), however, have long since shown that educational systems tend to reproduce and perpetuate the existing social stratification, rather than change it.

Yet, as a result of the dominant construction of what education is about, the problem of school failure of children from poor and ethnic minority families is not considered as a problem of the school or of the educational system anymore. It is now considered as a problem of individual children and their families. Poor parents are, historically and at present, almost automatically associated with poor parenting (George, 2010). This deep, historically rooted mistrust of parents has led to interventions in the family, shaped parent support programmes, leading to the pedagogicalisation of parents (Popkewitz, 2003) and especially to their instrumentalisation. By this we mean that parents are expected to be involved insofar as this is 'helpful' for achieving the outcomes the school has set for the child, but not involved in discussion about these very outcomes.

The mistrust of parents also leads to the growing importance of the readying function of ECE, particularly for those children 'at risk', since the state is expected to take over where the parents fail. In the meantime, CSE can carry on with 'business as usual', meaning the education of the alleged *average* child. Indeed, the very concept of 'school readiness' becomes some kind of a standard or norm, a measure against which children are categorised, in the meaning Foucault (1975) gave to this concept:

> La pénalité perpétuelle qui traverse tous les points, et contrôle tous les instants des institutions disciplinaires compare, différencie, hiérarchise, homogénéise, exclut. En un mot elle *normalise*.[4]

The excluding mechanisms of the readying relationship between ECE and CSE affect not only ECE, but also CSE. Since the function of ECE is to make children 'school ready', CSE can start with the average child, the one that fits in the system. We can witness how CSE today is less well equipped to deal with diversity (see for instance the growing number of ethnic minority children who are referred to special education, the rising numbers of diagnoses of early autism, ADHD and other alleged dysfunctions). The average child, the one that fits, is presented as natural and 'normal', going well with the myth of meritocracy telling us that each one of us eventually gets what he or she deserves. As Freire (1970, p. 144) said:

> The people are manipulated by . . . yet another myth: the model of itself, which the bourgeoisie presents to the people as the possibility for their own ascent. In order for these myths to function, however, the people must accept the word of the bourgeoisie.

School readiness is a myth and a construct that is believed to be an individual quality of the child, influenced by her family background. In his introductory essay, Peter Moss explained how this affects ECE. We have to elaborate on this, showing how it also affects CSE as well as how it excludes particular groups of parents. We have attempted to counterbalance this by giving voice to some of these parents.

Listening to these parents, we suggest a possible alternative to the concept of school readiness: child (and family) readiness of the school. The 'child' in 'child ready' is not an average child. It is a unique child, a child that we do not know before we have met her and her family. A child that will have similarities *and* differences with the children we have met so far. A child with a family that will resemble *and* differ from families we know. A child, therefore, that is fundamentally unpredictable. Being ready for that child, therefore, means being ready for unpredictability and uncertainty and, consequently, being ready to search and to research what ECE may mean for this child and for his family.

This is not to say that ECE cannot have a function of readying children. For some families, this is precisely what they expect. Some immigrant families, for instance, do not choose child care as a 'home away from home', but precisely because it differs from the home: it is a place for learning the dominant language and for socialising their children, holding out the prospect of integration and social capital (Vandenbroeck *et al.*, 2009). But it is to say that whether ECE has this function or not, and especially *how* this function is shaped in practice, is the result of on-going negotiations between local communities, practitioners, management, policy makers – and parents.

In order to make these negotiations reciprocal, a series of conditions need to be fulfilled: reflective practitioners supported by a reflective system that gives them resources and time to document and discuss their practices; above all, a vision of education as a public good and as a transitional space between the private and the public spheres. As Arianna Lazzari (2011b) has shown in her well documented PhD study of early childhood teachers in Bologna, it is no coincidence that the inspiring pedagogues from northern Italy, such as Loris Malaguzzi and Bruno Ciari, reacted against the experience of fascism with a deep commitment to democratic aspects of education, education of, by and for the people. In her historical analysis of present-day professionalism in Bologna, Lazzari shows how this is embedded in civic traditions of solidarity and participation by citizens in the political life of their communities and in the development since the late 1960s in municipal ECE of *gestione sociale* or social management. Italian authors throughout the 1970s and 1980s describe early childhood institutions as *'laboratorio cultural'*, cultural laboratories in which 'all actors – policy makers, practitioners, families and citizens – were involved in the construction of a common project for social and cultural transformation' (Balduzzi in Lazzari, 2011) (for a fuller discussion, see Chapter 7).

Listening to parents, we learn that we cannot construct an image of the child without an image of the parent. It is not possible to respect the child without respecting the parent. The reciprocal negotiation with parents, however, is a risky adventure, as we expose some of our dearest assumptions to questioning. But so is democracy itself a risky adventure.

The Flemish experience, as we have analysed it, can be considered as a plea to at least take into account alternative meanings of the relationship between ECE and CSE. There is a case for a strong and equal partnership and for a meeting place. This is what actually happens in some municipal *kleuterscholen* in the city of Ghent, which acknowledge that the experience of child care services for the youngest children has much to offer to education. *Kleuterschool* teachers sit together with child-care professionals, and ask the latter to support them in working with parents from diverse origins, in order to discover new ways of experiential learning, in which the experiences of *all* children are taken into account. Notwithstanding the fundamental inequality in the relationship between child care and education (i.e. child-care practitioners have lower qualifications, lower salaries, more working hours and fewer holidays), these tentative meetings between the two professional groups offer some hope that the meeting place Peter Moss explained in his introductory essay may be possible, and remind us of the words of Freire (1970, p. 92)

> Men are able to transcend the limit-situations to discover that beyond these situations – and in contradiction to them – lies an *untested feasibility*.

Notes

1   *Kleuterschool* means 'school for toddlers'. Initially for children from 3 to 6 years of age, since the late 1970s children from 2 and-a-half years are admitted. Due to the shortage of child care for younger children and the fact that *kleuterschool* is free for parents (in contrast to child care), growing numbers of children from 2 and-a-half years are enrolled in *kleuterschool. Kleuterschool* is part of the education system. Together with *lagere school* (primary school) it forms the *basisschool* (basic education), although compulsory school starts at 6.
2   CoRe stands for *Competence Requirements in Early Childhood Education and Care,* a study commissioned by the European Commission Directorate General for Education and Culture. The study was jointly conducted in 2010–2011 by the University of East London and Ghent University and comprised a literature study, a survey in 15 EU countries and seven in-depth case studies. The data we refer to in this section are drawn from the survey.
3   We gratefully acknowledge the cooperation with Meryem Usta and Rosheen Demaret (city of Ghent). We also thank Katelijne De Brabandere (VCOK) for guiding the project, the Flemish Youth Agency for support, and especially Rudi Roose and Griet Roets from the Department of Social Welfare Studies for inspiring discussions about the meaning of this project.
4   The perpetual coercion that penetrates every point and controls all the moments of the disciplinary institutions compares, differentiates, hierarchizes, homogenizes, excludes. In one word: it *normalizes* (Foucault, 1975, p. 185; original emphasis; translation by the authors).

Part IV

Concluding reflections

Chapter 9

Citizens should expect more!

Peter Moss

The aim of this book has been 'to extend the space of educational contestation to include compulsory schooling and the relationship between ECE and CSE', making the relationship one of Chantal Mouffe's 'properly political questions', which 'always involve decisions which require us to make a choice between conflicting alternatives'. At a time when the educational 'dictatorship of no alternative' insists the relationship entails only a technical question – 'how best can ECE ready children for compulsory schooling?' – politicising the relationship shifts the terms of the discussion to the properly political question, 'what do we want?' I hope the book has contributed to that shift by insisting there are alternatives and delving into two in greater depth. For policy makers to talk of ECE 'readying' children for school or to learn, as if this was a neutral and self-evident statement of purpose, should no longer be acceptable or accepted. Citizens should expect more!

The book, therefore, is a contribution to renewing a democratic politics of education, a politics that thrives on properly political questions and the contestation of conflicting alternatives. The book, too, should be a contribution to educational debate beyond ECE. A recurring theme has been that the relationship between ECE and CSE can, and should, raise as many (political) questions about CSE as ECE: about purpose, pedagogy, values, ethics, the image of the child, and so on. Moreover, educators from ECE should engage with these questions about CSE as much as educators from the compulsory school sector itself, turning away from introspection to look across the whole field of education and having the confidence to contribute to a broadly-defined democratic politics of education.

The books in this series, but much else besides, provide evidence that ECE today has some of the most innovative thought and practice in the whole educational field; it is, as John Bennett describes, highly relevant to debates about education in the twenty-first century. ECE has a voice that needs to be heard, but that voice, as John adds sadly, is currently 'inaudible' in debates about current and future education. ECE needs then to ensure its voice is heard by those in other sectors of education – and one way of doing so is to insist on the contestability of the relationship between ECE and CSE and the challenge it poses for CSE.

Having re-iterated my hopes, I want, in this final chapter, to review my response to the chapters contributed to this book. First, how does the typology of ECE/CSE relationships look now? The three neat and abstract classifications – (I) readiness for school; (II) a strong and equal partnership; (III) the vision of a meeting place – do not survive unscathed the encounter with the messiness and singularity of real life. As Peder Haug observes, '[h]ybrids, combinations of different types, are very common'. Other authors share the view that the strong and equal partnership and the meeting place may be complementary rather than mutually exclusive; it is, as Arianna Lazzari and Lucia Balduzzi conclude, 'preparation for school that inevitably contrasts with the other two'.

From the experience of Norway, Peder suggests a fourth relationship – 'indifference and isolation' – whilst adding that this relationship is less likely today as ECE expands and assumes such a major role in national and international policies. Michel Vandenbroeck, Nadine De Stercke and Hildegard Gobeyn stand the readiness argument on its head by arguing for 'child (and family) readiness of the school', a readiness that is premised on welcoming 'a unique child, a child that we do not know before we have met her and her family ... a child, therefore that is fundamentally unpredictable' – a very different perspective to the normalising language of readiness *for* school. Sharon Lynn Kagan also questions the compulsory school when she observes that the 'schoolification' so often associated with relationship I 'might not be so bad ... if schools were truly child centred and pedagogically rich and exciting places for young children and their teachers'.

But compulsory education is, by and large, not like this. As John Bennett makes clear in his chapter but also in the *Starting Strong* reports he co-authored (see, for example, OECD, 2006, pp. 221–222), schools are too often impoverished and predictable places, subject-centred, working with simplified ideas of learning and discrete skills and knowledge items, increasingly bound by prescriptive outcomes and technical practice: purveyors of education in its narrowest sense. CSE is, in short, often a conservative force today, neither truly child centred nor pedagogically rich; and so, as Gunilla Dahlberg points out, the preparation for school discourse is accompanied by a simplified idea of learning 'as transmission of facts, of reproducing knowledge that is already known; rather than learning as a process of meaning making'.

Gunilla also emphasises that to contest this readiness discourse does not mean dismissing the importance of maths, language and science – but dismissing a simplified approach towards them and working, instead, with the grain of children's learning strategies.

But if we only looked and listened, we'd see, for example, that children in pre-school were using maths all the time. We prefer to test and diagnose at a distance rather than participate to better understand what children are actually doing, for example through pedagogical documentation. We then easily miss the possibility to challenge, deepen and extend children's learning processes.

The preceding chapters have also introduced some potentially useful concepts. Both Sharon Lynn Kagan and Margaret Carr refer to 'alignment' of ECE and CSE. Sharon proposes the need for pedagogical, programmatic and policy alignment; whilst Margaret refers to alignment of outcomes, which she sees encouraging signs of in recent curriculum developments in New Zealand, as well as alignment of 'mediational means', so far less apparent. Another concept is 'continuity', again in Sharon's chapter but also very central to the discussion by Arianna Lazzari and Lucia Balduzzi of Italian experience, in which *continuità educativa* has been an important idea. Both American and Italian authors refine the concept, distinguishing between 'vertical' continuity, across different stages in lifetime educational careers, and 'horizontal' continuity, which for Sharon is about creating 'linkages among health, education, parenting and protective services, as well as other supportive institutions and settings'; while for Arianna and Lucia the emphasis is more 'between learning experiences carried out by children in school and in out-of-school settings'. Within the Italian perspective, personified by the work of Bruno Ciari, there is also the idea that continuity can find expression through certain shared political values and goals: 'promoting democracy, civic engagement and cultural transformation.'

For Ciari, as Arianna and Lucia make clear, the concept of continuity also encompassed communities and families: 'horizontal continuity, so understood, is played out in the collaboration with families and in the integration of local agencies, which both involve reciprocal relationships between school institutions and the local community environment of which they are part'. The role and importance of families and communities in education in general and the ECE/CSE relationship in particular are also picked up by other contributors – though inexcusably overlooked in my own introductory essay. Gunilla Dahlberg talks of the need for parents to participate in pedagogical documentation, a means for everyone concerned to deepen understanding of learning processes, and which she emphasises can be applied as much to CSE as ECE. The 'borderland' between ECE and CSE must, Margaret Carr insists, be inhabited by families, a source of rich social and cultural capital. The innovative and highly regarded *Te Whāriki*, New Zealand's curricular framework for ECE, has 'emphasised the context-based nature of a curriculum that responds to its community, and did not see itself as a preparation for the then subject-based school curriculum'.

The centrality of families, especially parents, is the main theme of the chapter by Michel Vandenbroeck and his colleagues. With a focus on impoverished and marginalised families and on ECE's long-standing association with the 'prevention paradigm', they argue that social constructions of children should not be divorced from social constructions of parents – can you have, they ask, a 'rich' child but a 'poor' parent? They raise 'the democratic question about who is entitled to establish the educational goals', noting that families, and indeed practitioners, are rarely part of this process; parental participation is too often infused by instrumentality not democracy, concerned to garner parental support for outcomes, not welcome parental input to deliberation on political questions. And, using the case of Flanders, they show

> what may be the ultimate consequences of policies and practices that frame ECE as a preparation of CSE in a context of universal accessibility – extending compulsory attendance, *de jure* or *de facto*, to ECE. The consequence in Flanders is policing families to attend the service that 'we' have so generously developed for 'them', without 'them' being able to participate in the debate about what kind of education is to be provided, having no say in what they would wish for their children. It is indeed remarkable that the concern about equality has not led to discussions with parents about their expectations of education in general and ECE in particular. As a result, official concern about social *in*clusion, combined with the concept of a hierarchical relationship between ECE and CSE, has led to practices of coercion and *ex*clusion.

Nor, as I explained in my introductory essay, is the extension of compulsory attendance to ECE limited to Flanders; it is already apparent elsewhere in Europe and its further spread is only too possible in a discursive context that naively treats ECE as a sure-fire technical fix for social and economic ills, obviating the need for structural change, political commitment and participatory democracy. In the process, ECE risks becoming a site for pedagogical control and governing the soul, not a forum for democratic dialogue and emancipatory practice.

So where do these qualifications and elaborations leave my own thinking on the relationship between ECE and CSE? I fully accept the need for families and communities to be part of the relationship, and an important one. If, as I shall come back to, the vision of a meeting place is a preferred alternative, then participation in that process of constructing new understandings and practices should be as wide-ranging as possible, by practitioners and politicians, administrators and managers, parents and fellow citizens – not to forget children and young people. Widening participation in a meeting place may be easier said than done, but the principle should not be in question. The relationship is an issue of democratic politics, not of technical expertise. Indeed, if Peder Haug's conclusion is accepted, that 'the societal context at any time is very important when it comes to defining these relationships and how they are regulated', then it is all the more important to find ways of enhancing wide societal participation in formulating the relationship – actively intervening to shape the context, not simply treating it as a given.

I can also see that terms such as 'alignment' and 'continuity' may be useful additions to the vocabulary for talking about relationships. 'Continuity', for example, reminds us of the need to think broadly about education – beyond ECE or even beyond ECE and CSE – but also beyond the formal education sector to the many other relationships and environments where education occurs. However, both concepts always need qualification to clarify the meaning given to them in a particular context. Moreover, both define only one facet of the ECE/CSE relationship. They don't tell us on whose terms or by what process alignment or continuity has taken place. Is it the continuity of schoolification or of the pedagogical meeting place? Is it alignment as in bringing someone or something into line (with a dominant other) or as in two parties together drawing a new line?

I also acknowledge that there may be more than three types of relationship and that, in practice, at any given time and in any given place it is likely that we will discern elements of two or more types. Having acknowledged that, most contributors confirm the trend to Relationship I, readying the child for school with an attendant schoolification of ECE, and all share a deep apprehension about the consequences. An important point made here by Michel Vandenbroeck and his colleagues concerns the adverse effects of this shift on the educational system's capacity to respond to and welcome diversity: 'Since the function of ECE is to make children "school ready", CSE can start with the average child, the one that fits in the system. We can witness how CSE today is less well equipped to deal with diversity'.

Margaret Carr wonders if one reason for the more equal relationship apparent in New Zealand is 'because of our heritage as a nomadic people: the hybrid philosophy of Māori and, later, non-Māori migrants who have had to adapt to an environment different from home, seeking new possibilities and translating the known in a new context.' Diversity, according to her account, has had more constructive consequences in New Zealand than the more recent diversity in Flanders discussed by Michel Vandenbroeck.

Relationship II – a strong and equal partnership – seems to me to be a useful move away from Relationship I, with its recognition of the potential strengths of both ECE and CSE and the consequent potential for exchange and learning. Peder Haug illustrates an attempt to make this relationship work in Norway, when for a period the *barnehage* pedagogy was brought into the school, along with 6-year-old Norwegian children. In Italy, Ciari 'elaborated a new approach to CSE drawing on the inspiring experiences carried out in municipal ECE institutions.' While Michel Vandenbroeck and his colleagues describe another instance, in the relationship between 'child-care' and 'early education' services in Ghent.

> The experience of child care services for the youngest children has much to offer to education. This is what actually happens in some municipal *kleuterscholen* in the city of Ghent. *Kleuterschool* teachers sit together with child care professionals, and ask the latter to support them in working with parents from diverse origins, in order to discover new ways of experiential learning, in which the experiences of *all* children are taken into account.

This is not the only reference to the issue of the relationship between 'childcare' and 'early education' services, different sectors within a split ECE, which in most countries continues to be just as contestable as the relationship between ECE and CSE, and indeed has a bearing on that relationship. For as John Bennett notes, a 'schoolified early education sector is often matched by a childcare sector with limited educational goals and focused mainly on keeping children safe and well while parents work'. In such cases, the gravitational pull of CSE can readily pull early education for children over 3 away from 'child care' for under 3s, rendering the split in ECE wider and deeper.

There are then instances of attempting Relationship II, the strong and equal partnership. But the contributors raise questions about implementation and outcome. The examples given seem to show a one-way process rather than a mutual exchange. The partners are not equals, at least in terms of education, pay and status; and attempts at partnership seem limited either to a particular place, like the city of Ghent, or a short period of time, some 20 years in the case of Norway recounted by Peder Haug. Peder goes further, to question the very idea behind this type of relationship, that 'it is possible to "take" the best from different traditions and just mix them together...just like baking a cake. You take a bit of this and that and stir it together, and a new type of "education" grows out of it.' This idea, it seems to him, is fundamentally naive, ignoring the power of different educational traditions and the forces that have shaped them.

So I find myself still drawn, as in my introductory essay, to Relationship III: a relationship of new shared understandings and practices, constructed through a pedagogical meeting place – or meeting places, since it is apparent that we are speaking of a type of relationship that can and should take place in many and diverse forums. This is a relationship, too, that need not apply exclusively to ECE and CSE but to all sectors in the whole education system.

However my interview with Gunilla Dahlberg, the co-author of this relational concept, has led me to a better understanding of the significance of a point to which my introductory essay perhaps only pays lip service. That while this relationship needs to work at understanding differences between pre-school and school, it also needs to build a platform of 'a potentially common heritage of ideas', forming a basis for the development of the meeting place – in the Swedish case, these ideas prove to be 'a certain Enlightenment view of *bildung*, the progressive tradition in education and dialogue'. This in turn highlights the importance of a historical perspective, to search for concepts, projects and people from the past with which both ECE and CSE can identify.

The attraction of this relationship is enhanced by Gunilla Dahlberg's comment that 'meeting place' might perhaps be better translated as 'encounter', with the ethical implications of that term arising from Emmanuel Levinas's ethics of an encounter: 'The idea at the heart of Levinas's thinking – that the ethics of an encounter is about respecting the alterity of the Other, not grasping the Other and making the Other into the Same – was at the back of my mind when proposing a vision of an encounter in between pre-school and school'. So I see the 'vision of a meeting place' as being a vision of a meeting place inscribed with an ethics of an encounter, an ethics that supplies resistance to the grasping of 'schoolification' or any other attempt to make the Other into the Same.

But, having reflected on the previous chapters, I also find it important to be clearer than I was in the introductory essay about the relationship between a 'strong and equal partnership' and a 'meeting place'. It is, perhaps, too tempting to seek resolution of difference by saying they are two distinct yet complementary types of ECE/CSE relationship, so obviating the need to choose. I am clearer now that there is a clear distinction between them, calling for a choice to be made.

The 'strong and equal partnership', as discussed in the *Starting Strong* reports and in my introductory essay, is about a dialogue between the two sectors for mutual gain as each draws on the others' strengths. This, as noted above, seems hard to achieve, with a tendency for one sector to predominate in the dialogue and exchange; nevertheless, it is conceivable. The 'meeting place' relationship is, however, more transformational. As Gunilla Dahlberg puts the matter: 'Others said you should take and mix the best of both pre-school and school. But we said you should start out from analyses of dominant discourses and common traditions, deconstruct them – and then construct something totally new'.

Of course, it could be argued that this process of shared de-construction and construction would lead to a relationship between ECE and CSE that might be described as 'strong' and 'equal'. But that would be to give the words 'strong and equal' a different meaning from their use in the *Starting Strong* concept of 'strong and equal partnership' and risk blurring two very different processes: exchanging best practice and co-constructing new understandings and practices, albeit partly through an exploration of past traditions and current strengths.

Either form of ECE/CSE relationship seems to me to be a valid alternative to the stultifying discourse of 'school readiness', the choice a proper subject for a democratic politics of education. If I am drawn to one rather than the other, it is because the notion of the meeting place and the concepts within it are, as John Bennett puts it, 'very rich . . . the practice of a meeting place between early childhood and the compulsory school could revolutionise pedagogical thinking in both institutions'. This is undoubtedly the most transformative relationship, calling for both ECE and CSE to re-think and re-form. But it is also the one requiring most work if it is to be fully realised. For rich as it may be, John goes on to note that

> the vision of the meeting place is insufficiently operationalised, that is, it does not yet indicate where the meeting place or discussion might take place or in what form. At first view, it would seem plausible that research journals, training colleges and university research departments are obvious spaces for dialogue. But each location has its own difficulties and obstacles to surmount.

I am under no illusions about the difficulty of embarking on and sustaining such a relationship. As Peder Haug reminds us, the 'societal context is very important'; the current context, dominated as it is by instrumentality, economism, competition and simplified notions of education, favours a narrow concept of education and a narrow, Type I relationship. Change will call for a long struggle across many critical issues, a struggle that contests the present societal context and works, alongside other movements, to create a different context that will demand (recalling the work of Bruno Ciari, but also many other great educators) an education concerned with democracy, justice, equality, care and inclusion as lived values and practices. We should also remember that contexts are not universal, that resistances are possible to dominant discourses and that opportunities for change may occur locally, creating opportunities for local experimentation, such as those that occurred in Northern Italy in the 1960s and 1970s, described by Arianna Lazzari and Lucia Balduzzi.

Transformative change should not just be left to happen. The history of radical educational reform is littered with innovative and inspiring projects that faltered, fizzled and folded after just a few years, overly dependent on the energy of a few pioneers, before weariness, frustration or bad health took their toll. If we are serious about transformative change, then it seems to me that we have to give serious attention to the conditions that can help to initiate such change and then help to sustain it over many years.

The contributors to this volume suggest some of the conditions that may need taking into consideration. Thus Sharon Lynn Kagan, writing from a country (the United States) with a weak, unstable and fragmented system of ECE, emphasises the need to address structures and policies:

Efforts must concern themselves not only with differences in pedagogy and philosophy and with differences in the social construction of childhood; such efforts must also reach to the core of conventional ECE and its attendant structures. Such remarkable change is going to take more than developing a series of discussions or a common meeting place, although these themselves are critically important and signal a necessary shift in the dominant discourse. Complementing such efforts, there must be a set of actionable strategies and policies that are designed expressly to promote continuity within the ECE field and between the field and CSE. In short, to overcome contemporary schoolification, the inherent inequalities between ECE and CSE, and the structural reinforcements that have perpetuated distance between the two, demands nothing short of a well-conceived, well-articulated, well-funded frontal attack on convention. Discourse is a necessary, but insufficient condition to address the magnitude of the task at hand.

John Bennett, too, highlights the need for major structural change, arguing the case for a strong integrated ECE sector: 'in most OECD countries, early childhood systems were split between childcare and early education. This split still remains a formidable barrier to forging a strong identity for the early childhood sector'. A strong identity, he argues, is a necessary condition for the voice of ECE to be audible, without which there can be none of the dialogue that a 'meeting place' calls for. Gunilla Dahlberg also highlights the importance of ECE gaining a strong self-identity as well as societal legitimation, both essential for entering a relationship with CSE that is on equal not hierarchical terms – a precondition for a pedagogical meeting place.

Margaret Carr from the perspective of New Zealand, an exceptional example of an English-speaking country that has radically reformed its ECE addressing some of the structural issues highlighted by Sharon and John (Meade and Podmore, 2010), describes a meeting place as a 'place for dialogue: dialogue that constructs, reconfigures and transforms'. In the evolution of New Zealand's curricula for ECE and CSE, Margaret provides an instance of such dialogue contributing towards an alignment of the former's 'learning dispositions' and the latter's 'key competencies'. She further proposes three practices that 'can play key roles in developing, sustaining and deepening this dialogue ... teachers as researchers, a permeable curriculum on either side of the border, and documentation.' Margaret gives striking examples of such supportive practices from her own country, as do Arianna Lazzari and Lucia Balduzzi for Italy. These include local experimentation and research supported actively by progressive municipalities (of which Reggio Emilia is the best known but far from the only one); *istituti comprensivi* or school districts including a range or network of schools, which became sites for experimentation or laboratories for innovation under the management of a school director; discussing documentation within collegial meetings involving both ECE and CSE teachers; and local systems of 'pedagogical co-ordination', through which *pedagogisti* 'have played a crucial role in providing shared professional development opportunities for educators and teachers and in sustaining reciprocal professional exchanges through pedagogical guidance'.

Gunilla Dahlberg supplies further examples from Sweden of groups and projects that have provided meeting places where researchers, teacher educators and pre-school teachers have come together – though not, to date, many representatives from the compulsory school. Looking ahead, she sees a great potential in experimentation and pedagogical documentation.

John Bennett, with some reservations around current practice, suggests other potential meeting places, including research journals and higher education institutions. He raises, like others, the issue of the education of workers in ECE and CSE envisaging

> the education of both ECE and CSE teachers organised in common on certain general education topics, for example, the philosophy and history of education. The habit of CSE and ECE talking together, without hierarchy, should be formed as early as possible, complemented by a recognition of equal status through parity of pay and working conditions.

Examples of such overlapping education already exist, for example in Italy. Sweden moved recently to an integrated education for ECE and CSE teachers, but has now reverted to separate courses. Gunilla Dahlberg, while favouring integration in principle, is pleased to see the return of a separate and specific education for pre-school teachers, emphasising that an integrated education needs certain important pre-conditions if ECE is not to get lost in the process:

> the distinct features of pre-school teaching were getting lost in the integrated programmes. I think an integrated approach to teacher education is good in principle – but that before this can happen you have to legitimise pre-school education, which has to build a strong identity. At present compulsory school has the power and, therefore, the legitimisation, more so than early childhood education.

The education of educators must surely be part of a future meeting place between ECE and CSE – but there are clearly 'chicken and egg' issues to be thought through.

We have here a rich variety of examples of how meeting places might be initiated and sustained, enabling their work to go wider and deeper. Doubtless, too, there are many other possibilities, in theory or already in practice. What will form the supportive frameworks for transformative change will depend on local circumstances, the exchange of documented experience and the degree of support for change (for example, whether from all or just some levels of government): there is no universal blueprint. But it can be done, if the will is there and if equal importance is given to policy formulation and policy realisation.

On this last point, Peder Haug's comment on ECE/CSE relations in Norway is salutary:

> One of the most striking impressions that remains after this presentation of recent history is the weak implementation. It seems that little power has been handed over to local authorities and *barnehager* to make it possible to realize political intentions. The impression is that institutional reforms like these are supposed to happen by themselves, almost without any form of assistance: reform by words instead of reform by support and control.

In recent years, huge amounts of money and other resources have been poured into implementing neo-liberal and neo-conservative reforms in education, including the development of markets, the promotion of competitive private providers and detailed governing of children and educators through a range of human technologies. This has been a catastrophe, stripping education of its potential for creativity and joy, emancipation and future building; but a reminder, too, of the enormous power of the neo-liberal project and the means of enforcement at its disposal (see Ball, 2012, for a detailed analysis). If even a fraction of this treasure had been available to alternative educational projects – imbued with democratic values – then much could have been achieved.

While preparing this book, the relationship between ECE and CSE has been high on the policy agenda in my own country, England. Sadly, as indicated in my introductory essay, the dominating policy discourse has been about readiness for school or, slightly nuanced, ensuring children are 'ready and able to learn at school'. Battle lines have been drawn, with opposition coalescing into a campaign, Action for Early Childhood, which highlights 'the "schoolification" of early childhood with its over-assessment and excessive monitoring' (letter in the *Daily Telegraph*, 7 February 2012). Caught in the middle, the expert called in by the English government to review its early years curriculum recognises both the concerns that exist on this score and the competing concerns voiced about children insufficiently prepared for school – and seeks shelter from the conflict in another concept:

> I know that some people interpret the term 'school readiness' as implying that children can be pressured to learn to read and write at

inappropriately young ages. Others have a wider concern about leaving children free to enjoy their early years without pressure, and argue that schools should be ready for children, not the other way round. Balanced against this, some feel that we do children no favours if we fail to prepare them for the realities of the school environment, where skills such as literacy are at a premium.

To avoid the more ambiguous and emotive connotations of 'school readiness', I have considered it from the perspective of its opposite: school *un*readiness... Most children begin reception class [the first year of primary school] at age 4, and for most parents and carers this is when school life begins. If children are not ready for this transition or the move to Year 1 because, for example, they are not yet toilet trained, able to listen or get on with other children, then their experiences of school could present difficulties which will obstruct their own learning as well as other children's.

(Tickell, 2011, para 3.2, 3.3)

Ignore, if possible, the taken-for-grantedness of English children moving from ECE to CSE at the age of 4 years. Focus instead on the dead-end that is the '(un)readiness for school' discourse, leading only to a contest between the call for school readiness and the fear of schoolification. Consider what other discourses could have opened up, the new thinking that might have flowed from democratic deliberation on the diversity of relationships. Consider, too, how discussion of alternatives might have led to different questions; for example, how to welcome and sustain what Malaguzzi termed the 'rich' child, born with a hundred languages and initiating 'the search [for the meaning of life] right from the beginning of their lives' (Rinaldi, 2006, p. 64). In short, a child ready and able to learn from birth. Or, to take another example, how to rethink and reclaim the concept of the school, to still the fears of 'schoolification' and to create instead a vital public institution founded on principles of democracy and dialogue, creativity and care, respect for otherness and diversity. If we had such schools available from the earliest years through to 16 and beyond, then the notion of 'readiness', whether of child or school, would cease to have meaning since early childhood centres would comfortably wear the label of school without current connotations of narrowness and normalisation.

So the central question, it seems to me, comes down to this. In an age when most children, at least in rich countries, have several years in ECE before CSE, can the relationship between these two sectors – or indeed between sectors within CSE and between CSE and subsequent education sectors – be satisfactorily resolved without the construction of new shared understandings and practices through realising the vision of a meeting place?

References

Ainsworth, M. (1989) 'Attachment beyond infancy', *American Psychologist*, 44, 709–16.

Allen, G. (2011) *Early Intervention: The Next Steps* (http://www.dwp.gov.uk/docs/early-intervention-next-steps.pdf, accessed 15 March 2012).

Assessorato alle politiche sociali della Regione Emilia-Romagna (2004) *Identità in dialogo: scambi pedagogici*. Bologna: Regione Emilia Romagna, Servizio Politiche Familiari, Infanzia e Adolescenza.

Bakhtin, M. (1984) *Rabelais and his World*. Bloomington, IN: Indiana University Press.

Balduzzi, L. (ed.) (2006) *Nella rete dei servizi per l'infanzia: tra nidi e nuove tipologie*. Bologna: CLUEB.

Balduzzi, L. (2011a) 'Scuola dell'infanzia: femminile plurale', in P. Sorzio (ed.), *Apprendimento e istituzioni educative*. Roma: Carocci.

Balduzzi, L. (2011b) 'Promoting professional development in Early Childhood Education and Care (ECEC) field: the role of welcoming newcomers teachers', *Procedia: Social & Behavioral Sciences*, 15, 843–9.

Balke, E. (1979) Utvikling av barnehagen i Norge, in G. Simmons-Christenson (ed.), *Førskolepedagogikken historie. Norsk utgave ved Eva Balke* (pp. 130–41) Oslo: J.W. Cappelens Forlag a.s.

Balke, E. (1980) *101 førskolelærere om barnehagen: Barnehagens mål og innhold*. Oslo: Barnevernsakademiet.

Balke, E., Berg, B. and Fagerli, O. (1979) *Barnehage – heim – lokalsamfunn (Nærmiljø barnehage prosjektet – Rapport nr. 10)*. Oslo: Forbruker- og dministrasjonsdepartementet.

Ball, S. (2012) *Global Education Inc.: New Policy Networks and the Neo-liberal Imaginary*. London: Routledge.

Bandura, A. (1965) 'Influence of models' reinforcement contingencies on the acquisition of imitative responses', *Journal of Personality and Social Psychology*, 1, 589–95.

Barbagli, M. and Dei, M. (1969) *Le vestali della classe media: ricerca sociologica sugli insegnanti*. Bologna: Il Mulino.

Barbieri, N. (2011) 'Storia della scuola dell'infanzia e della scuola primaria',' in P. Sorzio (ed.) *Apprendimento e istituzioni educative: storia, contesti, soggetti*. Rome: Carrocci.

Bartlett, C., Arnold, C., Shallwani, S. and Gowani, S. (2010) 'Transitions: perspectives from the majority world', in S.L. Kagan and K.Tarrant (eds), *Transitions for*

Young Children: Creating Connections across Systems. Baltimore, MD: Paul H. Brookes Publishing Co.

Bateson, G. (1972) *Steps to an Ecology of Mind.* San Francisco, CA: Chandler Publishing Co.

Becchi, E. (1979) *Tempo pieno e scuola elementare.* Milan: Franco Angeli.

Benedetti, S. (2009) 'I coordinamenti pedagogici nella regione Emilia Romagna: un investimento sulla professionalità. Dal coordinatore al coordinamento pedagogico attraverso la progressiva costruzione di un'identità plurima in reti di relazioni', *Infanzia,* 1(3), 182–5.

Bénisti, J.A. (2005) *Rapport de la commission prévention du groupe d'étude parlementaire sur la sécurité intérieure.* Paris: Assemblée Nationale.

Bereiter, C. (1995) 'A dispositional view of transfer', in A. Mckeough, J. Lupart and A. Marini (eds) *Teaching for Transfer: Fostering Generalisations in Learning.* Hillsdale, NJ: Lawrence Erlbaum.

Bernard van Leer Foundation (2009) *Successful Transitions: The Continuum from Home to School* (http://www.bernardvanleer.org/partners/transitions, accessed 12 January 2012).

Biesta, G. (2007) 'Why "what works" won't work: evidence-based practice and the democratic deficit in educational research', *Educational Theory,* 57(1), 1–22.

Bodrova E. (2008) 'Make-believe play vs. academic skills: a Vygotskian approach to today's dilemma of early childhood education', *European Early Childhood Education Research Journal,* 16(3), 357–69.

Bond, J.T. (1982) *Project Developmental Continuity Evaluation: Final Report. Outcomes of PDC Intervention* (Vol. 1). Ypsilanti, MI: High/Scope Educational Research Foundation.

Bondioli, A. (1987) 'Verso un servizio per la fascia 0–6: un'esperienza di continuità', in A. Bondioli and S. Mantovani, S. (eds) *Manuale critico dell'asilo nido.* Milano: Franco Angeli.

Bourdieu, P. (1990) *The Logic of Practice.* Cambridge: Polity.

Bourdieu, P. and Passeron, J.C. (1970) *Le reproduction: eléments pour une théorie du système d'enseignement.* Paris: Editions de Minuit.

Bowlby, J. (1969/1982) *Attachment and Loss, Vol.1: Attachment.* New York, NY: Basic Books.

Braidotti, R. (1994) *Nomadic Subjects.* New York: Colombia University Press.

Bransford J.D. and Schwartz, D.L. (1999) 'Rethinking transfer: a simple proposal with multiple implications'. *Review of Research in Education,* 24, 61–100.

Brewerton, M. (2004) *Reframing the Essential Skills: Implications of the OECD Defining and Selecting Key Competencies Project* (http://www.tki.org.nz/r/nzcurriculum/whats_happening_e.php, accessed 20 February 2012).

Bronfenbrenner, U. (1974) *Wie wirksam ist kompensatorische Erziehung?* Stuttgart: Ernst Klett Verlag.

Bronfenbrenner, U. (1979) *The Ecology of Human Development.* Cambridge, MA: Harvard University Press.

Brooker, L. (2002) *Starting School: Young Children Learning Cultures.* Buckingham: Open University Press.

Brown, C.P. (2010) 'Balancing the readiness equation in early childhood education reform', *Journal of Early Childhood Research,* 8(2), 133–160

Brown, M.E. and Precious G.N. (1968) *The Integrated Day in the Primary School.*

London: Ward Lock Educational.

Bruner, J.S. (1981) 'Intention in the structure of action and interaction', *Advances in Infancy Research*, 1, 41–56

Calidoni, P. and Calidoni, M. (1995) *Continuità educativa: scuola materna, elementare, media e scuole comprensive*. Brescia: La Scuola.

Camaioni, L. (1980) *La prima infanzia*. Bologna: Il Mulino.

Cambridge Primary Review (2009) *Introducing the Cambridge Primary Review* (http://www.primaryreview.org.uk/Downloads/Finalreport/CPR-booklet_lowres.pdf, accessed 15 March 2012).

Cameron, C. and Moss, P. (eds) (2011) *Social Pedagogy and Working with Children and Young People*. London: Jessica Kingsley Publishing.

Canevaro, A., Balzaretti, C. and Rigon, G. (1996) *Pedagogia speciale dell'integrazione. Handicap: conoscere e accompagnare*. Florence: La Nuova Italia.

Cantillon, B. (2010) *Crisis and the Welfare State: The Need for a New Distributional Agenda*. Oxford: University of Oxford Press.

Carr, M. (2001) 'A sociocultural approach to learning orientation in an early childhood setting', *Qualitative Studies in Education*, 14(4), 525–42.

Carr, M. (2006) 'Learning dispositions and key competencies: a new curriculum across the sectors?', *SET*, 2, 23–27

Carr, M. (2011) 'Young children reflecting on their learning: teachers' conversation strategies', *Early Years*, DOI: 10.1080/09575146.2011.613805.

Carr, M. and Peters, S. (eds) (2005) *Te Whāriki and Links to the New Zealand Curriculum: Research Projects. Final report to the Ministry of Education*. Hamilton: University of Waikato.

Carr, M. and Lee, W. (2012) *Learning Stories: Constructing Learner Identities in the Early Years*. London: Sage.

Carr, M., Clarkin-Phillips, J., Beer, A., Thomas, R. and Waitai, M. (2012) 'Young children developing meaning making practices in a museum: the role of boundary objects', *Museum management and Curatorship*, 12(1), 53–66.

Carr, M., Smith, A.B., Duncan, J., Jones, C., Lee, W. and Marshall, K. (2010) *Learning in the Making: Disposition and Design in the Early Years*. Rotterdam: Sense.

Carr, M,. Peters, S., Davis, K., Bartlett, C., Bashford, N., Berry, P., Greenslade, S., Molloy, S., O'Connor, N., Simpson, M., Smith, Y., Williams, T. and Wilson-Tukaki, A. (2008) *Key Learning Competencies across Place and Time. Kimihia te ara tōtika, hei oranga mō to aō*. Teaching Learning Research Initiative Final Report (http://www.tlri.org.nz/key-learning-competencies-across-place-and-time/, accessed 20 February 2012).

Catarsi, E. (1992) 'Bruno Ciari e la continuità educativa', in E. Catarsi (ed.) *Bruno Ciari e la scuola di base degli anni novanta*. Firenze: La Nuova Italia.

Catarsi, E. (2004) 'Loris Malaguzzi and the municipal school revolution', *Children in Europe*, 6, 8–9.

Catarsi, E. (2011) 'Educazione alla lettura e continuità educativa: il ruolo delle famiglie e dei servizi per l'infanzia', in E. Catarsi (ed.) *Educazione alla lettura e continuità educativa*. Bergamo: Edizioni Junior.

Cerini, G. (ed.) (2000) *La scuola verticale. Istituti comprensivi e riordino dei cicli*. Tecnodid, Napoli.

Cerini, G. (2011) '*Armonizzazione*', in G. Cerini and M. Spinosi (eds) *Voci della scuola*. Naples: Tecnodid.

Children in Europe, Issue 6 (2004) *Celebrating 40 years of Reggio Emilia: The Pedagogical Thought and Practice Underlying World Renowned Early Years Services in Italy.* Edinburgh: Children in Scotland.

Ciari, B. (1972) *La grande disadattata.* Rome: Editori Riuniti.

Clandinin, D.J. and Rosiek, J. (2007) 'Mapping a landscape of narrative inquiry: borderland spaces and tensions', in D.J. Clandinin (ed.) *Handbook of Narrative Inquiry: Mapping a Methodology.* London: Sage.

Claxton, G. (2002) *Building Learning Power: Helping Young People Become Better Learners.* Bristol: TLO Limited.

Claxton, G., Chambers, M., Powell, G. and Lucas, B. (2011) *The Learning Powered School: Pioneering 21st century Education.* Bristol: TLO Limited.

Codignola, E. (1975) *La Scuola-Città Pestalozzi.* Firenze: La nuova Italia.

Coleman, J.S. (1966) *Equality of Educational Opportunity.* Washington: Government Printing Office.

Cowie, B., Hipkins, R., Boyd, S., Bull, A., Keown, P. *et al.* (2009) *Curriculum Implementation Exploratory Studies: Final Report.* Wellington: New Zealand Ministry of Education.

Cunha, F., Heckman, J.J., Lochner, L. and Masterov, D. (2005) 'Interpreting the evidence on life cycle skill formation'. *British Educational Research Journal,* 30(5), 713–30.

CORE (forthcoming) *Studio sulla continuità nelle scuole comunali dell'infanzia e nelle scuole primarie di Reggio Emilia* (http://www.reggiochildren.it/attivita/ricerca/core/, accessed 14 January 2012).

Dahlberg, G. (2000) 'From the people's home – *Folkhemmet* – to the enterprise: reflections on the constitution and reconstitution of the field of early childhood pedagogy in Sweden', in T. Popkewitz (ed.) *Educational Knowledge: Changing Relationships between the State, Civil Society, and the Educational Community.* Albany, NY: State University of New York Press.

Dahlberg, G. (2003) 'Det autonoma barnet och det entreprenöra självet. En ny form av styrningsstrategi?' ('The autonomous child and the entrepreneural self – a new strategy of governing?'], in E. Forsberg (ed.) *Skolan och tusenårsskiftet. En vänbok till Ulf P. Lundgren* (The school and the millennium: a festschrift for Ulf P. Lundgren). Stockholm: HLS Förlag.

Dahlberg, G. (2003) 'Pedagogy as a locus of an ethics of an encounter', in M. Bloch, K. Holmlund, I. Moqvist and T. Popkewitz (eds) *Governing Children, Families and Education: Restructuring the Welfare State.* New York, NY: Palgrave.

Dahlberg, G. and Åsén, G. (1994) 'Evaluation and regulation: a question of empowerment', in P. Moss and A. Pence (eds) *Valuing Quality on Early Childhood Services.* London: Paul Chapman Publishing.

Dahlberg, G. and Lenz-Taguchi, H. (1994) *Förskola och skola – om två skilda traditioner och om visionen om en mötesplats* (Preschool and school – two different traditions and the vision of a meeting place). Stockholm: HLS Förlag.

Dahlberg, G. and Bloch, M. (2006) 'Is the power to see and visualize always the power to control?', in T. Popkewitz (ed.) *'The Future is not What it Appears to Be': Pedagogy, Genealogy and Political Epistemology: In Honour and in Memory of Kenneth Hultqvist.* Stockholm: HLS Förlag.

Dahlberg, G. and Moss, P. (2007) 'Au-delà de la qualité, vers l'éthique et la politique en matière d'éducation préscolaire', in G. Brougère and M. Vandenbroeck (eds),

Repenser l'éducation des jeunes enfants. Bruxelles: Peter Lang.

Dahlberg, G., Lundgren, U.P. and Åsén, G. (1991) *Att utvärdera barnomsorg. Om decentaliserig, målstyrning och utvärdering av barnomsrogen och dess pedagogiska verksamhet* (To evaluate childcare: on decentralisation, goal governing and evaluation of the childcare system and its pedagogical activities). Stockholm. HLS Förlag.

Dahlberg, G., Moss, P. and Pence, A. (2007) *Beyond Quality in Early Childhood Education and Care,* 2nd edn. London: Routledge.

Darwin, C. (1877) 'A biographical sketch of an infant', *Mind,* 2, 285–94.

Deleuze, G. (1985) *Foucault.* Paris: Edition de Minuit.

Deleuze, G. and Parnet, C. (1987) *Dialogues.* London: Athlone Press.

Deleuze, G. and Guattari, F. (1999) *A Thousand Plateaus: Capitalism and Schizophrenia.* London: Athlone Press.

Depaepe, M. and Simon, F. (2005) 'De historiografie van het Belgische kleuteronderwijs nader bekeken', in M. Depaepe, F. Simon and A. Van Gorp (eds) *Paradoxen van pedagogisering: Handboek pedagogische historiografie.* Leuven: Acco.

Det kongelige kirke-, utdannings og forskningsdepartement (1996) *Læreplanverket for den 10-årige grunnskolen.* Oslo: Kirke-, utdannings- og forskningsdepartementet.

Det kongelige utdannings- og kunnskapsdepartement (2004) *St.meld. nr. 30 (2003–2004), Kultur for læring.* Oslo: Forfattaren.

Dewey, J. (1913) *The Child and the Curriculum.* Glasgow: Blackie and Son.

Dewey, J. (1939) *Creative Democracy – The Task Before Us* (http://www.faculty.fairfield.edu/faculty/hodgson/Courses/progress/Dewey.pdf, accessed 20 February 2012).

De Bartolomeis, F. (1972) *Scuola a tempo pieno.* Milan: Feltrinelli.

Donzelot, G. (1977) *La police des familles.* Paris: Les Editions de Minuit.

Di Maggio, P. J. and Powell, W.W. (1989) 'Introduction', in W.W. Powell and P. J. Di Maggio (eds) *The New Institutionalism in Organisational Analysis.* Chicago, IL: The University of Chicago Press.

Durkheim, E. (1977/1938) *The Evolution of Educational Thought.* London: Routledge and Kegan Paul.

Eisner, E.W. (2002) *The Arts and the Creation of Mind.* New Haven, CT: Yale University Press.

Eisner, E.W. (2005) *Reimagining Schools: The Selected Works of Elliot W. Eisner.* London: Routledge.

Elkind, D. (2007) *The Power of Play: Learning What Comes Naturally.* Cambridge, MA: Da Capo Press.

English Department for Education (2010a) *Business Plan 2011–2015* (http://media.education.gov.uk/assets/files/pdf/d/department%20for%20education%20business%20plan.pdf, accessed 15 March 2012).

English Department for Education (2010b) *Review of Early Years Foundation Stage* (http://www.education.gov.uk/inthenews/inthenews/a0061485/review-of-early-years-foundation-stage, accessed 15 March 2012).

English Department for Education (2012) *Statutory Framework for the Early Years Foundation Stage* (http://media.education.gov.uk/assets/files/pdf/e/eyfs%20statutory%20framework%20march%202012.pdf, accessed 10 April 2012).

Erikson, E.H. (1963) *Childhood and Society, 2nd edn)*. New York, NY: Norton.

Erikson, E.H. (1980) *Identity and The Life Cycle*, 2nd edn. New York, NY: Norton.

European Commission (2006) *Efficiency and Equity in European Education and Training Systems* (http://ec.europa.eu/education/policies/2010/doc/comm481_en.pdf, accessed 15 March 2012).

European Commission (2010) *Europe 2020: A Strategy for Smart, Sustainable and Inclusive Growth*. Brussels: European Commission.

European Commission (2011) *Communication on ECEC: Providing all Our Children with the Best Start for the World of Tomorrow*. Brussels: European Commission.

Featherstone, B. (2006) 'Rethinking family support in the current policy context', *British Journal of Social Work*, 36, 5–19.

Fensham, P. (2008) *Science Education Policy-making: Eleven Emerging Issues*. Paris: UNESCO.

Fielding, M. and Moss, P. (2011) *Radical Education and the Common School: A Democratic Alternative*. London: Routledge.

Finansdepartementet (1974) *St.meld. nr. 25 (1973–74) Petroleumsvirksomhetens plass i det norske samfunn*. Oslo: Finansdepartementet.

Foucault, M. (1975*) Surveiller et punir: naissance de la prison*. Paris: Gallimard

Foucault, M. (1977*) Discipline and Punish. The Birth of a Prison*. Hammondsworth, Middlesex: Penguin.

Foucault, M. (1988) *Politics, Philosophy, Culture: Interviews and Other Writings 1977–1984*. London: Routledge.

Foundation for Child Development (2009) *Pre-K–3rd: A New Beginning for American Education* (http://www.fc-dus.org/initiatives/initiatives_show.htm?doc_id=447080, accessed 12 January 2012).

Frabboni, F., Guerra, L. and Scurati, C. (1999) *Pedagogia: Realtà e prospettive dell'educazione*. Milano: Mondadori.

Freire, P. (1970) *Pedagogy of the Oppressed*. New York, NY: Herder and Herder.

Froebel, F. (1974) *The Education of Man,* revised edn. Clifton, NJ: Augustus M. Kelley. (Original work published 1826).

Foucault, M. (1988) 'Practicing criticism', in L. Kritzman (ed.) *Politics, Philosophy, Culture: Interviews and Other Writings 1977–1984*. New York, NY: Routledge.

Gardner, H. (1983) *Frames of Mind: The Theory of Multiple Intelligence*. New York, NY: Basic Books.

Genovesi, G. (1992) 'Bruno Ciari e la scuola di base degli anni sessanta', in E. Catarsi (ed.) *Bruno Ciari e la scuola di base degli anni novanta*. Firenze: La Nuova Italia.

George, S. (2010) 'Wasted childhoods? Beyond the pathologisation of poor children and their families', paper presented at the The Doors of Perception: Viewing Anthropology through the Eyes of Children conference, Department of Social and Cultural Anthropology, Vrije Universiteit, Amsterdam, 30 September–1 October 2010.

Giddens, A. (2005) *The New Egalitarianism*. London: Policy Network.

Giudici, C., Rinaldi, C. and Krechevsky, M. (eds) (2001) *Making Learning Visible: Children as Individual and Group Learners*. Cambridge, MA and Reggio Emilia: Project Zero and Reggio Children.

Gobeyn, H. and De Stercke, N. (2010) *Mag mijn kind naar het eerste leerjaar? Een onderzoek over kleuterparticipatie en ondergesneeuwde betekenissen van ouders.*

Onuitgegeven meesterproef. Ghent: Vakgroep Sociale Agogiek – UGent.

Green, J.A. (1969) *The Educational Ideas of Pestalozzi.* New York, NY: Greenwood Press.

Greene, M. (1995) *Releasing the Imagination: Essays on Education, the Arts and Social Change.* San Francisco, CA: Jossey-Bass.

Göthson, H. (1989) *Torget. Seminarier och lednings-och utvecklingsarbete i barnomsorg. Stockholm: Socialstyrelsen* (The Agora. Seminars and management and development work in early childhood education). Stockholm: Socialstryelsen.

Halvars Franzén, B. (2010) 'Barn och etik: möten och möjlighetsvillkor i två förskoleklassers vardag' (Children and ethics: encounters and conditions of possibilities in the everyday life of two pre-school classes). Doctoral thesis. Stockholm Institute of Education.

Hartley, C., Rogers, P., Smith, J., Peters, S. and Carr, M. (2012) *Across the Border: A Community Negotiates the Transition from Early Childhood to Primary School.* Wellington: NZCER Press.

Hattie, J. (2009) *Visible Learning: A Synthesis of over 800 Meta-analyses Relating to Achievement.* London: Routledge.

Haug, P. (1992) *Educational Reform by Experiment.* Stockholm: HLS Förlag.

Haug, P. (1994) *Formulering og realisering av utdanningspolitikk: om det politiske arbeidet med å innføre skulefritidsordningar og skule for 6-åringar.* Volda: Møreforsking Volda.

Haug, P. (2000) 'When to start school? The case of Norway', *Nordisk pedagogik,* 20(1), 30–45.

Haug, P. (2003) 'The Research Council of Norway Evaluating Reform 97', in P. Haug and T. Schwandt (eds), *Evaluating Educational Reforms. Scandinavian Perspectives.* Greenwich, CT: Information Age Publishing.

Haug, P. and Steinnes, G.S. (2011) 'Educated kindergarten teachers, a prerequisite of quality in Norwegian kindergarten?', paper presented at the Nordic Early Childhood Education and Care – Effects and Challenges conference, Oslo, 18 – 20 May 2011.

Head Start Bureau, Administration on Children, Youth, and Families (1996) *Head Start Children's Entry into Public Schools: An Interim Report on the National Evaluation of the Head Start/Public Schools Early Childhood Transitions Demonstration.* Washington, DC: Head Start Bureau.

Heckman, J.J. (2006) 'Skill formation and the economics of investing in disadvantaged children', *Science,* 312 (5782), 1900–1902.

Heckman, J. and Masterov, D. (2004) *The Productivity Argument for Investing in Young Children* (http://jenni.uchicago.edu/human-inequality/papers/ Heckman_final_all_wp_2007-03-22c_jsb.pdf, accessed 15 March 2012).

Hernes, G. and Knudsen, K. (1976) *Utdanning og ulikhet.* Oslo: NOU 1976: 46.

Hipkins, R. (2005) 'Thinking about the key competencies in the light of the intention to foster life-long learning', *SET,* 3, 36–9.

Hipkins, R. and Boyd, S. (2011) 'The recursive elaboration of key competencies as agents of curriculum change', *Curriculum Matters,* 7, 70–86.

Hipkins, R., Cowie, B., Boyd, S., Keown, P. and McGee, C. (2011) *Curriculum Implementation Exploratory Studies 2: Final Report.* Wellington: New Zealand Ministry of Education.

Hoëm, A. (2010) *Sosialisering-Kunnskap-Identitet.* Vallset: Oplandske Bokforlag.

Holland, D., Lachicotte, W., Skinner, D. and Cain, C. (1998) *Identity and Agency in Cultural Worlds*. Cambridge, MA: Harvard University Press.

Holmes, D. and Holmes, M.B. (1966) *Evaluation of Two Associated YM-YWCA Head Start Programmes of New York City: Final Report*. New York, NY: Associated YM–YWCAs of New York City.

Howes, C., Phillips, D.A., and Whitebook, M. (1992) 'Thresholds of quality: implications for the social development of children in centre-based child care', *Child Development*, 63, 449–60.

Hoyuelos, A. (2004) 'A pedagogy of transgression', *Children in Europe*, 4, 6–7.

Hubbell, R., Plantz, R., Condelli, L. and Barrett, B. (1987) *The Transition of Head Start Children into Public School: Final report* (Vol. 1). Alexandria, VA: CSR, Inc.

Hultman, K. (2011) 'Barn, linjaler och andra aktörer: Post-humanistiska perspektiv på subjektskapande och materialitet i förskola/skol'. (Children, rulers and other actors: post-human perspectives on the construction of subjectivity and materiality in prechool/school). Doctoral thesis. Stockholm University.

Ilg, F.L. and Ames, L. (1965) *School Readiness: Behaviour Tests Used at the Gesell Institute*. New York, NY: Harper & Row.

Innst. O. nr. 69 (1974–75) *Innstilling fra den forsterkede sosialkomité om lov om barnehager m.v.* Oslo: Stortinget.

Institut National de la Santé et de la Recherche Médicale (2005) *Troubles de conduite chez l'enfant et l'adolescent*. Paris: INSERM.

Jencks, C. (1972) *Inequality: A Reassessment of the Effect of Family and Schooling in America*. New York, NY: Basic Books Inc.

Jensen, J.J. (2011) 'Understandings of Danish pedagogical practice', in C. Cameron and P. Moss (eds) *Social Pedagogy and Working with Children and Young People*. London: Jessica Kingsley Publishing.

Johansson, I. and Moss, P. (2012) 'Re-forming the school: taking Swedish lessons', *Children and Society*, 26(1), 25–36.

Kaga, Y., Bennett, J. and Moss, P. (2010) *Caring and Learning Together: A Cross-national Study of Integration of Early Childhood Care and Education within Education* (http://unesdoc.unesco.org/images/0018/001878/187818e.pdf, accessed 15 March 2012).

Kagan, S.L. (1991) 'Moving from here to there: rethinking continuity and transitions in early care and education', in B. Spodek and O. Saracho (eds) *Yearbook in Early Childhood Education* (Vol. 2). New York, NY: Teachers College Press.

Kagan, S.L. (2007) 'Readiness – multiple meanings and perspectives', in M. Woodhead and P. Moss (eds) *Early Childhood and Primary Education: Transitions in the Lives of Young Children* (http://www.bernardvanleer.org/Early_Childhood_and_Primary_Education_Transitions_in_the_Lives_of_Young_Children, accessed 15 March 2012).

Kagan, S.L. and Neville, P.R. (1996) 'Combining endogenous and exogenous factors in the shift years: the transition to school', in A.J. Sameroff and M.M. Haith (eds) *The Five to Seven Year Shift: The Age of Reason and Responsibility*. Chicago, IL: University of Chicago Press.

Kagan, S.L. and Neuman, M.J. (1998) 'Lessons from three decades of transition research', *The Elementary School Journal*, 98(4), 365–79.

Kagan, S.L., Karnati, R., Friedlander, J. and Tarrant, K. (2010) *A Compendium of Transition Initiatives in the Early Years: A Resource Guide to Alignment and*

Continuity Efforts in the United States and Other Countries. New York, NY: National Centre for Children and Families.

Kagan, S.L. and Tarrant, K. (eds) (2010) *Transitions for Young Children: Creating Connections across Early Childhood Systems.* Baltimore, MD: Paul. H. Brookes Publishing Co.

Karlsson, M., Melander, H., Pérez Prieto, H. and Sahlström, F. (2006) *Förskoleklassen – ett tionde skolår?* (The pre-school class – a tenth school year?]) Lund: Studentlitteratur.

Katz, L.G. (2011) Opening Plenary: 20th National Institute for Early Childhood Professional Development, Providence, NAEYC

Kind en Gezin (2010) *Jaarverslag 2009 (Annual report 2009).* Brussels: Kind en Gezin.

Kjørholt, A.T. (1994) 'Institusjonalisering av barns liv – en barndom på avveier?', in P. Aasen and O.K. Haugaløkken (eds), *Bærekraftig pedagogikk.* Oslo: ad Notam Gyldendal.

Korpi, B.M. (2005) 'The foundation for lifelong learning', *Children in Europe,* 9, 10–11.

Korpi, B.M. (2007) *The Politics of Preschool: Intentions and Decisions Underlying the Emergence and Growth of the Swedish Preschool.* Stockholm: Stockholm: Regeringskansliet (Swedish Ministry of Education and Research)

Korsvold, T. (1998) *For alle barn! Barnehagens framvekst i velferdsstaen.* Oslo: Abstrakt forlag.

Kuhn, T. (1962) *The Structure of Scientific Revolutions.* Chicago, IL: University of Chicago Press.

Kunnskapsdepartementet (2006) *Rammeplan for barnehagens innhold og oppgaver.* Oslo: Akademika.

Kunnskapsdepartementet (2008a) *Fra eldst til yngst: Samarbeid og sammenheng mellom barnehage og skole.* Oslo: Kunnskapsdepartementet.

Kunnskapsdepartementet (2008b) *St.meld. nr. 31 (2007–2008), Kvalitet i skolen.* Oslo: Kunnskapsdepartementet.

Kunnskapsdepartementet (2009) *St.meld. nr. 41 (2008–2009), Kvalitet i barnehagen.* Oslo: Kunnskapsdepartementet.

Kunnskapsdepartementet (2011) *Meld. St. 18 (2010–2011) Læring og fellesskap.* Oslo: Kunnskapsdepartementet.

Lauglo, J. (1993) 'Policy Issues in Vocational Training', in L. Buchert (ed.) *Education and Training in the Third World: The Local Dimension.* The Hague: Centre for the Study of Education in Developing Countries (CESO) in Cooperation with the Centre for Development Research, Copenhagen.

Lazzari, A. (2011a) 'Continuing professional development of the early years workforce: Italian case study', Munich: Deutsches Judendinstitut, unpublished Report.

Lazzari, A. (2011b) 'Reconceptualizing professional development in early childhood education: a study on teachers' professionalism carried out in Bologna', PhD thesis, Bologna University.

Lazzari, A. (2012) 'Reconceptualising professionalism in early childhood education: insights from a study carried out in Bologna', *Early Years.*Published online 20/02/2012 at DOI: 10.1080/09575146.2011.651711..

Lega, L. (1999) 'Un laboratorio per l'innovazione: l'istituto comprensivo'. *Insegnare,* 10, 42–46.

Lenz-Taguchi, H. (2007) 'Deconstructing and transgressing the theory-practice dichotomy in early childhood education', *Educational Philosophy and Theory*, 19(3), 275–90.

Lenz-Taguchi, H. (2010) *Going Beyond the Theory/practice Divide in Early Childhood Education: Introducing an Intra-active Pedagogy.* London: Routledge.

Le Collectif (2006) *Pas de 0 de conduite pour les enfants de 3 ans.* Ramonville Saint-Agne: Erès.

Lie, S., Kjærnsli, M., Roe, A. and Turmo, A. (2001) *Godt rustet for framtida? Norske 15-åringers kompetanse i lesing og realfag i et internasjonalt perspektiv.* Oslo: Programme for International Student Assessment og Institutt for lærerutdanning og skoleutvikling, Universitetet i Oslo.

Lillard, A. (2005) *The Science behind the Genius.* New York, NY: Oxford University Press.

Lind, U. (2010) 'Blickens ordning. Bildspråk och estetiska lärprocesser som kunskapsform och kulturform' (The order of seeing: pictorial language and aesthetic learning processes as forms of knowledge and culture), Doctoral thesis, Stockholm: Liber Förlag.

Love, J.M., Logue, M.E., Trudeau, J.V. and Thayer, K. (1992) *Transitions to Kindergarten in American Schools: Final report of the National Transition Study.* Portsmouth, NH: RMC Research Corp.

Luke, A. (2011) 'Generalizing across borders: policy and the limits of educational science', *Educational Researcher*, 40(8), 367–77.

Lundgren, U.P. (1977) *Frame Factors and the Teaching Process: A Contribution to Curriculum Theory and Theory on Teaching* (Göteborg Studies in Educational Sciences, No. 8). Göteburg: Göteborgs Universitet.

Lundgren, U.P. (1991) *Between Education and Schooling: Outlines of a Diachronic Curriculum Theory.* Geelong: George Deakin University.

Maharey, S. (2007) *Letter Accompanying The New Zealand Curriculum.* Wellington: New Zealand Ministry of Education.

Malaguzzi, L. (1971) *Esperienze per una nuova scuola dell'infanzia: atti del seminario di studio tenuto a Reggio Emilia il 18–19–20 marzo 1971.* Roma: Editori Riuniti.

Malaguzzi, L. (1995) 'La storia, le idee, la cultura.', in C. Edwards, L. Gandini, and G. Forman (eds) *Il cento linguaggi dei bambini.* Bergamo: Edizioni Junior.

Målrettet arbeid i barnehagen (1982) *En håndbok.* Oslo: Universitetsforlaget.Manini, M., Gherardi, V. and Balduzzi, L. (eds) (2005). *Gioco, bambini, genitori: modelli educativi nei servizi per l'infanzia.* Roma: Carrocci.

Mantovani, S. (1986) 'Continuità nella specificità fra asilo nido e scuola materna', in V. Cesareo, C. Scurati and Centro per l'Innovazione Educativa Comune di Milano', (eds) *Infanzia e continuità educativa.* Milano: Franco Angeli.

Mantovani, S. (2007) 'Early childhood education in Italy', in R.S. New, and M. Cochran *Early Childhood Education: An International Encyclopedia.* Westport, CT: Praeger Publishers.

March, J.G. and Olsen, J.P. (1989) *Rediscovering the Institutions.* New York, NY: Collier Macmillian Publishers.

Marcon, R.A. (2002) 'Moving up the grades: relationship between preschool model and later school success', *Early Childhood Research and Practice*, 4(1), Article 1.

May, C.R. and Campbell, R. (1981) 'Readiness for learning: assumptions and realities', *Theory to Practice*, 20(2), 130–4.

May, H. (2009) *Politics in the Playground: The world of Early Childhood in New Zealand*, Rev. edn. Dunedin: Otago University Press.

May, H. (2011) *I Am Five and I Go to School: Early Years Schooling in New Zealand, 1900–2010*. Dunedin: Otago University Press.

McNaughton, S. (2002) *Meeting of the Minds*. Wellington: Learning Media.

Meade, A. (ed.) (2005, 2006, 2007, 2010) *Catching/Riding/Cresting/Dispersing the Waves: Innovation in Early Childhood Education*. Wellington: NZCER Press.

Meade, A. and Podmore, V. (2010) *Caring and Learning Together: A Case Study of New Zealand* (http://unesdoc.unesco.org/images/0018/001872/187234e.pdf, accessed 15 March 2012).

Meier, D. (1995) *The Power of Their Ideas*. Boston: Beacon Press.

Melhuish, E. (2011) 'Early years research and implications for policymaking: the UK experience', in Norwegian Ministry of Education and Reserch (ed.) *Nordic Early Childhood Education and Care-Effects and Challenges*. Oslo: Norwegian Ministry of Education and Research.

Meisels, S.J. (1999) 'Accountability in early childhood', in R.C.Pianta, M.J.Cox and K.L.Snow (eds) *School Readiness and the Transition to Kindergraten in the Era of Accountability*. Baltimore, MD: Paul Brookes.

Morabito, C. (2011) 'Analysis of the relations between 'equality of life chances' and 'early childhood care and education, as foundations for social justice and human development: a case study of Mauritius', unpublished document. Ghent: Ghent University.

Moss, P. (2007) 'Bringing politics into the nursery: early childhood education as a democratic practice', *European Early Childhood Education Research Journal*, 15(1), 5–20.

Moss, P. (2009) *There are Alternatives! Markets and Democratic Experimentalisation in Early Childhood Education and Care*. Working Paper No.53. The Hague: Bernard van Leer Foundation and Bertelsmann Stiftung.

Mouffe, C. (2005) *On the Political*. London: Routledge.

Nafstad, H.E. (1976) *Barnehagen som oppvekstmiljø og arbeidsplass*. Oslo: INAS/Tiden.

Nelson, K. (1978) *Children's Language, Vol. 1*. New York, NY: Gardner Press.

Newman, D., Griffin, P. and Cole, M. (1989) *The Construction Zone: Working for Cognitive Change in School*. Cambridge, MA: Cambridge University Press.

Nigris, E. (2007) 'Teacher training', in R. New and M. Cochran (eds) *Early Childhood Education: An International Encyclopaedia*. Westport, CT: Praeger.

Nordin-Hultman, E. (2004) 'Pedagogiska miljöer och barns subjektsskapande' (Pedagogical environments and children's construction of subjectivity), doctoral thesis, Stockholm: Liber Förlag.

Nuttall, J. (ed.) (2003) *Weaving Te Whāriki: Aotearoa/New Zealand's Early Childhood Curriculum Document in Theory and Practice*. Wellington: New Zealand Council for Education Research.

NZ (New Zealand) Ministry of Education (1996) *Te Whāriki. He Whāriki Mātauranga mō ngā Mokopuna o Aotearoa. Early Childhood Curriculum*. Wellington: Learning Media.

NZ (New Zealand) Ministry of Education (2002) *Curriculum Stocktake Report*. Wellington: New Zealand Ministry of Education.

NZ (New Zealand) Ministry of Education (2007) *The New Zealand Curriculum for English-medium Teaching and Learning in Years 1–13*. Wellington: Learning Media.

NZ (New Zealand) Ministry of Education (2009) *Ka Hikitia. Managing for Success: Maori Education Strategy*. Wellington: Learning Media.

NZ (New Zealand) Ministry of Education ECE Task Force (2011) *An Agenda for Amazing Children: Final Report*. Wellington: New Zealand Ministry of Education.

NOU (1988) 28. *Med viten og vilje*.

O'Connor, N. and Greenslade, S. (2011) 'Co-constructed pathways of learning: A case study'. *Early Childhood Folio*, 15, 2, 30–34.

Oberhuemer, P., Schreyer, I. and Neuman, M.J. (2010) *Professionals in Early Childhood Education and Care Systems: European Profiles and Persepctives*. Opladen: Verlag Barbra Budrich.

Ohlsson, J. (2004) *Arbetslag och lärande* (Working-team and learning processes). Lund: Studentlitteratur.

Okon, W. and Wilgocka-Okon, B. (1973) *The School Readiness Project*. Paris: UNESCO.

Olsson, L.M. (2009) *Movement and Experimentation in Young Children's Learning: Deleuze and Guattari in early childhood education*. London: Routledge.

Olsson, L.M. (forthcoming) 'Reading and writing beyond representation', *Contemporary Issues in Early Childhood*.

Opheim, V. (2004) *Equity in Education*. Oslo: NIFUSTEP, rapport nr. 7.

OECD (Organisation for Economic Co-operation and Development) (2001) *Starting Strong I: Early Childhood Education and Care*. Paris: OECD.

OECD (Organisation for Economic Co-operation and Development) (2006) *Starting Strong II: Early Childhood Education and Care*. Paris: OECD.

OECD (Organisation for Economic Co-operation and Development) (2007) *PISA 2006: Science competencies for tomorrow's world. Executive Summary*. Paris: OECD.

OECD (Organisation for Economic Co-operation and Development) (2011) *Pisa in Focus 2011/1*. Paris: OECD.

Palmer, A. (2010) 'Att bli matematisk. Matematisk subjektivitet och genus i lärarutbildningen mot de yngre åldrarna' (To become mathematical. Mathematical subjectivity and gender in early childhood teacher education), doctoral thesis, Stockholm University.

Perrenoud, P. (2001) 'The key to social fields: competencies of an autonomous actor', in D. S. Rychen and L.H. Salganik (eds) *Defining and Selecting Key Competencies*. Gottingen: Hogrefe and Huber.

Persson, S. (2008) 'Forskning om villkor för yngre barns lärande I förskola, förskoleklass och fritidshem' /(Research on conditions for children's learning in pre-school, pre-school class and leisure-time centre). (http://www.cm.se/webbshop_vr/pdfer/VR2008_11.pdf accessed 15 March 2012).

Peters, S. (2010) 'Shifting the lens: re-framing the view of learners and learning during the transition from early childhood education to school in New Zealand', in D. Jindal-Snape (ed.) *Educational Transitions: Moving Stories from Around the World*. New York, NY: Routledge.

Peters, S., Hartley, C., Rogers, P., Smith, J. and Carr, M. (2009) 'Supporting the transition from early childhood education to school: insights from one centre of innovation', *Early Childhood Folio*, 13, 2–6.

Peters, T. and Walgrave, L. (1978) 'Maatschappelijk- historischeduidingen bij het ontstaan van de Belgische jeugdbescherming', *Tijdschrift voor Criminologie*, 20, 57–70.

Pontecorvo, C. (ed.) (1989) *Un curricolo per la continuità educativa dai quattro agli otto anni*. Firenze: La Nuova Italia.

Pontecorvo, C. and Formisano, M. (1986) 'Continuità e discontinuità nell'educazione di base', in V. Cesareo, C. Scurati and Centro per l'Innovazione Educativa Comune di Milano (eds) *Infanzia e continuità educativa*. Milano: Franco Angeli.

Popkewitz, T. (2003) 'Governing the child and pedagogicalisation of the parent: a historical excursus into the present', in M. Bloch, K. Holmlund, L. Moqvist and T. Popkewitz (eds), *Governing Children, Families and Education. Restructuring the Welfare State*. New York, NY: Palgrave.

Rambøll. (2010) *Kartlegging av det pedagogiske innholdet i skoleforberedende aktiviteter i barnehager*. Oslo: Rambøll.

Ramey, S.L., Ramey, C.T., Phillips, M.M., Lanzi, R.G., Brezausek, C., Katholi, C.R., *et al.* (2000) *Head Start Children's Entry into Public School: A Report on the National Head Start/Public School Early Childhood Transition Demonstration Study*. Birmingham, AL: Citivan (http://www.acf.hhs.gov/programs/opre/hs/ch_trans/reports/transition_study/transition_study.pdf, accessed 12 January 2012).

Ravitch, D. (1978) *The Revisionists Revised: A Critique of the Radical Attack on the Schools*. New York, NY: Basic Books.

Rawls, J. (1971) *A Theory of Justice*. Cambridge, MA: Harvard University Press.

Reedy, T. (1995/2003) 'Tōku rangatiratanga nā te mana-mātauranga: Knowledge and power set me free', in J. Nuttall (eds) *Weaving Te Whāriki: Aotearoa New Zealand's Early Childhood Curriculum Document in Theory and Practice*. Wellington: NZCER.

Rinaldi, C. (2006) *In Dialogue with Reggio Emilia: Listening, Researching and Learning*. London: Routledge.

Ritchie, S., Clifford, R.M., Malloy, W.W., Cobb, C.T. and Crawford, G.M. (2010) 'Ready or not? Schools' readiness for young children', in S.L. Kagan and K. Tarrant (eds) *Transitions for Young Children: Creating Connections across Early Childhood Systems*. Baltimore, MD: Paul. H. Brookes Publishing Co.

Roemer, J. (1998) *Equality of Opportunity*. Cambridge, MA: Harvard University Press.

Rogoff, B. and Lave, J. (eds) (1984) *Everyday Cognition: Its Development in Social Context*. Cambridge, MA: Harvard University Press.

Roose, R., Roets, G., Vandenbroeck, M. (forthcoming). 'Democracy is what happens while you're busy making other plans: from research *on* parents to parents *as* researchers'. *Action Research*.

Rose, N. (1999) *Powers of Freedom: Reframing Political Thought*. Cambridge: Cambridge University Press.

Rychen, D.S. and Salganik, L.H. (eds) (2001) *Defining and Selecting Key Competencies*. Göttingen: Hogrefe and Huber.

Rychen, D.S. and Salganik, L.H. (2003) *Key Competencies for a Successful Life and Well Functioning Society*. Cambridge, MA: Hogrefe and Huber.

Sameroff, A. and Haith, M. (eds) (1996) *The Five to Seven-year Shift: The Age of*

Reason and Responsibility. Chicago, IL: University of Chicago Press.

Schleicher, A. (2011) 'The quality of childhood: evidence from the Programme for International Student Assessment (PISA)', in C. Clouder, B. Heys, M. Matthes and P. Sullivan, P. (eds) (2011) *Improving the Quality of Childhood in Europe, Vol. II,* Stourbridge, European Council for Steiner Waldorf Education/Alliance for Childhood European Network Group.

Schultz, T.W. (1961) 'Investment in human capital', *American Economic Review,* 51(1), 1–17.

Schweinhart, L.J., Montie, J., Xiang, Z., Barnett, W.S., Belfield, C.R. and Nores, M. (2005) *Lifetime Effects: The HighScope Perry Preschool Study through Age 40* (Monographs of the HighScope Educational Research Foundation, 14) Ypsilanti, MI: High Scope Press.

Scuola di Barbiana (1967) *Lettera ad una professoressa.* Firenze: Libreria editrice fiorentina.

Scurati, C. (1986) 'La continuità tra scuola fra scuola materna e scuola elementare', in V. Cesareo, C. Scurati and Centro per l'Innovazione Educativa Comune di Milano (eds) *Infanzia e continuità educativa.* Milano: Franco Angeli.

Sen, A. (2009) *The Idea of Justice.* New York, NY: Allan Lane.

Shaffer, H.R. (1977) *Mothering.* London: Open Books.

Shonkoff, J.P. and Phillips, D.A. (2000) *From Neurons to Neighborhoods: The Science of Early Childhood Development.* Washington, DC: National Academy Press.

Silvern, S.B. (1988) 'Continuity/discontinuity between home and early childhood environments', *The Elementary School Journal,* 89(2), 147–159.

Sinko, P. (2006) 'Pre-school in Finland', PowerPoint presentation, Morelia, March 2006.

Siraj-Blatchford, I. (2010) 'Learning in the home and at school: how working class children 'succeed against the odds', *British Educational Research Journal,* 36(3), 463–82.

Sjølund, A. (1969) *Børnehavens og vuggestuens betydning for barnets udvikling.* København: Sosialforskningsinstituttets publikationer 38.

Skolverket (Swedish National Agency for Education) (2004) *Pre-school in Transition: A National Evaluation of the Swedish Pre-school.* Stockholm: Skolverket.

Skolverket (Swedish National Agency for Education) (2008) *Ten Years after the Pre-school Reform: A National Evaluation of the Swedish Pre-school.* Stockholm: Skolverket.

Smet, P. (2009) *Samen grenzen verleggen voor elk talent. Beleidsnota Onderwijs 2009–2014.* Brussel: Vlaams Parlement.

Smith, A.B. (2011) 'Relationships with people places and things: Te Whāriki', in L. Miller and L. Pound (eds) *Theories and Approaches to Learning in the Early Years.* London: Sage.

Smith, Y., Davis, K. and Molloy, S. (2011) 'Assessment of key competencies, literacy and numeracy: Can these be combined?' *Early Childhood Folio,* 15(2),15–19.

Solheim, R.G. and Tønnessen, F.E. (2003) *Slik leser 10-åringer i Norge. En kartlegging av leseferdigheter blant 10-åringer i Norge 2001.* Stavanger: Senter for leseforskning.

Stebbins, L.B., St. Pierre, R.G., Proper, E.C., Anderson, R. B. and Cerva, T. R. (1977) 'Education as experimentation: a planned variation model', in *An Evaluation of*

Follow Through (Vol. 4-A). Cambridge, MA: Abt Associates.

Swedish Ministry of Education and Science (1998; English translation) *Curriculum for pre-school (Lpfö 98)*. Stockholm: Swedish Ministry of Education nand Science

Thirion, A.M. (1973) 'Evaluation des programmes d'éducation compensatoire', in G. De Landsheere (ed.) *Recherche en éducation. Recherches sur les handicaps socio-culturels de 0 à 7–8 ans*. (pp. 37–54.). Bruxelles: Ministère de l'Education nationale et de la Culture Française.

Tickell, C. (2011) *The Early Years: Foundations for Life, Health and Learning.* (http://media.education.gov.uk/MediaFiles/B/1/5/%7BB15EFF0D-A4DF-4294-93A1-1E1B88C13F68%7DTickell%20review.pdf, accessed 27 March 2012).

Tobin, J. (1995) 'The irony of self-expression', *American Journal of Education*, 103(3), 233–58.

Tobin, J., Hsueh, Y. and Karasawa, M. (2009) *Preschool in Three Cultures Revisited: China, Japan and the United States*. Chicago, IL: The University of Chicago Press.

Tönnies, F. (2001) *Community and Civil Society* (ed. Jose Harris). Cambridge: Cambridge University Press.

Unger, R.M. (2005) *What Should the Left Propose?* London, UK: Verso.

UN Committee on the Rights of the Child (2005) General Comment no. 7: Implementing child rights in early childhood. (http://www2.ohchr.org/english/bodies/crc/docs/AdvanceVersions/GeneralComment7Rev1.pdf, accessed 15 March 2012).

UNESCO (2008) *Overcoming Inequality: Why Governance Matters* (Education for All Global Monitoring Report 2009). Oxford: Oxford University Press.

UNICEF Innocenti Research Centre (2008) *The Child Care Transition (Report Card 8)*. Florence: UNICEF.

Urban, M., Vandenbroeck, M., Lazzari, A., Peeters, J. and Van Laere, K. (2011) *Competence Requirements for Early Childhood Care and Education*. London and Ghent: University of East London and University of Ghent.

Vandenbroeck, M. (2003) 'From crèches to childcare: constructions of motherhood and inclusion/exclusion in the history of Belgian infant care', *Contemporary Issues in Early Childhood*, 4(3), 137–48.

Vandenbroeck, M. (2006) 'The persistent gap between education and care: a "history of the present" research on Belgian child care provision and policy', *Paedagogica Historica. International Journal of the History of Education*, 42(3), 363–83.

Vandenbroeck, M. and Bouverne-De Bie, M. (2006) 'Children's agency and educational norms. A tensed negotiation', *Childhood*, 13(1), 127–43.

Vandenbroeck, M., Roets, G. and Snoeck, A. (2009) 'Mothers crossing borders: immigrant mothers on reciprocity, hybridisation and love', *European Early Childhood Education Research Journal*, 17(2), 203–16.

Vandenbroeck, M., Coussée, F. and Bradt, L. (2010) 'The social and political construction of early childhood education', *British Journal of Educational Studies*, 58(2), 139–53.

Vandenbroucke, F. (2007) *Maatregelen ter stimulering van de participatie aan het kleuteronderwijs*. Brussel: Ministerie van Werk, Onderwijs en Vorming.

Vandenbroucke, F. (2008) *Meer kleuters nar de kleuterschool, en liefst zindelijke kleuters*. Keynote speech of the Flemish Minister of Labour, Education and Training, Antwerp University, 23 September 2008 (http://ond.flanders.be/beleid/toespraak/080923-zindelijkheid.htm, accessed 12 January 2012).

Vatne, B. (2006) 'Leik', in P. Haug (ed.) *Begynnaropplæring og tilpassa undervisning – kva skjer i klasserommet?* Bergen: Caspar Forlag A/S.

Vatne, B. (2010) 'Towards an "Academic day" in Norwegian kindergartens? Issues of educational policy and educational activities in Norwegian kindergartens', paper presented at the European Society on Family Relations Conference, Milan, September 29–October 2, 2010.

Vecchi, V. (2004) 'The multiple fonts of knowledge', *Children in Europe*, 4, 18–21.

Vecchi, V. (2010) *Art and Creativity in Reggio Emilia: Exploring the Role and Potential of Ateliers in Early Childhood Education*. London: Routledge.

Ventura, G. (1986) 'Servizi formativi e territorio', in V. Cesareo, C. Scurati and Centro per l'Innovazione Educativa Comune di Milano (eds) *Infanzia e continuità educativa*. Milano: Franco Angeli.

Vygotsky, L.S (1978a) *Mind in Society: The Development of Higher Psychological Processes*. Cambridge, MA: Harvard University Press.

Vygotsky, L.S. (1978b) *Thought and Language*. Cambridge, MA: Harvard University Press.

Visalberghi, A., Maragliano, R. and Vertecchi, B. (1978) *Pedagogia e scienze dell'educazione*. Milano: Mondadori.

Wenger, E. (1998) *Communities of practice: learning, meaning and identity*. Cambridge: Cambridge University Press.

Wertsch, J.V. (1991) *Voices of the Mind: A Sociocultural Approach to Mediated Action*. Cambridge, MA: Harvard University Press.

Wilkinson, R. and Pickett, K. (2009) *The Sprit Level: Why More Equal Societies Almost Always Do Better*. London: Allen Lane.

Winsvold, A. and Gulbrandsen, L. (2009) *Kvalitet og kvantitet: kvalitet i en barnehagesektor i sterk vekst*. Oslo: Norsk institutt for forskning om oppvekst, velferd og aldring.

Wright, J. and Molloy, S. (2005) 'Case study 9: cross-sector professional development – what can we learn about relationships?', in M. Carr and S. Peters (eds) *Te Whāriki and Links to the New Zealand Curriculum: Research Projects. Final Report to the Ministry of Education*. Hamilton: University of Waikato.

Wylie, C. (2011) *Competent Learners @ 20: Summary of Key Findings*. Wellington: New Zealand Ministry of Education.

Wylie, C. and Hogben E. (2011) *Forming Adulthood: Past, Present and Future in the Experience and Views of the Competent Learners @ 20*. Wellington: New Zealand Ministry of Education.

Woolfolk, A. and Perry, N. (2012) *Child and Adolescent Development*. Boston, MA: Pearson.

W.K. Kellogg Foundation (2008) 'Linking early learning and the early grades to assure that children are ready for school and schools are ready for children – a SPARK legacy (SPARK Working Paper) (http://www.wkkf.org/knowledge-center/resources/2008/09/WORKING-PAPER-Linking-Early-Learning-And-The-Early-Grades-To-Assure-That-Children-Are-Ready-For.aspx, accessed 12 January 2012).

Zigler, E. and Kagan, S.L. (1982) 'Child development knowledge and educational practice: Using what we know', in A. Lieberman and M. McLaughlin (eds) *Policy Making in Education: Eighty-first Yearbook of the National Society for the Study of Education*. Chicago, IL: University of Chicago Press.

Index

curriculum codes 81

Dahlberg, Gunilla: academic influences
77–8, 80, 81; *bildung*, concept and
use of 28–9, 83–4; childhood
education, evaluation of 73–7, 80;
educational labeling 20, 75;
government commission 4–5, 19,
20, 72–3; 'meeting place' for shared
values 27–8, 30, 42–4, 63–4, 200;
opportunities for dialogue 88–90;
policy change, realisation of 81;
reform and shared understandings
24–7, 82–5; Reggio Emilia, influence
of 78–9; 'schoolification',
consequences of 19–22, 75; social
construction of the child 22–3, 64–5,
77; Stockholm project 85–6, 88–9;
team working, evaluation needed
34–5; unanswered questions 47
Deleuze, Gilles 39, 181
democratic experimentalism 70, 96
democratic participation: 'meeting
place' concept 27, 45, 70, 96, 168;
potential for change 48, 67, 105–6,
190–1, 197–8; realisation of 152–3,
156, 158
Denmark 8, 147
Dewey, John 71n, 84
dialogue pedagogy 84
documentation: progress reports, basis
for evaluation 76–7, 79–80, 153;
public visibility and accountability
26–7, 66, 86–7; teaching resource
26, 27, 66, 102, 110–11, 164
Durkheim, Émile 112

early childhood education (ECE): child-
centred learning 22, 54–5, 94–5, 99;
childrens' rights and access to 3–4,
54, 70–1, 152; co-constructive
learning 109, 160; collaborative
action research (NZ) 106–7;
conditional attendance 181–2;
cultural identity through learning
96–8, 110; economic investment
9–10; fundamental differences with
CSE 135, 139–40; learning
dispositions 97, **100**, 101; legitimacy
and self-identity 56, 86–7, 202, 203;
parental support, influence of
103–5, 145, 147, 164, 171n;
partnership option, wider usage

60–1, 146–8, 165, 172–3n, 198–9;
partnership with compulsory
educators 14–19, 24–5, 41–2, 121–5,
128–9, 163–4; 'schoolification',
consequences of 19–22, 32, 36;
'schoolification', factors for 138–40;
school readiness 10–14, 23, 47,
182–3, 189–90; shared
understanding and values 27–8, 30,
42–3; social investment 177–9;
social prejudice 181, 188–9; socio-
emotional development undermined
62–3, 183–5; split pre-school
provision 6–7, 52–3, 56–8; state
support, lack of 141–2; structural
context 6–9; traditional schooling,
critiques of 38–41; transitional
curriculum 8–9, 16, 58–9, 107, 111,
124–5
early childhood research: educational
continuity 159–62; limited national
debate 69; opportunities for
dialogue 88–90
Early Years Foundation Stage (EYFS)
12
education systems: evidence-based
policy 179–80; hierarchical
relationship 4; 'meeting place'
concept, potential of 42–5, 47–8;
orientation differences 135; policy
change, detrimental 166–7; policy
change, realisation of 201–2, 204;
split pre-school provision 7, 52–3;
transition, new supportive approach
144–8
Eisner, Elliot 62, 95–6
England 7, 12, 204
En skola för bildning (A school for
Bildung) 83–4
Erikson, Erik 132
European Commission 10, 183

Finland 53, 59
Flanders: community participation
190–1; compulsory learning, early
provision 176–7; *Experimental
Education* movement 59; parent led
research 186–7; schooling,
conditional attendance 181–2
Follow Through programme (US)
135–6
Foucault, Michel 21, 36, 48, 77, 78, 189
Foundation for Child Development 134